Chinese Intellectuals on the World Frontier

Chinese Intellectuals on the World Frontier

Blazing the Black Path

J. A. ENGLISH-LUECK

BERGIN & GARVEY
Westport, Connecticut • London

Library of Congress Cataloging-in-Publication Data

English-Lueck, J. A. (June Anne), 1953–
    Chinese intellectuals on the world frontier : blazing the black
path / J. A. English-Lueck.
        p.   cm.
    Includes bibliographical references and index.
    ISBN 0–89789–510–X (alk. paper)
    1. Intellectuals—China.   2. China—Intellectual life—1976–
3. China—Social conditions—1976–   I. Title.
HM213.E54   1997
305.5′52′0951—dc21   96–40906

British Library Cataloguing in Publication Data is available.

Library of Congress Catalog Card Number: 96–40906
ISBN: 0–89789–510–X

First published in 1997

Bergin & Garvey, 88 Post Road West, Westport, CT 06881
An imprint of Greenwood Publishing Group, Inc.

Printed in the United States of America

The paper used in this book complies with the
Permanent Paper Standard issued by the National
Information Standards Organization (Z39.48–1984).

10 9 8 7 6 5 4 3 2 1

To John Rader Platt (1918–1992), teacher and friend

Contents

Acknowledgments

Many people helped me with the task of constructing this tome. Many thanks go to my husband, Karl David Lueck. He was supportive during the years of data collection, valiantly mastering computer programs and transcribing over half of the interviews. He listened carefully to each successive draft of the text and gave me pertinent comments. Most of all, he understood my need to write this book, even at the cost of a sane social life. He cheerfully took our infant Eilene on walks when I needed a bit of uninterrupted time. My daughter Miriam has shown patience and understanding beyond her years of her mother's peculiar obsession.

My family and friends must be congratulated on their patience and kindness. Thanks to Karen, Peter, Robert and Florence Michaelsen, Darrow and Sharon English, Grace and Sandy Kline, David and Joan Lueck, Denise and Tim Aedan, Barbara Leavitt, Pat Hansen, Neil Websdale, George Guilmet, Joel and Linda Zimbleman, Dirk van der Elst and Joanne Kipps. Ruhama Veltfort also earns my respect and thanks for her editorial expertise and many hours of discussion.

I am grateful to Dr. Jen Shien-min for patiently working to give me entrée into China. Paul Bohannan deserves accolades for taking the time to read previous drafts and then making insightful suggestions that I hope I have enacted. Further intellectual stimulation by John Platt, Robert Textor and my San Jose State University colleagues—Charles Darrah, Soo-Young Chin, James M. Freeman, Chris Jochim, Thomas Layton, Miro Valach, Carol Chapnick Mukhopadhyay and William Reckmeyer—enlivened my knowledge of anthropology. I give my special thanks to David Miller for organizing the Oklahoma Symposia on Comparative Frontiers—the input and knowledge of the participants were invaluable. Dr. Staci Ford of the University of Hong Kong graciously gave her time and effort to give me the perspective of a women's historian and has continually inspired me to reach out to her discipline. The usual proviso prevails. Only I am responsible for my errors and lacunae; my colleagues are blameless.

Thanks also go to my various institutional homes—California State University Fresno, The University of Puget Sound and San Jose State University. I also want to thank the Council for the International Exchange of Scholars and the University of Hong Kong for choosing me for a Fulbright grant in 1993–1994 allowing me to continue my comparative studies in American and Chinese cultures. The Center for Asian Studies seminars, the history and sociology departmental seminars and the Hong Kong Anthropological Society lectures provided a venue for my thirst for knowledge.

Most of all, I want to thank my colleagues, students and friends in the People's Republic of China for giving me this opportunity to taste—if only a morsel—the flavors of the rich Chinese culture.

1

Of Maps, Metaphors, Perils and Precautions

This book is a story of journeys. Mine was to China to live, teach and learn. Chinese scholars sojourn to America, Europe and Australia, in person or along information highways, to follow similar agendas. China itself is on a journey, skirting the borderlands of the Westernized, globalized social realm, in search of "modernization." Its intellectuals, scientists and engineers are the pilgrims in that quest.

Many books, in diverse narrative styles, can and have been written about China. They may cover vast periods of time from macroscopic cultural overviews spanning three thousand years or focus on microscopic analyses of policy in a single decade. This volume was assembled with some specific issues in mind. In the style of post-postmodernism, this book has a concrete research focus—the choices and constraints of nonestablishment Chinese intellectuals at the end of the twentieth century as they establish a new identity for themselves, and perhaps even for China.

From August 1988 to January 1990 I lived in a university compound in southwest China, which I visited again in 1994. Out of that sojourn, taken in the tumultuous year that surrounded the events of Tiananmen Square, evolved the research that led to this book. My daily association with my Chinese colleagues, students and friends brought me in touch with an emerging social category in the People's Republic, nonestablishment intellectuals, who are neither political leaders nor dissidents. Interviews about the future of Chinese education, science and society allowed me access to their visions, values and personal vignettes.

This group finds itself at the cusp of change. The socialist state monopoly on academia, scientific and technical research is yielding to market pressures. Universities must be, at least partially, self-sustaining. Entrepreneurial niches, outside of state control, are opening for intellectuals as industry privatizes. The entire society has shifted its focus from ideology to material wealth. These dramatic changes have forced choices on China's "thought workers" that need to be explored.

The construction of this book required some stylistic features usually associated with a more interpretive style of anthropology. Devices such as fictional characterization, reflexivity and metaphor have been used to suggest subtle layers of meaning in Chinese discourse that may be lost in a direct, technical style of writing. Metaphorical evocation is considered preferable, more "alive" to the Chinese, than direct statement (Young 1994, 101). These literary tools need to be explained.

This chapter is a map designed to help you, the reader, traverse the stories contained in this book. One of cultural anthropology's key contributions to social science is that it tends to reject simple answers, highlighting the complexity of human interactions. Human behavior becomes multidimensional. People do not just behave, rather they behave in particular environments amid shifting patterns of meaning. In ethnography a wealth of perspectives and voices emerge to enrich our understanding. Yet complexity carries a risk that you will get lost as you travel through the pages. Chapter 1 provides a few signposts to aid the reader's literary sojourn.

The first section of the chapter defines the research focus of this book—questions of identity, both of Chinese intellectuals and China itself. It also discusses the range of issues and topics that need to be explored in order to answer these questions.

The second section of this chapter is explicitly designed to help you negotiate the logic of this narrative. It points out the "literary tricks" that have been used to present the different perspectives.

A QUESTION OF IDENTITY

The status of "intellectual" is being radically redefined. Intellectuals find themselves at the fulcrum of critical areas of change in education, economics and culture. Their prestige in the larger society was repeatedly challenged as the twentieth century unfurled. While they were initially a key to industrialization in the new socialist state, they were, as a group, subjected to suspicion and revilement during the tumultuous early decades of the People's Republic. Today, again, they represent the key to modernization, a process dependent on cultural contact between China and the West. Modern Chinese intellectuals find themselves at the cultural borders of Chinese dominion, assimilating Western modes of knowledge, passively as part of the world culture of science, or actively contacting foreigners and going abroad.

The changes in Chinese education, economics and culture have implications for what it means to be Chinese in the twenty-first century. I found the opportunity to investigate the population so central to these transformations irresistible.

The cultural transformation of the intellectuals provides the context for the research questions that emerged as I designed, conducted and analyzed the research data. The first question I addressed is the most descriptive—*How do the intellectuals define and redefine their niche in Chinese society?* Changes in the economic, educational and scientific sectors would be illuminated by such definitions. The second question is aimed at investigating the cultural changes that have been taking place and understanding the processes by which people "outwitted the state." *How do the intellectuals understand what it means to be Chinese—both in the abstract and in action?* Finally, I wanted to place the current round of changes within a larger picture of Chinese intercultural interaction along its frontiers. After all, although the scale of interaction may differ, cultural information has permeated Chinese borders in the past. This group may number tens of millions, but the true significance of this population lies in their power to transform the core identity of the larger population. *How then, does this process of intellectual self-definition affect the larger nexus of Chinese identity?*

To even begin to approach these questions, I had to observe the dance of choice and constraint that defines intellectuals' relationship with the society. Through interview, participant-observation and multidisciplinary literature review, I investigated the many contexts that influence their lives. Each individual intellectual is embedded in a variety of shifting roles. Most obvious is the intellectual role itself, but age cohort, gender and family role were also of critical importance. Educational policy and structure would clearly be relevant, as was the sociology of Chinese science. Policy and institutional structure are set against the background of the ever changing political economy. In turn, because of the transformations wrought by the Cultural Revolution and the subsequent market innovations, connections between rural and urban sectors have been recast. These spheres might intersect through the lives of individual intellectuals. A now urban electrical engineer might well utter "my mother and father were peasants." Another might spend his Sundays as a consulting entrepreneur working for a rural industry. Such erosion of boundaries might have significant implications for cultural identity. Each of these topics—education, science, political economy, social role—illuminates different aspects of the research questions. Intellectuals' identities cannot be defined outside of these important contexts.

NAVIGATING THE NARRATIVE

In this book, metaphors play a marked role in conveying ideas and suggesting emotional tone. Such metaphors have been used in traditional ethnography, and are essential in Chinese conversation and literature. To neglect metaphors would do damage to the integrity of this work.

Moreover, I am clearly present, not an invisible fly-on-the-wall observer. For example, in the second chapter I discuss my methods and methodological epiphanies as a narrative in which my own discoveries—often presaged by disconfirmed expectancies—are highlighted. Finally, I wanted to create a format that both personalized and disguised individual intellectuals. Too often Chinese are conceptualized en masse, masking individual differences. I wanted to present individual human voices. This is difficult to do without compromising their anonymity. To resolve this conflict I constructed fictitious characters that represent differences in age and gender.

The admittedly unusual format is designed to provoke multiple modes of mind, by employing poetic or historical allegory as well as the rhetoric of social science. Anthropological ethnographies have had a legacy of allegory—whether intended or unintended—that evoke "fables of identity" or "'cosmological' patterns of order and disorder" by the use of tone or reasoning (Clifford 1986, 119). This text places the allegory up front to make the message accessible to those for whom social science writing is opaque.

My methodology lends itself to metaphorical analysis. My interview technique asks scholars to discuss the future of China. Discussing distant and impersonal democratization, while tense, is not as risky as directly addressing the issue in real time. Politically or socially sensitive opinions, as well as the values that sustain them, can be indirectly approached by using the future as a metaphor.

Historic analogy, a favorite Chinese rhetorical device, will illustrate the patterns of marginality, accommodation and innovation that emerge in the lives of contemporary Chinese intellectuals. I used historical literature to look for patterns of intercultural interaction. Han dynasty frontier history metaphorically describes the uncomfortable necessity of China's cross-cultural associations. I saw parallels between China's past and present that stemmed from my own perception of frontier dynamics. Frontiers possess the potential to create new cultural knowledge, innovating where state control is weakest. By employing the Chinese technique of seeing history as metaphor, I came to realize that the modern pioneers of Chinese science and technology had more in common with the inhabitants of the historic Chinese frontier than I could have imagined. As I pursued this topic, I realized that the "comparative frontier" paradigm was a rich source of social theory. I also came to see that Chinese frontier dwellers had long struggled with the questions similar to those that face modern Chinese scientists and form the core questions of this project: What does it mean to be Chinese? What should be taken from the "other" and by whom? How can the differences—sources of potential spiritual contamination—be contained for those Han Chinese that must interact with foreign others?

Each chapter uses a Chinese allegorical verse of the Monkey King pilgrimage saga as an epigrammatic guidepost to the theme of that chapter. This technique is meant in the spirit of Chinese traditional drama, which uses characters to evoke an emotion, to suggest a frame of mind rather than present a factual representation (Vizenor 1987, 7).

The Journey to the West, Xiyou Ji, is a fantasy about the seventh-century Tang dynasty pilgrim Xuan Zang and his mythical companions. The saga suggests essential themes of the journey undertaken by Chinese scholars in the late twentieth century. The story, novelized in the Ming dynasty, in the 1570s, reflects a wide array of allegorical symbolism, and includes themes from Chinese popular culture, Buddhism, Taoism and Neo-Confucian morality.[1] Even though *Journey to the West* is a "comic fantasy," it "captures a sense of complex reality" (Hsia 1968, 18).

While the nominal protagonist is the Tang Priest, it is the ever artful disciple Sun Wukong, the Monkey King, who is the key character. The versatile Sun Wukong is not just one character but many. He is adventurous, optimistic and loyal to his family. He can embody many virtues, yet he is often criticized and stigmatized. Whether his tale is unabashed comedy or allegory, certain cultural themes emerge. The Monkey King's various entanglements illustrate the quandaries of the late-twentieth-century Chinese sage.

This character is complex, consisting of myriad images and conflicting personalities (see Wang 1992, 20, 223). On one level he is a classic trickster, a fool-sage, whose hubris is ridiculous and monstrous, and yet it is his insight that repeatedly saves the day. Simultaneously, he is the pilgrim who transforms his chaotic monkey mind, dominated by a lust for power, flitting from vanity to vanity, to that of a legitimate, disciplined and enlightened Buddhist consciousness. The allegorical tale reveals a struggle in which, having lost his power, his face and his freedom, Sun regains all, albeit in a new and unexpected form, by "persisting in the face of obstacles" (Overmeyer 1984, 320).

The metaphorical power of the character Sun Wukong is made apparent by the range of people who identify with him. Mao Zedong likened himself to the popular Monkey King, as did Chinese kindergartners in my daughter's work unit affiliated preschool. Chinese Americans view Sun as a projection of themselves, as illustrated by Maxine Hong Kingston's *Tripmaster Monkey*. Other American sinophiles rewrite Sun along more Western lines.[2] Most importantly, Chinese intellectuals themselves playfully admire and identify with his stamina and ingenuity, seemingly elevating his antics to wistful role model. That sentiment inspired me to choose the Monkey King's saga as the prime allegory for the experience of contemporary Chinese intellectuals.

The Journey to the West is a pilgrimage tale. The task of the Tang Priest is to bring the sacred Buddhist *sutras* from India to the court of the Tang Emperor. Xuan Zang is homesick for the Tang court, which today is viewed as a zenith of the Chinese past. The Tang Priest acquires supernatural disciples who become linked to him through the dual ties of necessity and *guanxi*, the intricate system of personal connections that is essential to Chinese society.

Sun Wukong, once king of the monkeys on the Mountain of Flowers and Fruit, must serve the priest to atone for his hubris. Sun is imprisoned under the Five Elements Mountain for having challenged both the court of the King of Heaven and the Buddha himself. Xuan Zang releases Sun, but just in case he rebels, he can command the tightening of a golden band on the immortal Sun's head, causing excruciating pain. All the disciples—Zhu Bajie, Friar Sand, the Spirit Horse and Sun—are heavenly manifestations who were bound to undertake the journey to make amends for their past misadventures. In the course of their sojourn, they encounter twisted monks, hungry spirits and martial devils who hinder their quest. Repeatedly, Monkey saves the day, but often by defying the strictures of his pious and non-violent master, thus tricking not only the enemy, but also his master. Yet as the adventures progress, the disciples learn to submit themselves to the quest, thereby reforming their errant natures. In the end, they secure the sutras and reach Enlightenment. The golden band disappears, and Sun gains his autonomy.

Out of the complex set of roles that Sun assumes, I have drawn on verses and events to evoke a frame of mind at the onset of each chapter. Monkey King's myriad characterizations set the tone for the issues to be explored. In the vignettes in this book, Sun acts as the intermediary who struggles with the barbarian demon Red Boy in order to serve his master. He is also the bold "Great Sage Equaling Heaven" who has rebelled against an unjust Heaven and is imprisoned, awaiting his reformer. He is the independent optimistic youngster who seeks his destiny and thirsts for knowledge. Yet Sun is also the patrilineal leader and name-giver of his primordial monkey family. He is their protector, even when he must leave them to perfect his own skills. He is ultimately a trickster who can use his special knowledge to transform himself to meet the needs of an unpredictable and changing situation. Sun Wukong is a mass of conflicting roles, competing obligations and a master of the ingenious transformations necessary to adapt to the unexpected. He embraces the contradictions necessary to evoke the complex multiplicity of emotions, values, and attitudes associated with intellectuals in modern China.

The themes of *mianzi* (face-work) and *guanxi* (connections) are played out in both the ancient fable and the modern narrative. The relationship of master and disciples reflects the ambiguity of Xuan Zang and his magical, somewhat reluctant converts. In the broadest sense, the goals of the master are the goals of the disciples. Yet the hierarchical bonds that tie them together also forever separate them. In a similar fashion, the Chinese government agonizes over its ambivalent relationship with its intellectuals. Scholars are traditionally honored, a legacy of the Confucian past. Yet a mere fifteen years ago, they were just emerging from the Cultural Revolutionary stigma of being *chou lao jiu*, "stinking number nines," grouped with such social dregs as landlords, counter-revolutionaries, rightists, renegades, enemy agents and capitalist roaders (Du 1992, 62).

The tradition of Chinese scholarship is bound up in a host of authoritarian ties—ties based on status, prestige and *guanxi*. The entry of women, peasants, and workers into the educated elite highlights the changes brought by the Liberation, but at the same time, inequality persists. A woman may become a mathematician, but a host of other structural barriers remain intact. Thus, she may end up doing the accounts for her work unit instead of pursuing the field of high-level control theory for which she was trained. The importance of technical expertise places a strain on the traditional system of seniority that has continued to be the basis for promotion and success. Armed with foreign training, a young scientist may bypass the usual years of waiting to reach a position of authority—or he may never make that leap, perhaps because he was not home building the *guanxi* connections necessary to advance.

Ultimately, the ties that bind the disciple to the master may be based on rules of status and authority, but they are also personal. Such patronage, vertical *guanxi*, between scholars and individual officials keeps the scientific and educational system working even when it is assaulted by radical structural changes, such as the Cultural Revolution (1966–1976) or the subsequent economic reforms, which have disrupted all modern Chinese institutions.

The twin themes of *mianzi* and *guanxi*, that is, face-work and connections, are reflected in the many stories of Chinese scholars, but they are not unique to the Chinese. As an academic sojourner in China I found myself enmeshed in the same web of rank, power and personality that bound my colleagues. This book is also my story.

My journey from raw to half-cooked, to use a Chinese metaphor for the process of being sinocized, reflects issues that my American readers might find compelling. The same American assumptions that thwarted my initial understanding might stump my readers. I wanted the text to be explicitly comparative. The book is a joint venture, featuring Chinese scholars, but also Western readers (and a Western author who has studied American culture) who all bring a wealth of assumptions, misapprehensions and interpretations to the reading of the text. Link points out that Americans automatically compare the Chinese experience to their own, often with massive distortion (1992, 301). To some extent, this is inevitable. Indeed, in the anthropological tradition, there is a recognition that ethnographic treatments of "others," exotic and otherwise, are intrinsically comparative—as the culturally distinct reader and author consider their own experiences and worldview (Barnes 1987, 119). The trick is to lead the reader to an *appropriate* comparison.

Using the reflexive mode, I can explore life in a Chinese university from the perspective of a participant. Although my experience cannot match that of a Chinese intellectual, I was more than a casual observer. Methodologically, my use of participant-observation techniques augmented the information I acquired from the hundred plus interviews I collected. In a parallel way, the reflexive miniature "autobiography" in Chapter 2 amplifies the fictional interviews that follow it.

Use of interview material in creating this book posed narrative challenges. Anthropological ethical tradition mandates anonymity. In some cultural accounts, merely changing the names of people and places can accomplish that goal. That is really not sufficient for work on potentially sensitive issues in modern China. Another approach would be to raise the discussion of the data to a level of abstraction, causing the individual people to fade into the background. That too presented a problem, for I was unwilling to sacrifice a sense of personal presence. I wanted to include "the smiles and dimples" that so often must be sacrificed for confidentiality (see Link 1992, 19–20). My solution was to merge the interviewees and informants into a trio of invented personae drawn from their aggregate characteristics. The result, though fiction, is truer to the reality of living people than isolated statements could be.

These literary techniques also serve to protect the confidentiality of the intellectuals. The first, and most obvious, obstacle I had to overcome was political. Writing about China required balancing criticism and diplomacy, a feat sometimes difficult to achieve. I needed to be careful that no assertion I made would reflect badly on my Chinese friends and informants. Opinions acceptable in 1990 may not be tolerated in 1997. Since political acceptability is an often shifting criterion, editing the interviews required careful attention. Even offhand comments about history might create peril. This dilemma is echoed in the often quoted observation that the "difficulty in China is not predicting the future, it is predicting the past" (Lin 1981, 46).

The ethical consideration was paramount. The presentation of the interview material and participant-observations *could not* compromise the anonymity of my hundred plus Chinese interviewees, or the several hundred people in my social circle, yet their viewpoints still had to be presented. The standard techniques of renaming or offering only small vignettes were not sufficient to the task, particularly in the post-Tiananmen era.

Each chapter in this book has key lessons to offer, and contributes fundamental information to the question of Chinese intellectuals and Chinese identity. This chapter is designed to guide you through the narrative. The next chapter introduces the historical context—the year surrounding the conflict at Tiananmen Square—and the methods I used to explore the nature of contemporary Chinese intellectuals. Chapter 3 continues to provide background information, briefly outlining some features of China's frontier pattern and reviewing pertinent elements of modern Chinese history vis-à-vis intellectuals. The structure of Chinese education, the creation of age cohorts, the status of intellectuals and their relationship to the open door policy are all issues of significance.

Chapters 4, 5 and 6 introduce the fictional characters, Wang, Zhou and Li, who reveal diverse aspects of life in their composite interviews. The words are drawn from the Ethnographic Futures Research (EFR) interviews, informal interviews and casual conversations.[3] Within my sample of intellectuals, generational experience and gender were the meaningful divides.

Given that I wanted to present a lively representation without identifying any single "voice," I created three fictional voices to speak for the hundred plus interviewees, using a composite of their responses. Each voice will represent and speak for one of the three categories: the middle-aged scholar, his younger colleague and a woman scientist. Together the "fictionalized" interviews of Wang, Zhou and Li provide the framework for presenting the diverse images of China's future.[4] I would also place myself in these fictional interviews, and so I would be able to question, comment and consider points of view that were both comparative and interpretive. This technique would allow me to expand the compressed shorthand of interview data, integrate conversations and observation, and incorporate discussion and analysis *in situ*.

Chapter 4, Wang's story, sets up the format of the composite interviews. The Ethnographic Futures Research interview proceeds as it would in actuality, consisting first of a background interview, followed by discussions of the best, worst and most probable scenarios. Set in the months before Tiananmen, Wang, a middle-aged scholar, outlines many of the key issues of interest to all intellectuals—their ambivalent status, their faith in science and hope for a substantial Chinese presence in global science and their worries about the changing values wrought by materialism. Wang also explores issues characteristic to his group—the preference for basic research, the desire for predictability and a particular careful style of self presentation. He has a clear vision of the scientist's difficulties in a system that favors secrecy over collaboration.

Wang's younger colleague Zhou, captured in Chapter 5, is more daring. He is less marked by the Cultural Revolution and more clearly subject to the rhetoric of modernization. He revels in competition, applied research and the potential for entrepreneurial success. At the same time, he expresses a romantic vision of Chinese tradition that his elder counterpart echoes only faintly. He worries about crime and his own ability to succeed in a system geared toward seniority. Set in the months following Tiananmen, his interview reflects a more constrained optimism and is more elliptical.

Both Wang and Zhou differ from Li, the subject of Chapter 6, a woman whose approach to science differs markedly from theirs. Her visions, her metaphors of the future, are more socially aware. She fervently hopes that the "students returning from abroad" can transform an ailing educational and scientific system. She is articulate about technology's potential social uses and social costs. She is particularly concerned about potential moral erosion. Unlike Zhou, she views competition with suspicion, fearing it will lead to individuation and isolation. She worries that excessive materialism will undermine China's strength, reflecting an assumed respect for education. She hopes for gender equality, but does not hold much confidence in that regard. Her interview is actually a dual interview set both in the months prior to and the days following Tiananmen. This time frame surely colors her remarks.

Chapter 7 dissolves the fictional personae and explores the range of choices made by individual intellectuals regarding their education and research. Again, their choices highlight the constraints placed by the system. Returning once again to the three research questions, intellectuals' self-definitions are reexamined. Their self-confessed Chinese virtues and vices illuminate their visions of "Chineseness." Finally the chapter addresses the connection between these intellectuals and the greater reformation of Chinese identity. In order to outwit the state, intellectuals have been forced to reconceptualize their goals—synthesizing service to the state and individual survival. They have learned to minimize sacrifice without abandoning a larger purpose. They are willing to traverse new frontiers—ranging from forays into the rural interior to extended travel abroad. In so doing they have pioneered new conceptual territory, instrumentalizing Western knowledge in a way that has evaded the powers that be. They have the potential to master Western cultural forms and retain deeper Chinese processes, creating a new model for the twenty-first-century *Zhongguo ren*, Chinese person.

2

Journey to the East

The pilgrim who was seeking the sutras
Was torn with nostalgia for the Great Tang
The disciples accompanying their master
In a rest-home found happiness in their dream

(Wu Cheng En, *Journey to the West*, 1:530)

This book is my journeyman's work. I am an anthropologist, a "young scholar." That means that I am too young to be part of the senior sector of academia but old enough to have firmly rooted my identity in the discipline of cross-cultural inquiry. This Chinese venture was my first major foreign fieldwork since I had earned my doctoral credentials as a cultural anthropologist. The study of anthropology is itself a kind of journey in which a scholar submits herself to alien cultural stimuli in order to gain illumination and insight into the nature of culture.

Although I had previously traveled to Holland and the rain forests of Surinam in order to dislocate my cultural biases, most of my fieldwork had been among the complex natives of the United States. I had studied members of various social movements, including the environmental, holistic and women's health movements (see English-Lueck 1990a). My teaching had brought me in touch with the multitude of ethnic cultures of America, particularly the Asian and Native American. Yet I yearned to have that intellectual splash in the face that cross-cultural living provides.

In 1986–1987 a friend and I presented a paper at the annual tribal gathering of anthropologists (English-Lueck and Marchetti 1987). We grandly expressed the belief that we anthropologists, with our self-proclaimed traditions of respecting diversity and appreciating the cultural lessons of daily living, would be supremely qualified to study American culture. One of our points was that, unlike those scholars who focus solely on American history, society and beliefs, anthropologists are expected to have experience and knowledge of widely differing cultures. That perspective would allow ethnographers to perceive the unquestioned assumptions and actions that permeate American life.

Later that year, I sat in my office shamelessly eavesdropping (an occupational compulsion) on a colleague who was discussing the advantages of teaching in the People's Republic of China. I experienced a moment of truth. How could I tout the advantages of the comparative perspective from my California haven when my cross-cultural knowledge came from dimming memories and second-hand reading? I decided then to take my family and go east to China.

A TALE TOLD BY AN IDIOT

One of the "advantages" of cross-cultural living, part of the mystique of anthropological fieldwork, is the experience of being a highly educated literate being who is suddenly transformed into a village idiot. I felt this in Surinam, when I asked a young Kwinti maroon girl, in halting *taki-taki*, "What do you call a 'bowl?'" She responded with great hilarity, "Don't you have those in America?" To be culturally ignorant was bad enough, but to appear ridiculous was worse. That feeling of ignorance compounded by foolishness was to be greatly exaggerated during my experience in China, *Zhongguo*, the millennia old Middle Kingdom, an ancient fount of civilization. With such a lengthy and distinguished past, the channels of cultural inertia run deep. The Chinese placed a high value on behavioral conformity and cultural propriety in everyday interactions, and these involved innumerable unstated expectations of what was "proper." As a consequence, many potential pitfalls, both great and small, awaited the sojourner. The insights those *faux pas* engender are an integral part of the favored anthropological tool, participant-observation. By trying to live the rules of another culture, and failing, the rules of the anthropologist's home and host cultures become apparent.

On the broadest level the overt high status of the "Foreign Guest" is overshadowed by a deep suspicion that non-Chinese are not quite human. In daily life I would make countless transgressions against Chinese normality. I could hardly have anticipated the sharp intake of breath from my students that accompanied my first action as a teacher—writing my name. I had streamlined my name to avoid the questions of maiden-married hyphenation, nicknames and contractions. What had elicited such a universal response? Should I have known that writing with my left hand would violate my Chinese students' sense of the predictable?

Like anyone planning a sojourn, I had tried to prepare myself for the unknowable. In the year that separated my decision to go to China from the actuality of stepping on the plane, I had tried to learn all that I could about China, as well as secure a post, all the while continuing my professorial teaching duties. I discussed possibilities for research with my colleagues, knowing that in coming to China as a teacher, I would not be expected—or perhaps even allowed—to pursue a study. At the very least I could study the sojourner experience, the life of a foreign teacher within a Chinese university, but first I had to get there. The road to obtaining a post as a visiting scholar was strewn with cultural lessons.

My culture shock, and my concomitant cultural exercises, began before I left for China. In penetrating the local American Chinese community for the apparently simple task of language practice, I encountered the omnipresent effect of status and *guanxi*. As an instructor, I could unofficially audit classes with relative ease, simply by asking the teacher's permission. But obtaining conversation partners required a more Chinese approach. I sought out visiting scholars who could teach me about their lives as well as their pronunciations. This simple strategy turned out to be more delicate than I had expected, and shattered my egalitarian expectations. As a professor, even a lowly one, visiting students might be uncomfortable with me, just as visiting professors would be uncomfortable with American student conversation partners. The status difference was a problem. The Chinese solution was for my culture-broker colleague to arrange introductions to visiting professors. We could then mutually share our languages and cultures, a solution that met the requirements of Chinese propriety.

My first partner was from Taiwan and later suggested his acquaintance, an engineer from a Southwestern province in the heart of the People's Republic. My first impulse was to call the engineer directly, an approach doomed to founder as I encountered another aspect of the complexities of *guanxi*. The culturally appropriate action was once again to call on my high status colleague to arrange an introduction. This gesture turned out to be a critical move.

Securing a position turned out to be another experience of pre-departure culture shock. Using the "standard" application procedure—sending a letter of intent, credentials and references—elicited virtually no response. Only by using the connection with my eminent Chinese-American colleague could I begin to enquire about a position. He had taught in Hunan province, and we assumed that would be my destination. My husband and I corresponded with one institution that had already accepted one of my former students as an English teacher. We were given tentative acceptance. I accelerated my language lessons and departure plans. We got passports, and shots, and arranged for the HIV antibody test required by the Chinese. Then came the letter saying the institution would not be ready for us in the fall of 1988, but perhaps in the spring of 1989 instead. More uncertainty prevailed until we received another invitation from a technical institute of somewhat lower status. The position sounded challenging, and it was far less tentative. I intensified my practice conversations with visiting Chinese scholars, including the engineer from the Chinese Southwest. He graciously offered to forward my resume to his university, in case the other opportunity should fall through.

In July, I was scheduled to make my annual trek from California to the Pacific Northwest, where I taught summer school. Awaiting me was a telex from the engineer's "key" university. Both my husband and I could teach in the language institute, a well-regarded organization designed to prepare scholars going abroad. We accepted the positions, scrambled to pack our belongings, arranged—with help from my Chinese-American colleague—for our visas and boarded the plane by August. We received our visas via express mail the day before we left. Thus came our first lesson in Chinese sojourning: never underestimate the power of personal connections, *guanxi*. When the ordinary channels of bureaucracy fail, personal relationships provide a way.

Armed with a handful of storybooks on travel to entertain our then three and a half-year-old daughter, we boarded our eighteen hour flight. In Hong Kong, we boarded the Civil Aviation Administration of China (CAAC) hopper to Guangzhou where we would wait to catch our final flight five hours later to our southwestern destination. Welcome to culture shock, first class. When we arrived in Guangzhou, Canton, there were virtually no cars in the airport, only bicycles. It was the first time I had ever seen bicycles in an airport. The air was hot and heavy with humidity—it smelled organic, of coal and humanity. I did not realize at the time, but I missed the "proper" smell of sun-transformed fumes from combustion engines. Intellectually, I knew that ethnocentrism, the sense that one's own culture was "right," was a visceral reaction, but I had not realized it was so powerfully olfactory.

What was worse, my Chinese dialect would have been more appropriate 500 kilometers to the north. After several failures at communication, I eventually spoke Chinese to a young girl who actually understood me. We talked about my daughter, Miriam, who was soon given the Chinese nickname "Mimi"—"kitty, kitty." Throughout our journey, she proved to be the key that opened doors for us. She made us human. Through her, connections could be made. Eventually presents would be given to her, establishing a *guanxi* link with us. In the Guangzhou airport we were getting our first glimpse at the stir she would create. We had a certain entertainment value, judging from the reactions of those around us. This jocularity was another facet of the "village idiot" phenomenon. We did not walk, talk or eat properly. We were high-status foreigners who knew less than kindergartners. The fact that one of us was a kindergartner only exaggerated the effect.

We wandered back into the main waiting area of the airport, the only foreigners, probably because the more seasoned travelers had gone into the air-conditioned area we knew nothing about. After many hours we figured it was time to check in; we could have done so long before. The shock of procedural ignorance was highlighted at the Guangzhou airport. Even in American airports I had been struck by the mysteries of pre-flight activity, a marvelous example of implicit culture. How did uninitiated travelers know how to find "gates" and where to check in? Even if most airline passengers were vaguely familiar with the events surrounding preflight activity—baggage and ticket check-in, seat assignment, security check, gate assignment—how did they discover the sequence? There are no explicit lessons, only the inexplicit rules that hint at lines, counters, monitors and niches for competing airlines. Having mastered American and European "models" of action, it had never occurred to me that the Chinese system would be so different. Gone were the diverse airlines, to be replaced by one state system. Gone was the computerized verification that one was in the right place at the right time. My usual cues had vanished. I was further dismayed to discover that just as Chinese internal currency, *renminbi*, could not be exchanged for hard American dollars, our "international" tickets were not valid and would serve only when converted to the proper domestic flight tickets.

We recognized our city on the loudspeaker and miraculously made it into the right line with the right tickets, but we did not accomplish this feat alone. A Taiwanese businessman, amused and helpful, initiated us into the mysteries of Chinese airport behavior. We also met a foreign teacher from New Zealand who had lived in Fujian as a student, and was now going to Sichuan to teach. Such old China hands, or a least young China fingers, provided a lifeline for us during our journey. They could explain what would be perfectly obvious to the Chinese, who would naturally find it hard to explain in detail what were, to them, ordinary "natural" actions.

Aboard the plane, olfactory culture shock continued. On the plane the air conditioning did not work as we were accustomed, and the fragrance of garlic, sweat and tobacco was intense. We were given crackers that looked like Ritz, but were actually "Fancy Smell Biscuits," certainly an acquired taste. That moment of biting into the cracker, expecting the familiar sweet and salty, and getting instead herbal savory, exemplified the culture shock experience for me. It may *look* Western, but it *is* not.

Upon our arrival we took up abode in a "foreigners'" compound on our university's campus, dubbed with that village idiot tone again—the "Panda House." Cement and square, surrounded by iron work, it combined the grim functionalism of Soviet-style architecture with a greener, "Chinese garden" atmosphere. On the bottom floor was the dining hall, open to visiting Chinese and foreign faculty. Past the reception checkpoint, a single stairway led up the four floors to the top of the building. Most apartments had one bedroom, one living room, a kitchen and a bathroom. The end units, of which ours was one, had two bedrooms. The building was backed by taller units that housed the permanent Chinese faculty and their families. Across the street a new compound, more hotel than apartments, would be built during our stay, to house the influx of foreign and visiting Chinese students. A short walk down this lane led to the back gate of the university. Outside that gate was a flourishing peasants' "free" market, not as thrifty as the massive *daxue lu* (University Street) market a kilometer away, but more convenient. Eventually, we would learn the necessary hand signals, appropriate prices (eavesdropping was again useful) and the tricks of buying live chickens. Initially we astonished, and greatly amused the local peasants by buying fruit with "FEC," foreign exchange certificates available only to those foreigners—foreign experts, tourists and businesspeople—with hard currency to exchange.

We arrived in the Panda House as the latest members of a multinational team of educators. There were six other Americans, three British experts and a rotating entourage of visiting Westerners. Some had extensive Chinese experience, but others lacked even our purely scholastic knowledge. Most were language teachers in either the Foreign Languages Department or the more entrepreneurial language center. The select elite were visiting scholars—European, North American, overseas and native Chinese with valued technological expertise. This ephemeral collection of expatriates and visitors comprised the core of our day-to-day social life. Their illnesses, cares and anxieties became our own.

Equally important were our local Chinese colleagues—fellow instructors or professional intermediaries from the foreign affairs office—who taught us the parameters of our jobs, often by riding herd on this collection of unpredictable foreigners. Some of these people, along with other intellectuals in our university, became friends and cultural guides, instructing us in the rhythms and daily practicalities of life in a Chinese megalopolis.

Students completed the final major element of our newly invented social life. The chance to teach the teachers, to sinicize, however marginally, their Western instructors, seemed to be an overpowering challenge in which they took great delight. Those interactions formed the basis of enduring bonds.

Our associations with students were diverse, ranging from tightly controlled classroom experiences to the informal pleasures of food and friendship. The students would meet us in classrooms for structured exercises. Chinese pedagogical technique is biased toward "skill and drill," favoring lectures, repetitive exercises and practice examinations. Depending on the kind of program and concomitant examination, students would favor different approaches to language pedagogy emphasizing writing, academic skills or speaking. Those who were expected to work with visiting scientists were interested in understanding the possible cultural pitfalls inherent in intercultural interactions. Many students were simple intrigued by the opportunity to talk to living, breathing aliens. For my ethnographic purposes, the verbal exchanges were the most fruitful.

Such cultural discussions could reveal a wealth of information. Penetrating questions about America would reveal my unconscious assumptions. Discussion about Chinese customs would be informative. Beyond the verbal content, the manner and style of discussion could point to sensitive issues in contemporary Chinese culture. For example, I would be grilled about the practice and meaning of various Western holidays. In the same vein I could inquire about Chinese holidays. These topics would then spill over into casual discussions on other social occasions. In one class that discussed "Western holidays" I innocently asked my students to discuss the rituals and meanings of the chief holiday, *chunjie*, Spring Festival, or Chinese New Year, as the overseas Chinese world calls it. In my naivete I did not consider this question to be a particularly politically sensitive, for the rituals for family worship had existed, in some form, since the third century B.C. (Goodrich 1991, 29–72). The era of ultraleftist condemnation of traditional Chinese culture ended with the 1970s. In response to my inquiries, I heard the standard litany about food, travel and fireworks (the last-named since banned). I asked if this were a "family holiday" in the sense of the recently studied Western Christmas—a time when family is expected to gather. Indeed, yes, it was. Then a curious hesitancy appeared. One person added, "sometimes the ancestors are remembered." He looked around at his peers. "With pictures." Another added, and "sometimes we . . . bend our knees." There was a pause and once more the room was examined to judge peer reactions. Another added, "Yes, we kneel." Yet another voice said "And then we touch our heads to the floor," and another chimed in, "Three times." Amid laughter, there was then a cascade of descriptions. Braving censure, several scientists admitted following "superstitious" and clearly patrilineal rituals. What struck me was both the need to hesitate and the enthusiasm with which the discussion was later conducted. Nor were they particularly worried about my reaction; it was peer judgment that was at issue.

Becoming able to recognize these moments of significance is the point of participant-observation. A classroom incident such as this could touch off days of casual discussion. One tidbit that emerged was that *chunjie* was far more important than *guo jing ri*, National Day. After all, New Year's celebrated thousands of years of being Chinese, whereas National Day only celebrated mere decades of being socialist. Such comments would provide a vital clue to deep-seated values of Chinese identity.

In our day-to-day life as educators, we had to comprehend the consequences of the "stratigraphy of Chinese universities,"[1] (a feature to be discussed in greater detail in the next chapter). The educational institutions of China in the late 1980s were built on layers of shifting policies. The foundation was the Confucian institution, existing only to prepare candidates for the all-important exams that would make or break fledgling officials. In the early part of the twentieth century, this structure was transformed by Christian missionaries who brought an influx of educational ideas from the West, particularly Dewey's seminal theories on education and democracy. After the 1949 revolution, the Soviet model of education produced the next layer—narrowly focused, ideologically pure, practical disciplines. The role of ideology became paramount in the next dark layer, the Cultural Revolution. *Guanxi* increased in importance as the traditional infrastructure disintegrated.

The most recent layer was formed by the Four Modernizations, which continue to change the politics and scope of intellectual life. The tectonic shifts of competing paradigms have jumbled the layers so that in any particular interaction, some part of each layer appears. In my conversations with students and colleagues, an air of respect, gentility and status awareness reflected the old Confucian ideal. Yet I might be talking to someone trained in the narrow Soviet model of engineering, who lacked a broad educational background, but who had suffered humiliation and dislocation during the Cultural Revolution for studying a clearly Western discipline. Now that same person, based in a university that was once a missionary school, must master the ways of the West to communicate with European, Australian or American counterparts who would provide facilities and expertise for his research.

Specific contradictions inherent in this multilayered multicultural system would pop up in daily teaching life. Every Thursday, program staff would meet to discuss the oral classes and general administrative problems. The meetings were occasionally quite lively, with agendas and memos flying. The act of giving grades provides a useful illustration of cultural discontinuities between Western expectations and Chinese realities. The scores I gave, based on tests and class assignments, would only be approximations or suggestions of the final grades. The main office would assign final grades based on a variety of issues, including a student's rank and *guanxi*. Someone with good *guanxi* might well receive a higher mark than a competent student with less important connections. It is akin to the American academic practice of granting athletes special academic consideration.

Another typical conflict occurred when it was found that the students knew official test dates before the foreign teachers did, which caused the "experts" to lose face. From the European and American point of view, this flew in the face of academic protocol. It was, however, consistent with the idea that the Chinese should be privy to information before the "outsiders," academic status notwithstanding.

Our students were not passive objects of the instructors' and administrators' policy, but exerted a profound influence. Students not only had family connections to consider but were themselves influential individuals. The institute in which we worked contained money-making programs that recruited students who did not fit the youthful profile of the typical undergraduate. Our students were recruited from within the teaching ranks of our *danwei*, our work unit.[2] Students were recruited from local and national work units—other universities, technical institutes, engineering firms, hospitals, municipal and provincial agencies—yielding a broad canvas for creating connections.

The institute offered several separate programs, each with a different level of prestige. The bulk of my own students were established intellectuals with the highest prestige and English competency level. In theory we had a pre-departure program designed to prepare scientists for study and research abroad, but in reality the main purpose was to help the students pass their various exams. The most difficult exam required an interview with a native speaker of English. Topics would touch on the scholars' fields—physical science, computer science and math, social science, medicine and life science, or engineering—as well as family, home-town, and career. Such a format was unlike a standardized written English exam and made the students nervous, and therefore eager to practice speaking with a native speaker—that is, me. This later proved to be a critical factor in my research.

As I grew to know more Chinese people, I found myself questioning the highly charged literature on Chinese collectivity, and even the notion of collectivity itself as understood by behavioral scientists. Informed by the literature in psychological anthropology and cross-cultural psychology, my notion of Chinese "self" was abstract, monolithic and inaccurate. In Chinese society, lurking below the surface of conformity is a lively and chaotic array of individual actions and motivations. Just because the locus of control is elsewhere, that is, the government, individual Chinese cannot be said to be without clear opinions and feelings.

An axiom in the Western academic community states that the Chinese are a highly "collective" people, driven not by individualism[3] but by the welfare of the group. This idea is reinforced by the behavioral conformity observable from the outside—fifty synchronized disco dancers all doing the same steps at the same time, or kindergartners locked in classroom-wide uniformity (Mathews and Mathews 1983, 384; Tobin, Wu and Davidson 1989, 84). The Chinese themselves and a few social scientists (Pye 1991, 445; Yang 1986, 116) as well have mixed feelings about this notion, suggesting that Westerners might be attributing more group feeling than is actually warranted. The metaphor employed, courtesy of Sun Yat-sen, is that the Chinese are a "plate of sand." While it is true that the group is highly valued, and the state overtly praised, the essence of interaction within the group is idiosyncratic and *personal*, reflecting relationships between individuals and their intimates. The motivations, undiscussed and therefore invisible, might be far more individualistic than the official spoken versions would suggest.

The Chinese do not have one voice, but many. Uniformity of behavior need not reflect conformity of thought. As has been noted before, being Chinese is less a commitment to a collective notion than to one another. China is thus a network consisting of "billions of individual relationships" (Mathews and Mathews 1983, 5).

I had come to China expecting to find a laboratory for collectivism, but instead discovered that my own notion of the distinction between individualism and collectivism was inadequate. These are slippery terms, defined by vague parameters and composed of various differing components. Hui and Triandis (1986) tried to discover how anthropologists and psychologists use these terms. The professional stereotypes, and therefore the working definitions, are that a collective culture's primary orientation is directed to the in-group, stressing harmony and interdependence. The assumption is that collectivists "care" more about people (1986, 230–231). In contrast then, an individualistic culture is defined as one that focuses on self and nuclear family and minimizes in/out-group orientation (Gudykunst and Ting-Toomey 1988, 40–43).

This grand definition is too absolute and essentialist for my purposes. Studies that merge Singaporean, Hong Kong, Taiwanese, mainland and overseas Chinese into a single essential Chinese national character will miss the impact of shifting familial, bureaucratic and work structures on how people evaluate their experience, that is, create values. Even within a single polity, do peasants from rural Yunnan prioritize their reality in the same way as an urban Beijing intellectual? Do answers on an abstract form that asks us to rank whether we honor our elders really generalize to how we think, talk and treat our cranky uncles?

I do not propose to abandon the concept, but instead suggest that the abstraction of collectivism be *refined* and *contextualized*. Finer distinctions must be proposed (see Schwartz 1990). Do "the Chinese" always place a value on empathy, face and sharing? How are these values used to draw distinctions between the in and outgroups, to create identity? What are the values directed at the outgroup? Within a society, who is supposed to act on these community-oriented values? Everyone, or do different parts of the polity have different areas of authority, legitimacy or power?

We act differently in different circumstances. When I help a fellow American sojourner in trouble, I am responding to my heightened sense of ingroup identity. In that circumstance, my expression, my enactions of identity would seem quite collectivistic. Could the proper verbal expression of idealized collectivistic behavior be at odds with personally felt and enacted ideas, thus obscuring the meaning of an individual's values? Could a person "in a collectivist culture" show attributes of individualism in lived interactions within the group? Clearly, there were critical questions to be considered. I was faced with a new kind of culture shock: I had discovered my academic assumptions were too simplistic.[4]

Part of the confusion stemmed from the different approaches of psychology vis-à-vis anthropology, or even more fined tuned, some aspects of psychological anthropology vis-à-vis cognitive anthropology. There is a subtle distinction in anthropological research; an inquiry can approach a topic with an *emic* or *etic* perspective. If employing an *emic* approach, then the anthropologist should retrieve and convey the point of view embedded in the native perception. *Guanxi* is an example of a culturally specific and meaningful *emic* concept.

Once enough of those *emic* cultural models have been collected, an overall *etic* pattern can be discerned for the culture(s) or even the species. Thus, considering *guanxi* along with similar institutions in other cultures, we can draw a wider generalization regarding the function of obligation in Asian cultures. Comparison of different cultures is a solid path to such *etic* observations. Comparing Californians and southwestern urban Chinese models will yield theories that transcend the individual cultures.

In theory, the *etic* perspective yields information that neither group can see about itself. But there is a danger. The theorizing scientist is massively infiltrated with his or her own cultural models and can easily extend a homeland's or a profession's *emic* model to another culture and call that model "objective." This adds to the conceptual vagueness and distortion that so plagues discussions of individualism and collectivism.

One way to cope with that tendency to abstract is to augment the methods traditionally employed in quantitative research that force individuals into preexisting categories—abstract ranking and limited choice surveys. By asking open ended questions, matching uttered value statements with observed behavior and reflecting on the trials of learning and participating in a new culture, a more nuanced picture can be drawn of how individual people place themselves in the collective framework of both Chinese culture and the modern socialist state. Such an understanding is essential to understanding issues of identity. By rethinking collectivism and individualism, I had begun to deal with my conceptual culture shock, that the Chinese "self," and therefore Chinese identity, was not what I expected.

Back in my mundane life, I felt the culture shock acutely, even more than my daughter. Entering Chinese kindergarten with barely a *"ni hao"* (hello), she nevertheless suffered only two weeks of intense trauma before she began to look forward to her classes. In contrast, after several months, I still had moments of resentment over playing the village idiot. However, in the mysteries of qualitative research, culture shock is not a nemesis. Based largely on a psychological analogy of grief, culture shock is envisioned as a process—initial superficial adjustment, crisis and regained adjustment as the sojourner learns to select those aspects of home and host culture to enact (Bochner and Furnham 1986, 130–132). The difference between participant-observation and observation alone is that wretched sense of ambiguity in the crisis phase, placing unchallenged assumptions in the foreground. The struggle to learn and reshape personal identity highlights the features of surrounding social structures, and especially underscores their social meanings.

I watched my non-Chinese neighbors, friends and colleagues try to juggle alternating modes of either identifying with Chinese culture or rejecting it out of hand. Those who were deeply attached to Chinese culture suffered acutely from the knowledge that no amount of competence or empathy would bring them into the inner circle of Chineseness, to be *neiren*. I soon realized I could never "go native" and be Chinese. I would always be *waiguoren*, a foreigner.

Many elements of Chinese life were *neibu*, for internal Chinese consumption only, and I could not participate in them. For instance, I would not be going to the weekly political study meetings with my Chinese peers. With little access to Chinese peasants, other than fruit sellers, I had to create my own corridor through this society. Thus I created a community of expatriates, Chinese intellectuals and colleagues. That was the reality in which I had to live, and as a sojourner I knew I had to make peace with that knowledge. As part of that adjustment process, I resumed my primary role in life, as an anthropological researcher.

I knew that whatever research I chose would have to be intimately linked to my teaching life; the pressures of my work schedule precluded any other strategy. Yet through my university work, I had developed relationships with scientists and engineers from all over China. Would it be possible to get permission to interview them? I began to appreciate the cultural device of *guanxi*. I wanted a special favor, in a sense a delicate one.

Anthropology has not been a favored discipline in the recent history of Chinese academe.[5] When permitted at all, it has narrowly focused on archaeology and the study of China's fifty-six (or more) minority groups, not on issues of the dominant Han ethnic group, the Chinese equivalent of "white Anglo-Saxon." While Han urban anthropologists would like to extend anthropological inquiry to Han issues (Ruan 1993, 11–12), in the late 1980s this was somewhat problematical. The Chinese generally formed a distinction between anthropology and sociology, similar to one made in the United States. In the traditional academic conception, American anthropologists have studied exotic, marginal global cultures, ethnic others of the United States or obscure urban subcultures, but there has been resistance within both anthropology and sociology to recognizing anthropologists who study the Euro-American majority, in spite of widespread work. That sort of inquiry has been placed within the purview of sociology. Similarly, the Han national majority traditionally has been placed within the domain of Chinese sociology; anthropologists study minorities or marginal rural peasants (see Guldin 1990, 5).

In the mid-1980s, foreign anthropologists would not ordinarily be given access to urban Han Chinese, for they are not "primitive" or exotic. Going through the "front door," asking direct permission before entering China, would be less successful than adopting a "nonanthropologist" role such as foreign teacher. In that role, once in China, I could bargain with my currency in the *guanxi* market. I was a native speaker of English, and I could provide my interviewees an opportunity to practice and get feedback on their spoken English.

I submitted my research questions and procedures to the office of international affairs, which was responsible for my interactions with the Chinese, and to my administrative superiors. So the bargain was struck. If I made myself available to anyone who wanted the interview "experience," I would be free to conduct interviews. I agreed wholeheartedly, hoping for ten, maybe twenty participants. I hardly suspected that more than fifty people would grace my doorstep by the Spring Festival (Chinese New Year), and over a hundred would come by the following year.

Ad hoc research design is consistent with the spoken narratives of anthropological fieldwork, if not strictly in conformity with the scientific methods of sampling I had learned. And sampling strategies, no matter how well designed, have a way of being distorted by circumstances in the natural world. No matter what I might have thought I would study, reality would remold it. If I was not free to pick the population to answer my pre-fieldwork questions, I could adapt my approach to increase its inferential power. I had to ask myself the question, "What meaningful questions could be asked of *this* accessible population?" My initial query was descriptive—I wanted to identify what cognitive models of reality Chinese scientists held about their own education, science and society. What elements of their society did they see as helpful in creating a strong scientific sector? What elements were less helpful?

I employed a threefold strategy. First was the classic anthropological tool of participant-observation. I lived and taught in a community filled with scientists and engineers and interacted with them, both within and outside of the academic setting. I could see directly how people actually defined and solved their daily problems, not simply the methods they *said* they used to cope. I learned the hazy outlines of the social rules by trying to be human by local standards.

Second, I collected over one hundred interviews with Chinese intellectuals using the Ethnographic Futures Research [EFR] technique. These interviews elicited the scholars' abbreviated life history and their best, worst and most probable scenarios of the future of Chinese science, education and society.[6] This provided an "ecology of the imagination" as people discussed their emotions and reasons—hopes, fears, decisions and justifications. Again, the indirect, metaphorical nature of the questions allowed people to comment on today's reality in a way that is less threatening.

The technique posed some difficulties. Past, present and future represent a lineal vision of time embedded in Indo-European languages, such as English, but are not necessarily the same in languages such as Chinese that express the future tense more obliquely. In Chinese, there is not a future tense, but auxiliary words, such as *yao* or *xiang*, added to an utterance, which can express intention or desire (Newnham 1987, 112–113, 133). While this structure implies a future, it does not reify it in the same way English does. For English speakers, the future is a place, perhaps unformed, that is subject to all sentences that contain "will." Chinese grammar speaks of the future in a way that emphasizes continuity and connections (Young 1994, 59). This difference in linguistic structure may change the way this interview technique functions. For the English speaker discussing future scenarios is predictive; for the Chinese speaker it is more editorial. I had to bear this distinction in mind as I analyzed the interviews.

The interviews were conducted in my "office," that is, my living room. Tape recorder to the side, I would invite my interviewee guest to sit on the large overstuffed black vinyl chair provided by the *danwei*. As per Chinese custom, I would repeatedly offer cups of tea or coffee, which would mostly be refused. After describing the project and making other introductory remarks, I would ask a series of questions about age, marital status, educational, residential and professional history.

In asking about these personal sagas, I pursued the theme of choice—of tertiary educational institution, academic subject, workplace, research topic. What were the critical moments of decision making, and who made the decisions? How were these decisions then understood, justified or criticized in later life? How did this particular person come to do research in materials science in a university in the Northeast? How was the *danwei* position determined? This was a sensitive line of questioning, delicately balanced with anonymity. *Danwei* designations were a key part of individual identity formation. Although I explained that names and work unit designation were to be avoided during the interview to ensure anonymity, *danwei* names were invariably mentioned, even though people found it easy to avoid using their own individual names. The use of English during the interviews provided an additional screen of privacy.

In discussing the scenarios for the future, I used a chart showing possible tracks of development for science, education and society between now and 2020 in terms of the most desired and least desired outcomes. The interviewees would describe the most extreme possible outcomes in each area and then locate the most probable future between "best" and "worst." Each interview was then followed by a general discussion.

Finally, this "ground-level" research was augmented by a literature search (primarily in English) on modern Chinese history, particularly as it related to scientific and educational policy in the New China.[7] Although I had access to some of this literature before and during my stay, the a priori topics I thought would be at issue in potential interviews were left undiscussed while others grew in importance. Thus I did much of this research after my return to America in 1990 or during my Hong Kong sojourn in 1993.

As the interviews progressed, the pattern of answers allowed me to refine my questions. Issues such as the locus of control—who "calls the shots"—began to emerge. Basic assumptions and values about progress, justice and the role of technology came into focus.

But most of all, the context of the inquiry changed dramatically over time. Up until the early spring of 1989, my Chinese acquaintances were concerned but optimistic about the future. The "open door" was widening, particularly for the people I met. There were critical underlying concerns, but the whole flavor of the moment was auspicious. That changed at the end of spring, after the demonstrations and the tanks rolled into Tiananmen. Ultimately, I collected another set of interviews, in December 1989 and January 1990. The stark contrasts and the even more striking similarities of the two sets of interviews were in themselves invaluable data, forcing me to look at the value of historical context and realpolitik.

In the spring of 1989, I had been wrapped up in my own sojourner experience—traveling, teaching and surviving an illness that required major surgery in the local hospital. I was anxious to get well and return to full-time teaching, and to the promise of yet more interviews.

History did not cooperate. Hu Yaobang died in April 1989, and students through-out China, from Beijing to the Southwest, were concerned over the implications. He had previously been heir designate to Deng Xiaoping until he was disempowered for his sympathies with student demonstrators earlier in the decade. He was strongly associated with social and educational reforms that had not materialized. Then came May 4. This day marked the key historic anniversary of a previous generation of intellectuals who protested the 1919 betrayal of China by Europe to the Japanese in the Treaty of Versailles, 70 years before (see Fairbank 1987, 182–203; Spence 1990, 310–319). These early twentieth century protests had marked a movement away from classical Chinese orthodoxy toward an exploration of Western cultural and political styles.

As the current unrest intensified, I began to feel acutely isolated by my journalistic illiteracy in Chinese. Even for my Chinese colleagues and students, confirmed information was scarce and rumors abounded. Had Beijing cut off the telephone lines to the outside? Were there going to be massive protests demanding reform and a halt to political corruption? Posters appeared on campus and around the city.

Then student protestors occupied Tiananmen Square in Beijing.[8] Local student and worker support was visible everywhere. The hunger strike in Beijing set off debates. Would the old guard now realize that "China belongs to 1.1 billion people, not just a handful of old men?" Or were the students young and foolish, calling down destructive forces they were not old enough to remember? Would this lead to another Cultural Revolution? The worst case scenario under discussion was that some of the hunger strikers might die, and this was unconscionable. No one mentioned the possibility that troops might fire.

The first nocturnal protests began on campus, calling for support from the sleeping professors and students. Euphoria was high and widespread. Hotel workers staged supportive parades. Even remote mountain villages had demonstrations. The student strikes crept into our university. My colleagues and students, a more sedate lot, were deeply concerned and watchful, but, at least with me, were more focused on personal and professional events. Through it all, we, both faculty and visiting students, kept working. I arranged for my second set of interviews. The first person in this group was scheduled to begin June 4, 1989.

On the morning of June 4, my British neighbor rushed into our living room. She had heard the news on her shortwave—tanks were rolling into Tiananmen and students were dying. Soon the entire expatriate population was on the balcony of the Panda House, frozen with shock. Many of my friends were from Beijing—what must they be feeling? By noon I knew.

I actually managed to complete five interviews in the next few days, one a retrospective on an earlier interview. I decided not to continue. I was not a ghoul; I did not want to exploit the pain they expressed. Moreover, it was increasingly becoming clear that with the riots and deaths in my own city, and my own university, xenophobia was rising. Rumors were the only source of information, whether they came from the Beijing grapevine, the Chinese press, the Voice of America or the BBC. No source could be entirely trusted. Tests were canceled. Foreign teachers who were part of organized European or American programs were pulled out and sent home. Chinese friends apologized if they seemed unfriendly, but the price of casual association with foreigners was uncertain. The loudspeaker denounced the lies of the foreign press. In the hallways the phrase "civil war" was bandied about, hotly denied by some, tentatively whispered by others.

Our administrators met with the remaining foreign staff. They told us that they would understand if we left, for the American consulate had advised us to do so. We packed our bags and waited.

Having a timid soul, I kept a low profile. Running away seemed tempting indeed. I have been repeatedly asked, especially by anxious relatives, why we did not leave. What would we do if we came back to the United States, unemployed and broke? Running to a Hong Kong filled with panicked refugees seemed more frightening than staying in our work unit, where we belonged and would be protected. And how could we be sure we could protect our informants' anonymity if our untranscribed tapes were confiscated at the border?

Mostly, however, we stayed because we believed in the open door. If we and others like us left, China's door would be open only to those who felt no ties, no *guanxi*, with the Chinese people. We had obligations to our students, colleagues and friends to remain. Our reasoning was not very American, if you will, for the debate back home was filled with absolute ideas of human rights, justice and making a stand. But for us, sitting in our guest hotel and standing in front of our classrooms, that rhetoric was not appropriate. We had personal ties with these people, and we could not deny our commitments.

As "foreigners who stayed," we knew we could easily become the subjects of propaganda. Although our colleagues and friends welcomed us, the daily discourse became decidedly anti-Western. More importantly for this story, the public media debates became anti-intellectual as well.[9] My informants—the scholars, scientists and technologists—once again had gone overnight from being heroic models for the future to being suspect troublemakers.

We survived. On June 1, I had begun to teach in a new program in which I had far greater control over the curriculum than I had earlier. I was responsible for designing and integrating the program. It had a varied multicultural teaching staff—Chinese, American, Canadian and British—and the weekly assignments were to be thematically integrated so that the students would learn English while learning about American culture. Each week my husband or I gave a lecture on American culture, and topics for English skills courses would revolve around the cultural focus. The circumstances were difficult; June 5 was our first real day of class. I knew that I should be as neutral as I could, being a source of Western culture for those who wanted it, while maintaining a discreet silence on *neibu*, internal political issues. I was constantly aware that talk was cheap. I could loudly disapprove of the political situation around me—but then, I could always go home and leave others to pay the price for my indulgence.

By August break I was weary. I wanted to gratify my wanderlust and explore areas of China that had captured my admittedly romantic imagination. Our locale in the Southwest was the "St. Louis" of the Chinese frontier—the formerly distant province that was nonetheless thoroughly dominated by the Han majority nationality. I had a passion for archaeology, another subfield of anthropology. What better use of my limited free time than to travel to the far western province, Xinjiang, to the sites of the old "Silk Road"?

THE ROAD TO COMPREHENSION

This journey proved to be a transformative experience. Until then, I was only aware of the issues facing my intellectual informants, as I had focused only the data from my interviews. Their dilemma was that while, as intellectuals, they were necessary to modernization their very contact with global science and technology put them dangerously close to the "spiritual pollution" of the West. I could see that this pattern of precarious acceptance had been repeated throughout this century. Yet the larger cultural process eluded me.

When I had worked with American social movements, I could place the events and interactions I observed within the framework of theories of social change. I could trace the role of ideology, and the patterns of recruitment and transformation and clearly mark their connections to the theories of Margaret Mead, John Platt, Virginia Hine, Luther Gerlach and, of course, the ever present Max Weber.

While that body of understanding could be applied to the "democracy movement" in China, it did not quite fit with what the interviews revealed. A deeper pattern of marginalization was at work. While the European, American or even Papuan movements I had observed or studied often had the implicit goal of redefining their collective identity, the Chinese situation appeared to be operating with a distinct historical template. What was that difference? They were clearly negotiating their cultural *boundaries*. What would it mean to be Chinese in the twenty-first century? Nothing less was at stake. Was there a more general cultural process, a deeper set of Chinese cultural values, in effect?

This enigma hovered in the back of my mind as I took my combination of planes, trains, buses and donkey carts along the ancient crossroads of Asia. Being an old hand at field courses, I did not just travel, but threw myself, and my family, into the history and cultural geography of the Chinese analogue to our "Old West." My beleaguered family heard endless discourses on Uighur history, Manichean kingdoms and ancient Buddhist entrepreneurs.

Riding by the decaying Han dynasty remnants of the Great Wall, contemporaneous with the Roman Empire, I realized that the essence of the current drama being revealed in my interviews and in the historical events that engulfed me was an expression of an ancient pattern of the Chinese frontier. The modern "barbarians", that is, me and mine, were to be used and contained by a select group that occupied the inner frontier. That frontier buffer zone would filter the differences to protect the core and yet provide access to the material benefits on the hinterland. The buffer, since it was vulnerable to conversion, was suspect but necessary. I realized that my Chinese friends and colleagues, the Chinese scientists, constituted that inner frontier.

Science as a frontier is a virtual cliché in Western, if not global, folk images. That impression had crept into the popular Chinese discourse as well, although it was culturally a bit suspect. Yet perhaps the image carried more objective validity than I had realized. Were the dynamics of the frontier, especially the Chinese frontier, appropriate for the contemporary denizens of international scientific circles? That was a question that would have to wait until I could dip into English-language libraries once again.

I returned to my *danwei* in September, ready for work, to discover a surprising addition to my work schedule. In addition to my work with engineers, and my other responsibilities, politically tentative programs had been renewed. In the tense national climate, Chinese participation in international programs had been drastically cut. It had not been certain whether some programs would even continue and the students arrived a week before their teachers. The semester had been shortened and the students felt tremendous pressure to succeed, especially since the morale of intellectuals in China had become so grim.

Given this hectic schedule, I had all but abandoned the idea of further interviews. Yet when I broached the subject with my leaders, they were surprisingly cooperative. I confess that my mental state often alternated between exhaustion and paranoia. The interviews that were conducted from late 1989 to the beginning of 1990 were definitely more strained, both for me and for those whom I interviewed, although I certainly had many willing interviewees. Of course, we avoided certain delicate subjects by mutual, mostly unspoken, agreement.

In mid-January we returned to the United States. My husband had a credential to complete, ironically in education, and I had a desperate urge to visit libraries. My child spoke both English and Chinese fluently, but remembered little of American life—it was time to return. Most sojourners' tales would end here[10] but this had been only the first half of our journey. The experience of culture shock includes two equal parts, the venture outward to another culture and the homecoming, which can be more traumatic than the initial shift. After all, a person expects home to be familiar (Bochner and Furnham 1986, 131, 135; Weaver 1991).

We arrived, lusting for Cheerios, and our patient families must have thought us quite peculiar. All we could talk about was, "In China . . . , " and we would be outraged or laugh at attitudes and events that once were so obvious as to be unquestioned. Friends' denunciations of American news media or complaints about the smog seemed ludicrous. After all, there was ten *miles* of visibility here, unlike the coal-filled skies of China that obscured even neighboring tall buildings. A supermarket provided me with a spiritual revelation. Here were endless arrays of cereals, giving the illusion of wealth and choice, so essential to Americans' self-image.

The shock of return peaked nearly two weeks after our arrival, when we visited a friend and took our children to a suburban park. The sheer lack of people there was startling. Where were the ten extended families that should have been there? My daughter, in her default Chinese mode, found the one other family in the park and sat next to them. Conscious that the American norm would be to move as far from them as possible, I felt an odd sense of dissonance.

I was even more alarmed by the complete lack of understanding given to the Chinese perspective. Americans assumed that the Chinese should be listening to the right way to do things, the American way, and that they would "naturally" want to imitate the United States. The idea that the Chinese—even liberal ones feel quite complete without American kibitzing was never considered. This placed us in a difficult moral and cultural quandary. The values expressed by the American press and public did resonate with my own value system, yet the statements were so utterly idealistic, as if the speakers of this rhetoric were caught in a fantasy. The ideals had no connection with the realities of Chinese culture and Chinese life. This too is part of culture shock, a sign that my original intent, to see my native culture afresh, had been successful. It also meant that home was not the ideal haven I had envisioned.

Clifford Geertz, an icon of anthropology, makes much of the process of "being there" and "being here," the distinction between foreign fieldwork and the domestic academic experience. In the fashion of my intellectual ancestor E. E. Evans-Pritchard, the writing of this book is a key portrayal of my message. Just as he, according to Geertz, presented *Images Afriques* (1988, 55), so I seek to convey *Images Chinois*. The beauty of Evan-Pritchard's writing is that it carries this message: that the unfamiliar is not opaque, but "one of manifest vitality, distinct and immediate: recognizable, strangely reminiscent, familiar even, if but steadily enough looked at" (Geertz 1988, 69).

As in China, my research and teaching became my tools for readjustment. I now had access to those historical and theoretical tomes that held the key to the idea of the frontier. I could compare the written works on Chinese educational and scientific policies with the experiences I had documented in the interviews. I could work on cultivating my *guanxi* with the Chinese, both near and distant, and the scattered sinophiles, devotees of Chinese life. The excitement of cultural discovery began to replace the dreariness of reality in my memories of China. It became a struggle not to mentally reform China into paradise lost, or overindulge in shocking students with the exotica of Chinese differences. Through my teaching and research, I realized that not only was the frontier a fruitful metaphor, but also that it would prove useful to place the interviews within the context of values studies in cross-cultural psychology and the sociology of science.

By treating Chinese science as a virtual frontier, one that buffers intellectual, if not geographic, boundaries, I could place this experience in a broader context that would be more meaningful to the reader. This frontier pilgrimage is embedded in the narratives of the Chinese intellectuals. Although they might not have recognized it themselves, it is the historic saga of creating new identities and alternative realms of influence along the boundaries between cultures.

For scholars in contemporary China, the "pilgrim's path" is the open door policy, *kaimen*. Although China is increasingly equipped with graduate programs to train its scholars, it nonetheless still requires that they sojourn in "advanced countries," as the Chinese sometimes call the West, to acquire a higher level of technical expertise. Those scholars, like the Tang Priest and his disciples, must pass beyond their motherland's frontiers to achieve their collective and professional goals. Fueling these voyages is the sense that if China is to carve a dominant place for itself in the world, it must modernize. Chinese scientists and technologists see themselves as absolutely intrinsic to this process. Interviews, casual conversations and the media reveal the hope that the great days of the Tang dynasty will come again, days of unparalleled power and sophistication. Implicit in this hope is the possibility of a newly forged Han Chinese identity, one that will be revitalized by this global exchange.

3

Journey to the West

I remember when you left Great Tang,
And saved me from my torture in the cliff.
Demons have plagued you at each mount and stream;
Your heart was torn by countless pains and woes.
Sometimes you have eaten well and sometimes not;
You've spent your nights in forests or in farms.
Your heart was always set on the Achievement;
Who knows what agonies you suffer now?

(Wu Cheng En, *Journey to the West*, 2:173)

Speaking these words, midway through his journey, the Monkey King bewails the kidnapping of the Tang Priest by the barbaric Red Boy, the self-proclaimed Boy Sage King, amid the flaming mountains of Xinjiang on China's outermost frontier. In typical demonic fashion, Red Boy wants to dine on the flesh of the Tang Priest. Sun has already made several futile attempts to save the life of his Master. This incident nearly ends the quest for the Indian sutras. Sun Wukong wistfully remembers that, although the two have not always agreed, they do share the same goal. Priest and disciple have often bickered over Sun's ruthless strategies. Repeatedly, he has had to make choices, perilous choices, which must balance his unique, dangerously wild talent and his service to his Master. Monkey King may be exotic and difficult to contain, but he is not barbaric and he recognizes the superiority of the Great Tang. To rescue the Priest, the Monkey King must invoke divine intervention from the Bodhisattva Guanyin, the austere deity of compassion. He confounds the demon boy with his Daoist transformations. Together, Sun and the Bodhisattva convert the Red Boy to Buddhism, making him at least nominally controllable, and thus echoing China's historic pattern of frontier mastery.

ETHNOGENESIS IN THE CHINESE "OLD WEST"

The subject of this book is not just the "other"—Chinese intellectuals—but the global journey we all share in the fin de siècle. Many communities lie on cultural borderlands. In China these include not only the cities located on the industrial Chinese seaboard, but also other urban centers in Western China that have developed since Liberation. California's Silicon Valley, Ekaterinberg, Cambridge, Paris, Tsukuba and Singapore are other silicon centers of global interaction. Their border is a virtual one, with old order homelands on one side and interactive global networks on the other. Like all frontiers it is marked by chaos and innovation, as well as culture contact, restless trailblazers, and pressures from the homeland elite.

Living in contemporary China is an all-consuming process. In the midst of teaching and interviewing, I found myself obsessively trying to fathom the mysteries of Chinese policy. Yet, even as I understand their internal contradictions, delineating modern policies in isolation gave me an incomplete picture.

Coming from a society where an object becomes an antique after a mere fifty years, I was well aware that Americans tend to function in an ever-shifting present tense. An American student once named this characteristic "history impaired." But in China, historic parallels, poetic and instructive, permeate discussion, literature and political rhetoric. Such allegorical historiography most often focuses on the ends of eras, reflecting the current sense of "uncertainty . . . " that "anything could happen" (Link 1992, 166).

The frontier is a process, a chaotic journey from initial cultural contact that can lead to stable and often stratified relations. It can also result in ethnocide, the death of a culture. But the journey will effect some change in the cultures concerned. The human species has made this journey in many contexts, with widely varying details and outcomes. In China the modern tale of cultural contact and containment has been foreshadowed by prior contacts from the imperial Han through Tang dynasties. Both frontiers contain culture brokers that channel ideas back to the homelands.

The very discussion of "frontiers" has a markedly different moral context for the Chinese than it does for Americans. In China, where a sharp moral distinction is drawn between insiders, *neiren*, and outsiders, *waiguoren*, symbolic separation from the purity of Chineseness is filled with peril. The Chinese refer to that difference between insider and outsider in culinary terms. A proper Chinese person is "cooked," a barbarian is "raw." Some barbarians, such as the Vietnamese, are considered partially cooked (Braudel 1979, 40–41). In daily discussion, my Han Chinese colleagues and students would discuss an ethnic continuum extending from the Tibetans and Yi, at the raw end, to the Korean-Chinese who were nearly indistinguishable from the Han. Manchurians were very "cooked," but their historical political dominance made them unpalatable. Thus, a Chinese sojourner who must go out among the great "uncooked" is risking spiritual pollution.

In contrast, Americans embraced the "moral potential" of separating from their pasts. In 1892 Frederick Jackson Turner gave a presentation to a group of historians in Chicago. He postulated that the essential difference in the American historical experience was the *frontier*—that it broke down traditional class structures, democratized the West and provided a safety valve for the restless.[1] Turner's frontier thesis was optimistic, powered by a worldview that postulated a special frontier American energy and drive, marked by innovation and risk-taking. The thesis expressed some of the values that Americans hold dearly to this day.

In the last century, especially in the last few decades, Turner's frontier thesis has been debated as a historical approach and as a model. It has been applied in arenas from Australia to Zaire and tested for "fit." Historians, geographers, archaeologists and anthropologists have investigated it systemically and in various ethnographic contexts. It has, of course, been applied to China. The most potent theoretician in this regard has been Owen Lattimore, who influenced generations of scholars, myself included, with his powerful thesis of China's inner and outer frontier. Unlike those who classify China's western edge as a static frontier, Lattimore and other historians note that the border was in constant flux as ancient Imperial China gained control over areas from Gansu to Xinjiang. The Great Wall was less the ultimate defense than a symbolic marker of *neiren*, the inner people, who were surrounded by a buffer of sinicized ethnics and unusually broad-minded Han who could bear interaction with barbarians. Lattimore, like Turner, opined that this frontier was not a liability, but rather infused the Chinese system with revitalizing ideas, and at the same time helped China crystallize its own identity by giving it "others" to measure herself against. Beyond this vital inner frontier was the outer frontier, controlled by nomadic groups possessing valuable resources but who had little peaceful contact with the Han Chinese.[2]

Beginning in the Qin dynasty, twenty-two centuries ago, the Chinese formed a cultural core in which Han ethnic identity was the integral and defining feature. The centrality of a coherent core identity has remained a constant, although the characteristics that define it have changed. Once, being "Chinese" required Confucian patrilineal devotion; more recently, it mandated Marxist revolutionary fervor. In historic China, *landedness* was the defining factor. Both Han gentry and peasantry derived their identities from their relationship to land. The other defining feature was rank. To be Chinese meant being bound in a hierarchy of authority and obligations. Both landedness and a Han-like hierarchy were apparently lacking among the neighboring nomads, although that would periodically change with increased contact between groups. Nomads would adopt some features of the Han political system, just as the eighteenth-century Cherokee would adopt aspects of the British political structure. The distinction between the cultural systems was great enough to symbolically separate the Han from their neighbors.

Yet China was not an utterly closed system, the Han were not isolated from others. From the Han dynasty to the Ming, trade was an essential feature of Chinese intercultural interactions. With the trade came other sorts of interactions—military, religious and political—that joined the Han to a larger Asian system.

Creating cultural-political boundaries also reified—made real in contrast—what it meant to be Han, that is: agrarian, hierarchical, imperial or (at times) feudal.

Lattimore once observed that the Great Wall was not a barrier to the outside, but a "Great Mirror," reflecting the identity of the Han (1988, 240, 441).

In the ancient Chinese West, the Han core viewed brokers on the inner frontier with suspicion. While the inner frontier population was considered partially *nei*, all parties were aware that the borderlands were constantly vulnerable to the lure of the outside and the pressures to indulge the nomadic trade partner/enemies of the Han. The inner frontiersmen conveyed the needed horses to the interior of China proper, and funneled out the requisite silk and tea. As intermediaries, however, they lost their "proper" core identity.

Historic western China expressed its cultural distinction in religion—Manichaeism, Buddhism and Islam—and in creation of a way of life that centered on trade and materialism rather than on land and hierarchy. The Han elite were always in doubt as to whether the frontier populations were more loyal to the motherland, the cultural core or their own way of life.

This relationship between the homeland and the frontier has produced both conflict and creativity. In many historic frontiers, from colonial America to Australia, and certainly in colonial Africa, the needs of the homeland have had the highest priority. From the homeland's point of view, the frontier provides resources and a locale for dumping problematic populations—at the homeland's convenience. For those on the frontier, although raw materials may abound, familiar products from home may be scarce. Moreover, the sophisticated infrastructure that exists in the homeland is not transferred intact to the frontier. Carefully structured colonial hierarchies—be they Han or British—cannot be transplanted whole to the outback. These lacunae in the fabric of social structure force frontier people to relate to each other in new ways, and these innovations—adaptations to frontier life—widen the cultural gap between homeland and border.

Frontiers soon grow their own cultural identity; this process is called ethnogenesis, the birth of a new culture. These distant outposts then transmit elements of the new culture back to the homeland. Imagine an imperial China without cavalries, Buddhist monasteries or the animal zodiac with its "year of" the dragon, snake, rabbit, and so on. All of these were nomadic imports that were funneled through the inner frontier to become essential features of "Chineseness." Like Sun Wukong, the Monkey King, historic Chinese frontiers broke away from a mold of propriety, integrated new cultural elements and thereby revitalized both themselves and their homeland.

In this dynamic process, the frontier society creates its own goals, distinct from those of it parent cultures. Frontier values may overlap, but more often they contradict those of the homeland, thus generating uncontrolled social change. In modern China, where the political climate emphasizes control in order to create a strong unique national identity, this unpredictability and creativity poses a dilemma.

THE BLACK PATH

In contemporary China intellectuals are a key source of innovation. The Chinese word for intellectuals, *zhishifenzi*, the knowledge element of society, technically encompasses everyone who goes beyond a secondary degree in education. Among themselves they refer to the *gaoji zhishifenzi*, an emerging social classification of knowledgeable elite, embracing artists, acknowledged literary figures, and university graduates in the humanities, science and technology. They comprise between 1 and 5 per cent of the population of China, some tens of millions (Link 1992, 14; see also Judd 1984, 156). For the purposes of this book, further distinctions must be made.

Several factors shape the internal differentiation of intellectuals, chief among them being the relationship of the person to the state. Traditionally, Confucian literati were intrinsically bound to the state as bureaucrats, teachers and models of moral rectitude (Hua 1994, 93). The shadows of those roles linger over contemporary intellectuals. Some portion of modern intellectuals, especially the technically trained elite, could legitimately be called technocrats. They are establishment intellectuals who directly serve the state and are active players in the political arena. This bureaucratic role has a millennia-long tradition behind it, but unlike the Confucian literati before them, modern establishment intellectuals have a limited social role.

The modern technocrat is a weaker political player than his predecessor. His role as a teacher is secondary and he no longer serves as an exemplary role model for virtuous behavior (see Hua 1994, 92–93). Nonetheless, the technocrats are gaining power in the military and in regional power networks. There has been a massive shift among China's power elite, especially at the local level. They are younger and better educated (White 1994).

The second category of intellectuals may overlap with the technocratic elite or emerge from the nonestablishment educated who have no direct role in the political arena. Yet these intellectuals have distinguished themselves by vocally expressing dissent. Dissidents have deviated from the "norm" of self-censorship, uttered strong public opinions and become engaged in political discourse. They may be in the minority, as the state insists, or they may well be expressing sentiments that many others share quietly (Link 1992, 256–257). However, their very visibility sets them on a different social trajectory from that of their fellow intellectuals. Whether vilified by the state or venerated by students or workers, they no longer have the luxury of obscurity.

Somewhere between the establishment technocrats and visible dissidents are intellectuals who hover outside the arena of political power. They may share the burden of "worrying about China," but they do not have the means to engage directly in the power game. They must live and work in a reality shaped by those with power. This group of nonestablishment intellectuals is in the process of establishing a "new social base." That base must have a foundation outside the political arena. By bypassing or loosening ties with state-sponsored research, nonestablishment intellectuals can use "commodification" to establish a new medium for possible autonomy (Bonnin and Chevrier 1991, 569–570, 577). The voices in this book emerge from such innovative but marginalized intellectuals.

These intellectuals are in the midst of the turbulence created by the surface current of political power and the deep cross-current of cultural authority. This group is not an overt political player in the state. Neither are these intellectuals disconnected from the state. Far from it, they are bound to it by forces of tradition and realpolitik. They find themselves in a position to create strategies to "outwit the state" by bypassing state power and seeking instead to find the authority and legitimacy to create a new identity and set their own agenda. In his research on "outwitting the state," political anthropologist Skalnik suggests that the "powerless" use knowledge, empathy, consensus and compromise to create an alternative means to set and achieve goals (1989, 3–8). He suggests that a variety of tactics are used to create a legitimacy that provides protection from the state. The powerless can use reciprocity or submission to force acknowledgment by the state. They can try to create an alternative power structure or simply avoid the state. Finally the powerless can revive traditions, creating a new basis for legitimacy that cannot be easily challenged by the state (Skalnik 1989, 9–12).

That quest for legitimacy is the driving force behind the dreams, fears and actions revealed in the ensuing pages. Whether intellectuals are making decisions, justifying actions or speculating on the future of the Chinese educational and scientific landscape their legitimacy is at issue. It is not the technocrat or the dissident who vies for political potency, but the nonestablishment scholar/scientist who feels himself or herself to be the rightful guide to a new China. The old literati roles of bureaucrat, and perhaps even model, may not work for this group. But they do want to reclaim the right to teach, to create knowledge and to generate culture.

For modern Chinese scholars the twentieth century has set the stage for another story of marginalization. Recall the layers of the modern Chinese university—Confucian, Western missionary, Soviet, ultra-Maoist (during the Cultural Revolution) and recently, even quasicapitalist under the reforms of Deng Xiaoping. Each layer has posed challenges and constraints for China's scholars.

The Confucian tradition placed the elite philosophical scholar at the heart of the Han cultural core. From that exalted position the Mandarin scholar enjoyed privilege and respect. Yet, after socialism prevailed, the intellectuals became a potential "rival elite" and therefore came under suspicion. In addition, the nature of relevant knowledge changed. The once literary and philosophical doctrines central to core knowledge were less significant than scientific and practical information. Such information was part of a global, not Chinese, repertoire. The shift transformed the culturally pure scholars of yesteryear into persons who must necessarily interact with non-Chinese. In the last forty years, modern scholars have been repeatedly marginalized (Wang 1991), as purveyors of dangerous "rightist" ideas—expertise, consumer technology, educational restructuring and the unencumbered flow of information. Because of these internal contradictions the "intellectual class" defied categorization. Were they good or bad, predictable or unpredictable?

The very symbolic ambiguity of intellectuals made them subject to "spiritual pollution." For, as Mary Douglas pointed out in her seminal work, *Purity and Danger,* it is the violation of cognitive order that creates "pollution." Dirt is not dirty in a field, but is perceived as pollution in a kitchen (see 1966, 48). When the system is "at war with itself," the source of that social conflict is perceived as "polluting." For example, in societies that emphasize social, rather than legal, domination over women, women paradoxically gain power by being able to subvert that control. Women then, in their ambiguity, become the potential sites and sources of pollution (1966, 170–181).

The folk of the inner frontier, past and present, could be similarly "dangerous." The sinicized ethnics and marginal Chinese of the ancient inner frontier defied clear categorization. Their symbolic ambiguity led them to be viewed as objects of suspicion by the Han. On the modern global frontier, intellectuals—at once both repositories of economically valued and culturally impure knowledge—become the potential sites and sources of "spiritual pollution."

The years following the 1949 revolution have been filled with rhetoric that alternately recognizes their value or their danger. China's policies toward its scientists, who by their very nature must be intercultural, have thus varied widely between relaxation, *fang,* and repression, *shou* (Bonnin and Chevrier 1991, 572). These reversals come unpredictably and are both symbolic and quite substantial in effect. Statements of policy are utterances of *today's truth,* "as if stating that something is true really makes it true, and itself creates a new reality" (Ogden 1992, 3). The truth about intellectuals—their economic usefulness, ideological purity and moral safety—is constantly shifting.

The real-world effect of this symbolic marginalization is the economic and social deprivation of living intellectuals. In 1988, at the beginning of this fieldwork, a survey revealed that Beijing intellectuals deviated significantly from the average worker. They were paid 11 percent below average, but worked an hour and thirty-nine minutes longer per day. They slept fifty-one minutes less and recreated for about half the time. Seventy percent suffered from chronic disease. A national survey noted that for intellectuals the average age at death, 58.5 years, was nearly ten years younger than the national average (see Link 1992, 91).

The interviewed intellectuals were caught in shifting eddies of educational traditions, attitudes and policies that are themselves subject to larger political currents. It is useful to systematically examine those fluctuations, noting the ever changing political contexts, shifting educational policies and ensuing legacies for contemporary intellectuals.

The Confucian and Republican educational institutions of the early twentieth century set the stage for several of the conflicts and solutions of socialist China. The purpose of the Confucian system was to produce the scholar officials that would administer, teach and act as moral guides to the polity. The canon of Confucian texts was absolute, and only a narrow range of interpretation was permitted. Academic "disciplines" were irrelevant, the only salient distinction being between the worthy knowledge subject to imperial examination and a handful of applications in medicine, engineering and mathematics (Hayhoe 1987, 200). The fourteen-hundred-year-old examination system was the key—it determined the status and placement of successful scholars (Lin 1993, 49). This archaic system could not reflect the modernization of the early Republican era.

From 1912 through the 1927, European and American missionary influences vied to shift the academic content of Chinese education from moral to practical knowledge, reproducing their own cultural models. Disciplinary lines were drawn, and the influential European models emphasized the purity of knowledge, shying away from applied science. Cai Yuanpei, chancellor of Beijing University, was seminal in this transformation (Cooper 1994; Hayhoe 1987, 202–203). Late Republican and early Nationalist leaders stressed the American model, creating an educational system that advocated broad exposure to knowledge and emphasized applied and pure sciences "vital to economic modernization" (Hayhoe 1987, 203). During the 1940s, Shanghai came to play an increasingly significant role in higher education, a key channel for transferring technical knowledge to other parts of China (Hayhoe 1988, 258). These patterns would be repeated half a century later. In the emerging presocialist Chinese educational system, expertise, not traditional orthodoxy, became the measure of an intellectual's prowess.

Throughout the period of this shift from "moral" to "practical" education, the scholar continued to be venerated, even as he found himself disengaging from the cultural core. After Liberation, from 1949 to 1952, educational policy was driven by a Soviet model, echoing the European knowledge tradition—separating pure and applied disciplines, giving higher status to the pure. Comprehensive universities were made distinct from the polytechnics. Specializations in applied disciplines were narrowly defined, and disciplinary boundaries were made firm (Hayhoe 1987, 205–207). The formal foundation for the "key school" system was laid. Distribution of equipment, personnel and materials favored certain prestigious institutions. Admission was based on academic achievement, implicitly favoring intellectual and elite families (Ogden 1992, 301). After Liberation, overseas Chinese scientists had been encouraged to return and apply their skills to the new China. Chinese scholars were sent to the Soviet Union for advanced training, especially in technical fields.

By 1955, however, the emerging role of intellectual expert was to suffer a crushing blow. The basis of a core Han "authentic identity" was about to shift from educational elitism to a "leftist" ideal of rural proletariat ideological purity. In the largely politically motivated "Hundred Flowers" campaign of 1956, Mao Zedong encouraged intellectuals to express their observations and criticisms. In June 1957, when this criticism began to turn against him, Mao began an "antirightist" campaign, and some three to four hundred thousand intellectuals were jailed by the end of that year (Ogden 1992, 197). The scale of this "reeducation" campaign is staggering; perhaps 60 million people were in *fang xia* campaigns from Liberation to 1965 (Ogden 1992, 198).

The struggle between agrarian Chinese identity and accommodating alien ideology was intense. While trying to define a modern "cultural core," China has been buffeted by foreign influences. Even Marxism is inherently a foreign idea—born from the class struggles and evolutionary philosophies of nineteenth-century Europe. Mao Zedong thought was an attempt to give socialism "Chinese characteristics." This philosophy harkened back to the land-bound agrarian Chinese peasants and imbued them with a mystique of idealized earthiness and competence. In the late 1950s, the Great Leap Forward tapped into this agrarian population and relied on the notion of their patriotic proficiency. Peasants were expected to create efficient backyard industry and simultaneously increase farm yields on the newly organized communes. The result was widespread starvation, claiming 20 million lives between 1959 and 1962 (Spence 1990, 583). The social infrastructure fractured under the weight of "politically correct" deceptions and massive social restructuring. Sino-Soviet relations chilled rapidly, resulting in further hardships from the loss of trade and foreign aid. Rather than admit failure and lose face, the new revolutionary elite, including Mao Zedong, attempted to purge the alien pollution reputedly responsible for the chaos and purify the notion of core Chineseness.

Older scholars, often the parents of my interviewees, belong to a cohort that is deeply affected by the policies of the 1950s. As a consequence of the shifting political winds, they were left "confused, distraught . . . filled with self-doubt," desperately trying "to get rid of what others alleged were their 'rightist' thoughts" (Ogden 1992, 49). None of these individuals entered my interview sample per se, but their influence is felt in academic life since they are the influential senior staff. They also might be central to my interviewees' family politics—present as simultaneously disillusioned and canny parents.

The need for scholars to be "red" as well as expert intensified over the coming decade, culminating in the misery of the ten bad years from 1966 to 1976, or what the Chinese refer to now as the Cultural Revolution. Political orthodoxy, then the path to propriety among the Han, found its ultimate expression in that decade. The very semblance of competence and expertise became suspect and any bourgeois affiliation with the West was troublesome, if not lethal. The agricultural core of China, the peasantry, was the model of appropriate behavior. Worker and soldier ranks were self-contained and largely systemically closed. As in a caste system, social mobility was not encouraged. The legacy of a landlord grandfather or a bourgeois missionary-educated mother would mark individuals with an irrevocable stigma, an "inherited class nature," xuetonglun.

Universities were transformed by this era. Theoretical knowledge and mental labor were denounced. As theory weakened, disciplinary distinctions became meaningless. Planning, curricular design and materials disintegrated (Hayhoe 1987, 215–216). The newly founded Ministry of Education, the central arbiter of "correct knowledge," increasingly turned daily administration over to the Chinese Communist party in the years preceding the Cultural Revolution (Hayhoe 1987, 208; Ogden 1992, 298). Finally, the Ministry was suspended, along with university enrollments, in 1966 (Du 1992, 14). Redness was paramount over expertise. When classes resumed in 1970–1971, they were administered by revolutionary committees, selected for ideology, not administrative ability. The period of undergraduate education was shortened to three years, and degrees were abandoned as bourgeois. Examinations were abandoned, and "affirmative action" selection created a new kind of student—the *gong-nong-bing xueyuan*, the worker-peasant-soldier student. Even the word for student was transformed from *xuesheng* to *xueyuan*, implying egalitarian equivalence with the instructors, the *jiaoyuan* (Broaded 1991, 356–368).

The marginalization of intellectuals as "enemies of the people," was so profound that I can scarcely convey its magnitude. Intellectuals of the early 1960s, heirs to Confucian, missionary and Soviet educational philosophies, were the embodiment of all that the new Chinese cultural core rejected. They combined the elite elegance of the hated past with the missionary bourgeois values imparted by John Dewey's American democratic ideals. Even the remolding of Chinese higher education into the specialized practical disciplines of Soviet education was despised. By the early 1960s, Sino-Soviet relations had cooled considerably, and having "expertise" was seen as just another permutation of the hated Confucian elitism. The enthusiastic intellectuals of the 1950s, some overseas born or educated, were now the object of deepest suspicion and scorn. Scholars were redirected to work in factories and fields. From middle school[3] students to emeritus professors, intellectuals were "sent down to the countryside," *fang xia*. During the Cultural Revolution over 1,377,000 people were rusticated from Shanghai alone (Hayhoe 1988, 257).

Communities were torn apart as family members, friends and colleagues were separated or turned into informers. Books were burned, and politically incorrect arts were suppressed. Worse, no one knew the exact parameters of political correctness—devout young "Red Guards" could find themselves instantly recast as counter-revolutionaries. Activism was dangerous, but so was fence sitting. Intellectuals were targeted, humiliated and often beaten, some fatally.

The 1950s cohort, called the *Jiefang pai* ("Liberation brand," a pun on the ubiquitous Chinese-made truck) was born in the late 1940s through 1950s. The oldest were educated in the mid-sixties, before the universities shut down. Over 940,000 were recruited as *gong-nong-bing xueyuan* during the first six years of the 1970s. Others, many having been sent down to the countryside, sought their education as adults, long past the traditional age, when examinations opened the door to higher education in 1977. This cohort was socialized into values of "collectivism, redness and expertise, glorification of Mao, altruism and unquestioning acceptance of Party leadership" (Gold 1991, 599). They participated as both youthful Red Guard, rusticated youth or marginalized young staff. Their dissonance between uttered political rhetoric and the reality of lived chaos has led to an ability to "see through," *kantoule*, official truth. They became adept at using the twin tools of connections and the back door, *guanxi* and *houmen* (Gold 1991, 603). This cohort formed the interview pool from which Wang, featured in Chapter 3, was drawn.

There is a large literature on the devaluation of intellectuals in China over the last forty years,[4] especially during the Cultural Revolution, when intellectuals carried a social status lower than beggars. I find it difficult to navigate the "sea of bitterness," the wounded, *shanghen* literature of the ten dark years. The pain is palpable. My interviewees lived and echoed that pain, but in subdued tones—nor did I push them to elaborate. The memory of that cultural atrocity—that specific layer of university history—rested just beneath the surface.

The personal stories embedded in the interviews that follow this chapter clarify the ambivalent relationship between government and intellectuals. It is often hard to discern the quality of that interaction—hostile, submissive or approving—and that ambiguity is built into the dynamics of modernization. A.F.C. Wallace proposed that the process of modernization necessarily introduces new cultural ideas that must extend beyond the mere importation of technology creating a new worldview (1972). Wallace terms the adherents of this wider worldview the "paradigm core." We have met them already—the inhabitants of the inner frontier. This group comprises the culture brokers for imported cultural ideals.

Inevitably, according to Wallace's thesis, even a society pursuing only limited change will also import a new worldview. Innovations cannot be neatly contained, and they will provoke resistance and force accommodation from society's key decision makers. In other words, government leaders may promote *kaimen*, the open door policy, to get the power made possible by technological success. But they do not want the open mindset, *kaifang,* that science requires—innovation, creativity and candid information exchange (Schwartz 1987, 579–581). Those in power will try to resist that change while at the same time encouraging the growth that modern technology brings. Wallace considers this pattern to be the inevitable consequence of paradigm shift. The protestors of the May Fourth Movement of 1919 clearly recognized the connection between social and technological change when they linked together "Mr. D." (democracy) and "Mr. S." (science).[5] The political elite in today's China hope for technotransfer, not Westernization, and so have repeatedly tried to limit scholarship to narrow fields of "expertise," resisting the expansion of discussion and inquiry into broader issues.

While Wallace's interpretation clearly pertains to the historic ambivalence that the Chinese government has displayed toward its intellectuals, it does not convey the depth of confusion that this pattern creates among living, breathing individuals. Having been cast as both heroes and villains, today's Chinese scholars must reconcile their vision of the future with the more conservative vision of the political leaders. Like Monkey and the Tang Priest, both leaders and scientists see themselves acting in the China's best interests.

China has been caught in a structural contradiction that fueled its anti-intellectual episodes; it was trapped between the necessity for experts and the deep suspicion of those experts that was part of the dominant peasant worldview (Link 1992, 240). Americans, to a far less dramatic degree, have also been enmeshed in an ideology that elevated the "common man" to the level of icon and left a legacy of anti-intellectualism. Again, the structural contradiction of the modern egalitarian state— requiring expertise but distrusting the associated potential elitism—creates the war of "the system against itself." Using the logic of Mary Douglas, this contradiction makes the intellectual a potentially "tainted" spirit. In the United States this moral ambiguity plays itself out in playground scorn and a humiliation of the "nerds." On a political level, suspicion of intellectuals has been seen in the black lists of Joseph McCarthy and the contemptuous rhetoric of Jesse Helms. American intellectuals face a barrage of scorn summed up in the oft repeated phrase, "If you're so smart, why aren't you rich?" The forces that contain anti-intellectualism in America have also worked in post–Mao China. A society desiring technology, an effective bureaucracy and a literate public must have a functioning educated class. This inescapable fact has led to a partial rehabilitation of Chinese intellectuals.

With the ascension of Deng Xiaoping and his advocacy of economic reforms, the dynamics have again changed as a modern-day parallel to the "silk route" promotes technotransfer and trade. By 1978 the universities had opened again, and the door to the West was ajar. Deng Xiaoping's pragmatic saying—it does not matter if the cat is black or white, as long as it catches mice—expressed the new utilitarian tone.

By 1975 the direction of China was foreshadowed in Zhou Enlai's January speech advocating the "Four Modernizations," updating agriculture, industry, defense and science/technology (Volti 1982, 46). Deng, in 1978, could then recast "redness" to include expertise, leading the way for the rehabilitation of scientists and technologists who would be loving the socialist motherland by demonstrating "good performance in technical work" (Volti 1982, 47–48). The Ministry of Education was reactivated (Broaded 1991, 361). Undergraduate entrance examinations were restored with heavy academic content. Potential scientists and engineers would be tested on politics, Chinese, mathematics, physics, chemistry, biology and a foreign language (usually English). In the fall of 1977, 5.7 million people were simultaneously tested over the course of a few days (Broaded 1991, 364; Du 1992, 76–78). Graduate exams were reinstated after a twelve-year break (Du 1992, 80), and key schools were tentatively reestablished. By 1979 educational centralization had been reaffirmed as the state once again became the central arbiter of correct knowledge.

Earlier policy themes were reiterated in post–Mao educational reforms during the critical period of university restoration from 1977 to 1984. Some of these reforms reaffirmed an educational strategy that fostered the production of a technical elite. Key schools were tentatively put in place in 1978, setting students on a university "track" that required strict formal education (Ogden 1992, 307). By 1980 diplomas and degrees were reintroduced, separating the prestigious and popular four-year *benke* programs from the more vocationally oriented short-cycle *zhuanke* track. The *zhuanke* level was perceived by students as inferior and represented no more than 10 percent of enrollments (Du 1992, 81, 32). The state reinstituted graduate degrees—masters, by far the most numerous, and a smaller number of doctoral and nondegree programs (Du 1992, 31–32).

Other reforms addressed the need for mass higher education. The state fostered the increase of *zhuanke*-style specialized colleges (Du 1992, 33; Hayhoe 1987, 222–223). The state also expanded its adult education sector, promoting television "open universities," correspondence schools and various kinds of staff "universities" (Du 1992, 34–36).

By 1982 the first "exam-taking cohort" graduated, one portion of which were the older individuals from the 1950's cohort who had been forced to wait until adulthood to attend the university. Others came directly from senior middle school. All had to engage in intensive self-study to "makeup" for the gaps in Cultural Revolution-era education. Those 1982 graduates became the managers, lecturers and future graduate students of the 1980s.

The 1978–1982 period is significant. When the examination system reopened, it acted as a beacon to potential intellectuals, pointing to an emerging avenue to acceptance and success. The competition for university entrance was intense and included several older age groups, in addition to the traditional 18 year olds. One young man, just behind this important educational demographic blip, put it this way:

This benefitted many classmates, especially the graduates of 1982. Many of them are a little older than normal graduates. They are still specialized, but older, with a good education. Many of those college graduates became governors of a county [a rural township], many became managers as a result of this policy. Engineers became managers.

It is instructive to realize that "Wang," the subject of the next chapter, was drawn from a sample of just these people.

Because of the hiatus of the Cultural Revolution, competent faculty were lacking. Many of the brightest students were absorbed by their departments and transformed into teaching or research staff. More than 90 percent of new staff was recruited in this fashion (Du 1992, 67). This intellectual inbreeding posed an ongoing problem. Faculty were desperately needed. and such recruitment was an obvious solution; a former student was a known quantity with preexisting *guanxi* to his or her former teachers. This recruiting pattern also sidestepped the difficulties of changing residence permits. In the early 1980s it became clear that this strategy did have drawbacks—namely, that old knowledge was replicated and few new ideas were being introduced. To address this issue, promising students were selected to go to other institutions for graduate training or even nondegree work, either in an exchange between similar kinds of institutions or to a more prestigious university within China. Study abroad was considered the most desirable solution, and perhaps half of the key institutions would have faculty with some experience abroad (Du 1992, 67–69).

Curricular emphasis, as can be inferred from the selection of scholars going abroad, reflected the changing self-image of the state as it decided which subjects best served its needs. In the early 1980s the thrust of educational reforms was to "catchup" with the "advanced countries," making up for the time lost in the Cultural Revolution. In the years from 1978 to 1982, the emphasis was on building the basic scientific foundation necessary for the applied science that was cultivated in earnest after 1982. In 1983 another emphasis was added to applied science, favoring such subjects as economics, management, international trade and law reflecting the rise of market socialism (Hayhoe 1990, 299).

The rapid structural transformation of higher education begged the question of the ambivalent status of intellectuals. They were clearly necessary for the now prized modernization, but the stigma of earlier years of repression did not simply disappear. On the centennial anniversary of Karl Marx's death, Hu Yaobang, then heir apparent to Deng, gave an address that clarified the official position on intellectuals. He affirmed that the *zhishifenzi* were indeed part of the working class, the *gongren jieji*. He argued against the ancient Confucian sage Mencius, who stated that "those who work with their minds rule people: those who work with their hands are ruled by people." Hu contended that this attitude was a wrong-headed way of distinguishing mental and physical labor. Hu asserted that mental labor is more complex but not "more valuable." Nonetheless, Hu also asserted that the distinction between mental and manual labor will remain—the Marxist egalitarianism being some distance off in the future—and since mental labor is valuable to modernization, such workers should be cherished and given better conditions (Judd 1984, 156–157). Of course, implicit in this statement is not only a rehabilitation of intellectuals but also a warning against technocracy: the intellectual elite should not try to exert rule over the masses. This is particularly interesting given the introduction of "cadre schools" in the early1980s in which "technocrats," that is, establishment intellectuals, were being produced to manage state enterprises, who in turn competed with university graduates for official slots (Ogden 1992, 296). Thus the ambivalence toward intellectuals continued on a symbolic and structural level.

Within this milieu, the 1960's born cohort joined the 1950's born survivors to produce the intellectuals of the mid-1980s. The younger group differed markedly from their elders. These younger intellectuals had been politicized in their childhood years and as they came to adolescence and adulthood, the rhetoric of modernization had flourished. Obsessed with passing examinations and "overseas fever," that is, studying abroad, they focused on their own advancement and material well-being. They suffered from high expectations that were rarely to be fulfilled, leaving them feeling "aggrieved" (Link 1992, 241). This cohort, in their twenties and early thirties, comprised the section of my interview sample represented by the character "Zhou." This cohort came to their graduate training/job transition just as the key reforms of 1985 changed the basic rules of the educational iron rice bowl.

In May 1985 a new round of educational reforms was introduced. By June, the Ministry of Education was transformed and bureaucratically elevated, becoming the State Education Commission (SEdC)—coeval with the State Economic Commission and the State Planning Commission—with Li Peng as its leader (Du 1992, 22; Hayhoe 1987, 196–198, 223–224). The Commission had centralized authority over curricular decisions, enrollments and fiscal policy. It could establish new or eliminate old academic specializations which would in turn shape the direction of future scientific development. Applied disciplines were expanded and integrated with theoretical disciplines. The overall restructuring both emphasized central control and introduced a component of intellectual autonomy and flexibility. In spite of the intellectual "opening" these policies imply, it was made clear that just because the state advocated educational creativity, this did not mean that there was permission to act contrary to higher political authority (Hayhoe 1987, 224–225).

A structural effect of the 1985 reforms was to solidify the two-track system. Elite key middle schools could admit students with high scores or high fees—the children of intellectuals or high officials. Such schools could virtually guarantee university admission, since more than 95 percent of their graduates were admitted to higher educational institutions. Their prestige is such that some can simply bypass the examination procedure and send their best students directly to the university. The key middle schools have priority access to the limited resource pool; they receive best students, materials and staff, even inviting foreign teachers to augment their language programs. They can receive extra funding from provincial and municipal sources, unlike ordinary middle schools. This stratification leads to low morale among staff and students of the less fortunate institutions (Lin 1993, 52–60).

The educational allocation of China is around 10 percent, some 5 to 10 percent below that of other countries (Ogden 1992, 320). This funding is insufficient for the country's needs and has led to creative financing. Throughout the late 1980s the state increasingly encouraged alternative funding—enrolling extra students, collecting new student fees, contracting for research activities or even developing money-making university-based industries. Loans from the World Bank, and donations from enterprises and individuals, including overseas Chinese, supplemented the state funding. In 1987 Beijing University acquired over half of its funding from such alternative sources (Du 1992, 23–24). Unfortunately, not all institutions have *Beida's* reputation or resources, so many lesser universities are in dire financial trouble.

Students themselves are experiencing financial trauma. In the early 1950s, the higher education/job assignment package included tuition, housing and medical benefits. Grants were given to students who had difficulty paying board. In the expanding education sector, the state no longer could foot the bill. In 1987 grants were to be replaced by scholarships and loans. Students moving into unpopular regions or professions could have their loans paid by their employer. To encourage enrollment state loans to elementary and secondary school teachers could be forgiven outright (Du 1992, 82–83). A new policy advocating fees and tuition for university students was debated and as the 1990s approached, experimentally introduced. Even so enrollments in Agriculture had dropped from 6.3 percent in 1978 to 4.8 percent a decade later, while Medicine dropped 4 percent. Teacher training plummeted from 29.5 percent to 17.3 percent (Du 1992, 49). The statistics do not mention that the students who did go into those disciplines were low exam scorers, ethnics and women, whose perceived low status further lowered the prestige of these disciplines.

By the late 1980s, not only were students' finances no longer secure, post graduation jobs were becoming tenuous. Up until the late eighties a student could still rely on being assigned a job, even if the position was unsuitable or unpleasant. Although the job assignment system was resented, it nonetheless provided some measure of security. As the 1980s wore on, the centralized job assignment system became increasingly inappropriate for a market economy. Institutions began to arrange job fairs connecting students to enterprises (Du 1992; 84). Such flexibility favored young Han nationality males with degrees in popular disciplines and good connections, reinforcing the emerging structural inequalities.

The reintroduction of inequality is the key fact of life of the student cohort born in the 1970s. Undergraduates in the late eighties and early nineties aim to accumulate wealth (Gold 1991, 608), and indulge in what Link calls "postcynical nihilism" that views politics as irrelevant" (1992, 242). They are apathetic in their studies (Du 1992, 86), knowing that their connections, not their performance, will determine their life chances. Many of these assessments come from older generation pundits—the "Wang" and "Zhou" cohorts—who interact with these youth as their teachers, older siblings or even as their parents. The fate of the 1970's cohort is the source of much troubled speculation among their elders.

On the eve of the 1990s, the economic reform policies had created new possibilities, at least for some. Two groups have emerged with new roles in this social structure—the entrepreneurs (getihu) and the intellectuals (zhishifenzi). Both reflect ambivalent social status; where do they fit in the larger ranking of social positions? Like the frontier traders of earlier times, those culture broker scholars who want to interact with the "West" continue to be marginalized. This remains so even while technology, particularly consumer technology, is the key to China's development. One informant told me that the peasants and workers see intellectuals' work as the scurrying of insects, without much significance. I was told that workers have staged slowdowns to protest a wage increase for intellectual work. In the era of Deng's reform policy, the intellectuals' condition, linked to income, remains low. In a China where status is increasingly based on monetary prosperity, intellectual workers have few opportunities to improve their condition. Chances to do lucrative contract work beyond the regular work assigned by one's danwei are infrequent.

Yet if China is to have a wealthy and modern future, science and technology must play a dominant role in production and daily life. As peasants and workers are exposed to the conveniences of televisions, washing machines and the like, they will come to realize that intellectual workers, or at least engineers, do play an important role in the China's total prosperity. Thus technology, particularly mundane technology, is a key factor in raising the status of intellectual work.

The scope of modernization has been, and is being, contested. Visible strife was evident when workers and students began testing kaifang—cultural opening—in the Democracy Wall movement (1978), providing the subsequent governmental Spiritual Pollution campaign of 1982. Protests in 1985, 1986 and again in 1987 have continued to test the limits of democratization, the "fifth modernization," and have led to the purge of reformist Hu Yaobang. Zhao Ziyang, "friend of the intellectual" took over Hu's duties in the Chinese Communist party, only to fall with the turmoil in Tiananmen.[6] Within these large-scale shifts, immediate policies regarding promotions, travel, language preference and overseas studies have also undergone change.

The events of June 4, 1989, had many consequences. Some were immediately apparent, such as the placement of restrictions on exit visas given Chinese scholars, which now favored older and politically safer individuals. Official rhetoric was that overseas graduate research was largely unnecessary, since China had its own graduate programs. Anti-Western media comments proliferated. Scholars who had invested in the path that valued international expertise over political correctness were once again in an uncertain position.

The post–Tiananmen period saw changes that were simultaneously reversing structural and ideological reforms and continuing them. Moral and political education was restructured to reflect a concern with a "new orthodoxy" that vilified "peaceful evolution," a code name for the erosion of established party power by Western intervention. Such foreign interference included the donation of Western academic books and the encouragement of international scholarly exchange. The new official rhetoric repudiated individualism (Hayhoe 1993, 35–37, 40) as a potentially immoral basis for a Chinese Marxist state. There was a marked increase in political studies courses and publications, which emphasized, perhaps paradoxically, both the need for market socialism and ideological purity (Hayhoe 1994). History and political studies textbook contents echo Cultural Revolution discourse (Lin 1993, 2). The psychological atmosphere of post–Tiananmen higher education was tense and filled with difficult and often contradictory choices. Should there be a tightly controlled elite system, or should the state promote the much needed and wanted mass education? Should educational tracking reflect tight state control over academic majors and job assignments or the vagaries of a flexible market economy?

The 1993 Document of Reform transformed the job assignment system, funneling a minority of graduates into state-run enterprises. The reforms created new structural options. The majority of students were encouraged to seek "other avenues," namely, the private sector. Job mobility began to occur, and even the system of assigned residence began to loosen. Of course, with such structural changes, the rewards of formal education become less predictable, some individuals benefiting handsomely, and others not at all. Popular disciplines—engineering, law, economics—could charge high student fees with the promise of providing potentially lucrative careers. Yet normal schools could barely keep programs open to train the next generation of teachers. They dared not charge any fees, reducing their financial base yet further. This pattern is likely to widen the social gap between the wealthy and the intellectuals. The children of the financial elite—businessmen and miraculously wealthy cadres—will flow into elite professions, while the children of the intellectuals and the economically restrained officials will be the mining engineers, historians, agricultural and educational specialists of the twenty-first century (Hayhoe 1994).

In popular Chinese culture there exists an urban myth, a parable of choice. In this allegory, a young man—alas, not a young woman—must choose his life course. He can take one of three roads—the red, the gold and the black. These are the routes taken by officials, entrepreneurs and intellectuals, respectively (see Du 1992, 87). In this contest intellectuals are at a decided disadvantage. Intellectuals do not have access to the rewards of officials who have followed the "red" path of political orthodoxy within the Chinese Communist party. Nor can they take advantage of the financial opportunities available to the new entrepreneurial class following the "gold" road. Nearly all my interviewees see themselves as distinct from those establishment intellectuals or party functionaries who take the "red" path to political authority. They are ambivalent about entrepreneurs, hoping for financial success themselves but viewing merchants as rivals for the hearts of future generations. However, they are not wholly despondent about their own path. These scholars see themselves as harbingers of a new era of Han success, creating global scientific reputations and synthesizing traditional Han mysteries with Western materialism. They can, in their own minds, create a new Chinese cosmology.

By envisioning their own identity in this fashion, the Chinese intellectuals rationalize their own cultural outreach, reflecting the subtle difference between *kaimen* and *kaifang*. *Kaimen* means "open door," referring to the official policy wherein intercultural contact is used to permit only a tightly controlled trickle of technology and trade. It is directed solely to the homeland's culture core and is sharply exclusionary. *Kaifang*, "opening," embraces a movement that looks to the outside for new patterns, new ways of life, that are still Chinese, but include a broader range of foreign influences. The sojourners/frontiersmen make an irrevocable change when they turn away from their core homeland's orthodoxy as the model for the future. By invoking a future that depends on the open door, Chinese intellectuals create the potential for innovation, laying the groundwork for cultural synthesis and revitalization.

Modern trailblazers in China have created distinct cultural goals emphasizing flexibility, mobility, exchange of information, creativity and a host of features that outside pundits may lump together as "democracy."[7] Although marginalized, and often discouraged, there is no doubt that modern practitioners of science and technology see themselves as active creators of the future.

There are at least forty thousand Chinese scholars in the United States alone, not to mention those who have already returned home.[8] There are twenty thousand in Australia (Maslen 1992, A36), and thousands in Germany, France and Italy. Some will return to effect change. Many thousands more will never leave China, but will interact with the "sinicized barbarians" who come as foreign experts or teachers of English. Even more will read international journals and watch *Mi Laoshu* (Mickey Mouse) on Chinese television. Some Chinese find Western culture repulsive, but I would be surprised if even these were not profoundly affected by their culture shock, if only to identify those elements of Chinese life they hold most dear.

Culture brokers of China's scientific frontier do not merely mediate between an orthodox Han core and the cultures that interact at China's edges. They have created and are creating Chinese culture. I cannot predict what features of Western popular culture and transnational scientism will find a home in twenty-first or twenty-fifth century China, but I can predict that such a synthesis will occur. The citizens of China's inner frontier will give versions of their dreams of that pilgrimage in this book. Decades old predictions about Chinese culture may not materialize. Age and gender roles are already showing signs of change, but not as much as once predicted for this radical planned society. Individualism and its concomitant features—the desire for personal fulfillment, equity, creativity and personal achievement—will clearly be part of that synthesis. Egalitarian ideals, traditional obligations and a high degree of *communitas* might fall prey to change. The inner frontiersmen will mourn their loss and create innovative alternatives.

The Chinese scientific community does not consciously portray itself as a frontier, except as the scientific frontier image has been internationally implanted, but it displays the frontier ethic. The forces that act on intellectuals distinguish them from the Chinese cultural core. Chinese scientists, as active brokers with the West, function along a cultural boundary, acting as explorers and mediators. Their function is similar to that of European medieval monks, who have been described as "frontiersmen" in the historical literature; the monks too, were point men on a cultural interface, transforming worldviews from their cloistered enclaves (Sullivan 1979). Within this cultural environment of marginality and mediation, such frontier values as innovation and risk-taking are functional elements of a frontier worldview.

In China unlike the United States, however, those values are not used to promote or enhance their own identity, since those opinions are not particularly valued by Chinese core culture, but are instead viewed with suspicion as foreign spiritual pollution. Frontier images do, after all, intrinsically romanticize culture contact and change, the antithesis of an ideal of the cultural core.

As you read the interviews, the optimism they express is tangible. The mythic visions of life that these scholars construct are illuminated by hopefulness, sometimes dimly and sometimes in a blinding glare. For the Chinese intellectual this optimism has clearly traceable roots. The Confucian ethic built an attitude of self-cultivation and persistence in the face of adversity. That particular brand of optimism motivates the individual to act for self and family.

Marxism itself is steeped in nineteenth-century conceptions of evolution and the inevitability of progress (Smith 1987, 43). In the Marxist conception of history, "society," responding to economic and material forces, will progress from slavery through feudalism and capitalism to reach the socialist stage. I detected a distinct lack of faith in that historical formula. But the underlying assumption—inevitable struggle and eventual improvement—is part of the worldview of the interviewed intellectuals. The tone of progressive Marxism, with its millennial social promise, is part of the complex of optimism that permeates Chinese intellectuals' evaluations of their own distant future.

Finally, the Chinese scholars, scientists and engineers are members of a global fellowship who posit that science will provide the necessary solutions to life's dilemmas and that rationality is the most reliable of the available decision-making tools. This set of values, labeled "scientism," is not without caveats, as you will notice in the interviews, but the superiority of science remains an unchallenged assumption.

The concerns of the nonestablishment intellectuals reflect the cares of those on the inner frontier who must constantly try to reduce the ambivalence and hostility directed toward them by creating a new, more positive, identity. They must assess, as they do in their interviews: Who is in control? What forces are most significant in shaping and predicting the future? How can Chinese values be integrated with foreign materialism? Conversely, how can foreign notions of "rights" and "freedoms" be viably absorbed into the Chinese motherland?

The individual people you are about to meet are concerned with policy—economic, educational and scientific—and the ways in which that policy will shape their lives and their children's lives. By now you have seen that shifts in policy have dramatically shaped the directions of education and science, as well as the lives of intellectuals. These people express their concerns by the way they articulate their motivations, experiences and rationalizations. They choose paths and interpret their journeys along their cultural corridors with diverse hopes, fears and images. The composite interviews you are about to encounter in the next few chapters describe the personal journeys of individual Chinese intellectuals.

4

Sage on Trial

The monkey fiend was bold enough to rebel against Heaven,
But was subdued by the Tathagata's hand.
He endures the months and years, drinking molten copper for his thirst,
And blunts his hunger on iron pellets, serving his time.
Suffering the blows of Heaven, he undergoes torment,
Yet even in the bleakest time a happy fate awaits.
If some hero is ready to struggle for him,
One year he will go to the West in the service of Buddha.

(Wu Cheng En, *Journey to the West*, 1:128)

Early in the narrative of *The Journey to the West* the Monkey King rules his fellow monkeys on the Mountain of Flowers and Fruit. He has learned the secrets of immortality and, by tricking one of the dragon lords of the sea, has acquired the ultimate weapon, a magic gold-banded cudgel. Having heard somewhat distorted, but justified, complaints about the behavior of this wild immortal, the Emperor of Heaven commands the Monkey King to come to Heaven. The Jade Emperor then gives him a sham position in which he can be controlled and observed. Sun discovers the duplicity and rebels, declaring himself "Great Sage equaling Heaven." The Emperor of Heaven decides to punish him for his hubris. After a difficult conflict and another "honorary appointment," Sun Wukong, the Monkey King, revolts yet again. Defeated and ultimately contained by Buddha, Sun is placed under the Five Elements Mountain to await the Tang Priest, who will eventually release him for his fated journey to the West. Meanwhile he waits, his destiny uncertain.

When I began collecting my data in late 1988, China was in a time of flux. The introduction of market economy reforms had led to inflation, unemployment and a return of hucksterism. At the same time, there was widespread moral outrage at official corruption—the application of high-level *guanxi* by elite cadres for profit. Value shifts among youth, students, intellectuals and workers (in that order) were taking place at astonishing speeds. Although many people were cautious, the widespread sentiment was that China was taking a new place in the world. In this new worldview, the "Western" concept of individualism—or more precisely, humanism—was at issue. This value set was based on the idea that all human lives held worth and that human minds were capable of reasoned choices. In such a worldview, public opinion would be a valuable and necessary part of the body politic. This is the setting in which the projected scenarios—the future life stories of intellectuals—are imagined.

The information for this chapter derives largely from participant-observation and interviews, supplemented by the literature. The format of this chapter is based on the Ethnographic Futures Research interview. Understanding that method is essential to grasping the structure of the remainder of this book. The technique clarifies values by asking a person to create three clear and distinct futures—projecting three separate optimistic, pessimistic and probable future histories. The first assumes that social and structural problems will be solved to the greatest extent possible. The second assumes that the social and environmental obstacles will remain insurmountable. The third, a direct extrapolation of the interviewee's model of the present, confirms and prioritizes those problems that are most insoluble and those that are likely to fade in a generation.

The interview technique itself is biased toward optimism. After the initial background discussion that precedes the speculation, the "best" scenario is invariably the first to be fleshed out, while the interviewee's fervor is at its peak. So the basic structure of the future universe is designed in an architecture of optimism. Topics—population, policy, economic and social restructuring—are first mentioned in the "best" scenario and often define the discourse for scenarios to come.

Several forces within the New China augmented this preference for the "best" scenario. Proclaiming future Chinese greatness is part of the presentation of national "face." Political scientist Lucian Pye notes that "the desire to bring honor to the collectivity . . . inspires expressions of uncritical optimism" (1988, 62). He also notes that this optimism might be tempered by those who understand the world standard for "greatness." Moreover—and this is not to be taken lightly—optimism is difficult to construe as criticism of party politics. It is thus a relatively safe form of discussion. Of course, as you will see, some of the lines of projection, particularly in the first set of interviews, are inherently critical in that their optimistic scenarios predict significant social and political change.

Practically, interviews are difficult instruments to untangle. In the beginning, I scarcely knew what probes to use to clarify the fine points of the scenarios. The Chinese scholars were not accustomed to this strange form of communication. As you will see in the interviews, even well-disciplined scientists do not organize their thoughts in coherent rhetoric. I am unfortunately reminded of any game I have tried to play that uses a ball and a net—tennis, ping-pong or volleyball. At the beginning, such games involve much serving and missing. I ask questions that lead to seemingly disconnected answers. I ask another question, and thud—the train of thought does not connect. But when the volleys happen, it makes the game worthwhile.

I have been blessed with a few tightly reasoned, highly organized interviews, but most of us mere mortals shift topics, change our minds and contradict ourselves. Speculating about the best future might generate ideas for the worst scenario. A person might be trying to imagine the best possible changes in teaching methods, for example, and be reminded that such techniques require an infrastructure and openness that is unlikely in contemporary China, even in imagined futures. The interview's organizational structure—best, worst and most probable scenarios—was not systematically followed by each interviewee. Not everyone envisions the future as nice orderly alternatives, even with the EFR method.

The inability to imagine beyond daily life experience is another difficulty. While Chinese scientists may work with high-level theory and complex research technology, much of their daily life is overwhelmingly lived in "a low level of industrial development," which makes technological transformation difficult to imagine. A vivid image comes to mind. Early in our stay, we noticed the equivalent of a NASA office in our southwestern city, only to see a water buffalo pull a cart in front of it. Such are the contradictions of living in a modernizing China. This is played out in the interviews. "Exotic" technologies—such as computers—are rarely projected into daily life, banking, or family use. The technology remains firmly in the realm of "research tools." It is hard to imagine a social reality one has not experienced.

The future histories you will see in the rest of this book were based on the personal projections of 101 one people. In late 1988 and January 1989, I conducted my first set of interviews, fifty-four in all. Ten were women, forty-four were men, twenty-seven of those men were over 32 years of age. The older set, Chinese born before 1958, part of the "fifties cohort," were "conscious" through the seminal years of the Cultural Revolution. Many were "sent down to the countryside" as young intellectuals, an important transformative event in their lives.

I have already mentioned my ill-fated second set, which included only five people before I realized that my timing, while historically significant, was inhumane, if not risky. This set began the morning after Tiananmen Square had been forcibly emptied in Beijing, and just as students, workers, police and troops were becoming embroiled in my own city. Not surprisingly, the tone of these interviews is bleak. For once, the "worst" scenario was highly featured and optimism seemed to be in short supply.

The third set of interviews was collected in December 1989 and January 1990. Forty-two people participated; the bulk of them (thirty-one) were younger men, part of the "sixties cohort," and only seven were women. After the June lesson in realpolitik, I had expected far more pessimism, but was surprised to learn that the underlying substructure of optimism was still intact. Only the time frame for successful achievement had stretched to several generations. The atmosphere in which we conversed, however, was far more constrained. There were few bold words about any impending democracy. Both the interviewer—myself—and the interviewee were constantly aware that some topics were off-limits, to be referred to obliquely, if at all. This dance of political discretion will be evident, and it reminded me that I had a responsibility to ensure confidentiality.

Presenting these scenarios in a form that compromised no single person was a challenge and was met by creating fictional composite characters. To achieve this, I looked over the megabytes of raw interview material and asked myself, what distinctions are important to the Chinese intellectuals? Gender, age, graduation dates and historical experience emerged as the defining characteristics. Based on these patterns, I broke the sample into three personae, "average" composites that would use the actual words of the interviewees to express their worldview in the fictional interviews that you will soon read.

While this solution let me represent the modal point of view, it did not speak for everyone. In order to include unusual worldviews, I embedded those views into the questions I would pose in the fictional interview. For example, if someone had expressed an unusual speculation, I would ask in the text, "Your colleague thinks that the countryside will improve faster than the cities. What do you think?" The character would then respond with the majority opinion, in the authentic words of a real informant. Thus, I could include as many points of view as possible.

I compiled the comments of the hundred plus intellectuals, observations from informal interactions, along with my original interview questions, and organized them into topics, finally merging them into a single dialogue. This process resulted in slightly distorted composite interviews that might be broader in scope than most actual interviews. Few individuals can comfortably comment on such diverse topics as agricultural environmental engineering and artificial intelligence; most people confine their comments to their own discipline or vague "common knowledge." The interviews you will read are better organized than a typical verbatim interview, yet they are an accurate reflection of the interviews I actually conducted.

In this chapter you will meet scholar Wang. He is the composite of thirty-five older men, whose ages range from 31 to 45. Within this group of intellectuals were mathematicians, physicists, chemists, biomedical specialists and five social scientists. Notably, five of these men had more than one child—unusual in an era where one child had been mandated by the state for over a decade. Five were childless. Four were married to workers—nonintellectuals—a pattern not seen among the status conscious younger men. None was unmarried. Most had been "sent down to the countryside" during the Cultural Revolution and had been assigned throughout the country because of their critical job skills. Thus many had lived in more than one part of China (geographic mobility before the nineties was highly unusual). Legal residence was strictly fixed by law and policy. More came from Central China than any other region, followed closely by nearly equal numbers from the Northeast, Northwest, Southwest and Southeast. Over a quarter of them had lived or were living in Beijing, and a third had spent some time in Shanghai. While these older men provided the majority of the interviews in my first, pre-Tiananmen set of interviews, only four of them were interviewed afterward. Thus the fictional interview with the character Wang is set on the eve of 1989.

Wang is the average age of his group, nearly 37. He is an engineer but works in a research capacity, straddling the mysterious borderland between science and engineering. His work consumes his time; he could be described as "earnest" in his profession. He is well-read and well-informed, and has an air of cultivated self-possession I rather admire. He likes to discuss world events and is sometimes astonished and amused by my American perspectives. He plays *weiqi*, the original Chinese version of "go," an ancient game of pure strategy in which you surround and defend your territories and attack your opponent's stones. Mao Zedong was a devotee of this game and a master of its enactment in reality.

Wang is a devoted father and a husband. Like many intellectuals of his generation, he tries to live up to the ideal of gender equality as he understands it. He helps his wife with domestic work and is occasionally teased by his younger colleagues as "soft-eared"—henpecked. Back at his home *danwei*, he does the daily shopping, pedaling to the local free market to pick up vegetables and noodles. Once a month he splurges and buys a chicken. Each morning he drops his daughter off at the university's primary school. He is proud that she is learning to play the violin and studies English each day after school. He enjoys his child and is painfully aware that going overseas for an education will take him away from his precious daughter. His parental love is tangible.

His endurance is his most obvious quality. He endured the Great Leap Forward in his childhood. He endured the Cultural Revolution in which his father was tortured and he himself was sent to the alien countryside. He persevered to become an intellectual and is still working to further his scholarly ambitions by going abroad. He adopted a style that is conforming, careful and consummately shrewd.

BUILDING A GOOD WORLD

I prepare for the interview, setting two easy chairs at an angle, not face-to-face, but allowing some room for him to look away. I hope that we will not have too many interruptions, either from visiting students or my curious daughter. Wang knocks on the door and waits—his pre-departure program has trained him in this Western custom. He enters and I offer him his choice of tea or instant coffee, an expensive rarity. Wang looks wistfully at his mug and declines. It is shortly before Christmas, 1988, and the weather is cold, damp and perpetually overcast. I offer again, wondering how many offers I should make before I give up. I pour him some tea anyway, basing this on my understanding of appropriate Chinese behavior, and we begin.

I explain the purpose of the interview, reiterating that I am an anthropologist interested in Chinese science and education. Since my profession is rare in China and has been strictly focused on physical anthropology or the study of ethnic minorities, I note that my work bears great similarity to sociology. I describe the mechanics of the interview—a brief background inquiry followed by the construction of three scenarios describing the best, worst and most probable futures of Chinese science, education and society in 2020 some thirty years hence.

I assure him that the interview is confidential and anonymous. We both know that to some degree, such privacy is a fantasy. He is a Chinese scholar visiting an American social scientist, and although the "visitor's sign-in" at the gate of the Panda House is not strictly enforced at *this* time, his appearance is hardly unnoticed by the local staff. I tell him that I will not use his name or that of his *danwei*, work unit, and I would be careful to edit such material out of the transcriptions. I also tell him I will be taking notes—so I can focus on interesting or ambiguous answers, and so that I can give him feedback on his English communication skills. He speaks fluent English, quite sophisticated, but with the rhythms and sentence patterns of "Chinlish"—the Chinese version of English. I knew he would have problems with articles, tense, gendered pronouns and pronunciation—all common "Chinlish" errors. This feedback was part of the bargain I had struck with the university to be allowed to conduct the interviews.

We chat briefly about mutual friends and events in the university, then I begin the questions that will flesh out his background. I ask him about his age and his marital status, mainly to confirm what I already know. I note his gender on my questionnaire without asking—such a question would be obvious, embarrassing and perhaps even impolite. I ask him about his wife, her job, whether they have children, or more reasonably given current population policy, a child. Wang's wife is a physiologist, a teacher, and they have an 8-year-old daughter. I want him to think of his imagined scenarios in concrete terms, so I take the opportunity to mention that in thirty years, his daughter will be 36, almost 37—his age exactly. He seems startled by this revelation, or at least the American directness with which I ask him to leave the realm of the abstract of speculation for a concrete projection of his self into the future.

We return to the background questions. Can he tell me about his field, his specialty? I know this is a useful question for him to practice on, since when he goes abroad this will be the one inquiry foreign specialists will repeatedly ask him. Wang straddles the boundaries between optical physics and communications engineering. He has memorized a detailed "set piece" describing his work much like my own description of cultural anthropology as "a kind of sociology."

Then I ask him for a more detailed, personal, educational history. He had spent his late adolescence not as an undergraduate student, but in the countryside being "reeducated" by the farmers during the Cultural Revolution. "An interesting exper- ience," he adds wryly. He entered higher education at the earliest moment, 1972, but "no degrees were being offered in China at that time." Students were expected to learn from the workers and farmers; the granting of degrees was considered bourgeois, a symbol of elitist expertise.

Wang is a member of the "lost generation" of scholars whose education was disrupted and distorted by the Cultural Revolution. The group educated after the resumption of university life in 1971, the *gong-nong-bing xueyuan* (worker-peasant-soldier student), was particularly stigmatized as inferior to the examination-taking cohort that graduated in 1982 (see Broaded 1991, 353, 363). Those who did not become officials were largely shunted into subordinate positions as "technicians." Even those who returned for a supplementary fourth year of university were not perceived as equivalent to the post-Mao era graduates. Some of this generation found ways to evade the stigma. Lost generation scholars could gain legitimacy by showing competency in their *danwei* work. In addition, they could transform their questionable credentials by taking examinations to acquire one of the newly reinstated postgraduate degrees (Broaded 1991, 370–373). Wang did both.

The Cultural Revolution ended officially in 1976 with the downfall of the "Gang of Four," the associates of Mao, including his wife Jiang Qing, who were officially blamed for misleading the country's helmsman. Now that universities again offered examinations, Wang took the first chance he could to take the examinations for a graduate degree. He emerged with a master's of science in 1982. That year was a key year for many students in this cohort. It was a demographic blip of unusually old students who emerged from the newly resurrected university system to take positions of scholarly influence.

I want to know how Wang found himself in his current job. I ask him a hard question, one that many of his colleagues found difficult to answer. "How did you choose your field of study as an undergraduate?" He explains that he did not really make a choice, but that the government "placed him." He had never experienced the American phenomenon of declaring four different majors before settling on an interest area. He immediately skips to his pursuit of graduate work, which had been somewhat different in focus from his undergraduate training. His graduate work had been his first real opportunity to exercise choice, although even that choice was constrained by available openings in academic departments. Next, we discuss his educational and professional plans, which he hopes will include a doctorate from abroad. He is careful to point out that he plans to return to his *danwei* after he has gained the maximum education possible overseas.[1]

I ask him where he has lived in the course of his rather complex life. Born in Hebei province in central China, he had moved to Xian in Shaanxi as a child, largely because of his father's relocation. Initially educated in Beijing, he had spent six years in the Shaanxi countryside. Amazingly, he found his way to a graduate program in a prestigious institute in Shanghai, where he remained employed as a researcher and teacher. Such mobility is common among intellectuals. A worker or peasant would have a much simpler residential history, living an entire life tied to a single residential "assignment." Wang freely gave his opinions about the various regions he had lived in, ending on a positive note. Shanghai is a major center for technological development and he feels lucky to carry out his professional life in such a climate.

Shifting gears, we ease into the scenarios. We previously discussed the issues of the interview, at the time he agreed to participate. Now, I remind him of the futuristic setting, in which he is to imagine Chinese science and technology, education and society. We begin with my query: "In the best possible future you can imagine, within the bounds of realism, what do you see as the future of Chinese science and technology?"

Wang sits quietly for a moment and then responds, "Mankind must rely on advanced science and technology to develop. I accept this as true. This would give the best results for China. I am quite confident about that. Generally speaking, science itself is progressing. It has developed very fast after World War II, so I think science will make great progress in the next thirty years. I think in 2020, China will have some very advanced technology and science. There are many reasons for this. The first is after the smashing of the Four, after the Cultural Revolution, the people have more freedom to think. For a very long time our leaders refused to accept any other thoughts, especially from Western countries. But, as a matter of fact, every country has something useful to offer. We are now sending a lot of students abroad. China has an ancient culture and there are many good things about our inheritance. Chinese students are usually very good at doing research work in science, so I think science and technology may develop very quickly. Also, because the current young generation has the opportunity to study in the university and upper middle school, they have more basic scientific knowledge than their parents. I think the Chinese people are very industrious, and they know if we haven't developed enough we may not have gotten our position in the world. I find the future in thirty years hopeful."

This is a classic introductory statement, broad ranging and terse. Each statement is a topic sentence, implying, but not expounding, a tacit paragraph. He has placed a series of broad, quick calligraphic strokes, hinting at the total picture without revealing the details. Wang is implying a wealth of intersecting values—scientism, *kaifang*, national pride and modernization. Science will prevail. The West, now open to the Chinese people, will provide the catalyst to revitalize the Chinese scholastic tradition. The opportunities of modernization will provide the basis for improvements, creating a China that will take its place in the world.

Testing the parameters of that future, I ask, "In the best scenario, how will China stand in the world regarding science and technology? Some of your colleagues have thought that it will take one hundred or two hundred years to reach parity with the West, others have thought that parity in science and technology can be achieved in as little as thirty years. What do you think?"

"I hope the distance between China and the developed countries will be reduced. Of course this depends on many factors such as economics and government policies. I think the most important thing is government policies. If the government can continue the open door policy and the economic reform policy, I think science and technology will be developed very quickly."

I experience a curious sense of having heard all this before. Indeed, the same phrases had been repeated dozens of times in conversation and interviews.[2] I had come to recognize certain turns of phrase about modernization, technologies and education. Many came from essays in the newspaper; I could track them in the *China Daily* translations from the *People's Daily*. The language was formal, and the responses were nearly ritualized. *Tifa*, ways of mentioning, are part of a patterned style of speaking that is both prudent and proper. Improper behavior can be described as *buxiangyang*, "not resembling the pattern," or *buxianghua*, "not resembling the words" (Link 1992, 9–10). Words become the means by which propriety can be recognized. As Link notes, "official use of words, at its cleverest, resembled a go player's placing of stones: perhaps initially of opaque intent, yet well considered, sometimes sophisticated, and always with a final goal in mind" (1992, 8).

The conventional presentation may make the speaker seem stilted or insincere. Yet even in America, a conversational or editorial debate on sizzling topics, such as abortion or immigration, produces similar ritualized discourse. Rarely are original arguments generated on these culturally significant issues. However, the simple fact that an argument is culturally standardized does not mean it is not deeply held. Americans who believe immigrants hurt the economy do so fervently. Wang holds his opinion equally as dear and "places his stones" with great care.

"I hope the distance between China and the United States in science and technology will be reduced in twenty years or ten years, but I think it would be difficult to do in only ten years. The gap will not disappear, but it will grow smaller in a few areas. But because my country is so poor, a third world nation, I think our country can be as rich as Taiwan or Singapore now, but not as rich as Western countries, even in thirty years. While we are making up the gap, the Western countries are going even faster and faster."

To this point, the discussion has been fairly abstract, and I want to get a more direct opinion from Wang. He is in research, and I want to know how his point of view is reflected in his projections. In the United States and Japan, tighter funding has led to a systematic reorganization toward practical, not theoretical, projects that will yield short- or middle-range results. China is far more strapped for research funds, so I want to know if he has experienced a similar fate. Are the market forces that are changing the goals of global research at work in Deng Xiaoping's China? So I ask, "Will this change apply to both scientific research and the development of applied technology?"

"I think the Chinese system of science and technology is shifting from theoretical research to more practical research now, and will continue to do so in the future."

I echo his main point, trying to make sure I have understood him correctly and hoping for some elaboration. "So there will be more applied research? What is causing this change?"

Wang replies, "Yes, the managers of new enterprises are pushing practical technology. As you know, the economic reforms have created a new market system and the businesses must compete with one another. If they are able to create new technologies, they will succeed. Now we can see the impact of this process on research and development. Some scientists do not want to continue their basic research but want to change to practical research. There is already a shortage of scientists in basic research. Now, we are just at the beginning of this trend. So, I think the development of science will not be as good as technology's. I'm less confident about the future development of theoretical research. Basic science development depends on the efforts of leading scientists, but now their situation is poor."

"Poor in what way? Can you give an example?"

"In the sense of income. As a result of government policy, many engineers have an opportunity to earn money through private ventures. They can increase their living standard. But some research scientists work even harder than engineers. Their work is more complex than an engineer's, but you cannot see the results of their research in the marketplace. So they cannot get any extra income from their results. They can only receive a salary from the government."

"Will this pattern continue even in the best future?"

"I think this is a difficult question. It would be difficult to improve this situation. A few years ago we realized this unfortunate situation was occurring. We tried to improve the situation, but we haven't obtained good results. Once the reforms had introduced a market for inventions, but not basic long-term research, it became difficult to change."

Wang is describing the social trap that befalls all research. Once the reward system has been structured to reinforce short-term profit and production, the longer range generalities that generate new scientific paradigms are shorted. Such basic research may lead to too many unproductive "dead-ends" and tie up too many resources to be "cost-effective." Bell Labs, IBM and Apple have all made such decisions.[3] Apparently so has the central government of China.

He embarks on a litany of potential Chinese successes reflecting "common knowledge" about scientific culture. His list includes those subjects believed to be the special domain of Chinese genius—mathematics, artificial intelligence and genetic engineering. One arena, medicine, shows particular promise. It is an area in which Western rationalism can be blended with traditional Asian culture—increasing China's face in ways that both Han and foreigners would recognize as significant.

Wang notes, "If Chinese traditional medicine has a breakthrough in theoretical research, this would be significant. In fact, Chinese traditional medicine is very effective, I should say, especially in curing some chronic problems. Chinese traditional medicine is quite efficient, even for curing colds, but at this time there is no scientific or systematic theory system that can explain its effectiveness. But some people are doing research in this area in the Science Academy of China. They are doing research and trying to understand the meridian system of acupuncture. They are using instruments to detect this system, and they find that out it's quite similar to the traditional system we have inherited from our ancestors. This similarity may lead to a great breakthrough. Some Japanese scientists are very interested. They have similar cultural traditions and they are doing comparable research. If we can make a breakthrough in this field, it will be a great discovery for world medicine. Especially if we can combine traditional Chinese medicine and Western-style medicine."

I know from my previous research on American traditional medicine that China is trying to make the ancient paradigm of herbal, energetic holistic medicine mesh with the world of biochemistry and reproducible results. It has had mixed success, winning global fans from the traditional medical communities but leaving many rationalists unconvinced. Chinese medicine, however, is more than a matter of curing. It is a matter of national pride, reflecting millennia of experimentation and philosophy. If Western medicine could be merged with the honored traditions of acupuncturist and herbalist, then perhaps other syntheses are possible.

He waxes eloquent on his own field of optical physics and lasers for a few minutes; then his optimism is shaken as he considers the future of education—a field with which he is intimately familiar. He bluntly states, "The state of economics is such that there is not a whole lot more money to give to science education, or any education! The government at the moment can only gradually increase educational funding."

As this seems a shade less than optimal, I ask, "Even in the best possible future?"

"Yes. But I think if our economy improves, the situation in education will improve. Our government currently hasn't enough money to invest in the educational system, but if this situation can be changed, our whole educational system will be improved. We wait and do our best in the meantime."

"So the situation largely depends on educational funding? If education can get more money, it will do better?"

Wang then explains the connection between policy, money and educational fortunes, a complex relationship. "Recently, our government has issued some policies to encourage people to do business ventures. This new policy has a great influence on the students, and therefore on educational and scientific systems. Many, many students don't want to continue their studies, but instead want to pursue business. Teachers are becoming increasingly frustrated. I think it is very dangerous for the Chinese nation. I think this phenomenon is not natural."

His use of the word "natural" hints at a moral violation. Respect for education, despite his own personal experience of the contrary, is part of the proper cognitive order of his cosmos. It is a core value that he then goes on to confirm, "I think this phenomenon will be changed. I think this behavior is not suitable for the Chinese character. If you review Chinese history, you can see that the Chinese have always put education first—business comes last, sometimes second."

He has pinpointed a contradiction between two of the layers of the Chinese university. Confucian values placed education at the pinnacle, with mere mercantile prowess occupying a much lower position. However, the economic reforms of the 1980s and 1990s have promoted the value of wealth—"To get rich is glorious." This is a cultural incongruity that threatens the very identity of Chinese intellectuals.

"What will the situation be for university education in the best future? Could you give me some examples?"

"People will have a high modern standard of living. Perhaps any person who wants to go will have the opportunity to go into the university to receive a high level education. Because of the high-level of culture and knowledge, we would be more democratic—having more right to choose our own life course and lifestyles. We can do something we like, not what we are made to do. By that time maybe our government will give more respect to human rights."

I consider that in Wang's experience, much of his earlier life was devoid of personal choices. He had been "volunteered" to be resettled in the countryside. He did not choose his major, his residence or his job. His opinions reflect a strong reaction born of his own experiences. His words also reflect the vast demand for a shift from elite to mass education, a transformation that is expected to take place in the first decade of the twenty-first century (Hayhoe 1994).

Wang adds a personal note that reflects his own background: "Scientific education will be better than now, because our government will pay attention to this question. This is better than the Cultural Revolution when I went to the university—when just a few people went to university. . . . Just a few. So, in this, I say I am lucky. But by 2020 many people could go to the university. It would be better than now. Today, I think universities such as MIT in the United States and Cambridge in England are good. If people like me can study at places like these, it would be very good indeed."

"In what way will the universities themselves be improved?"

"I think perhaps in a lot of ways. The teaching methods will be improved. Nowadays we use ordinary methods—chalk on a blackboard and lecturing to the students. Teaching methods and teaching materials will certainly be improved more scientifically. Teachers will interact with students, and laboratory equipment will also be improved."

"More laboratory and practical teaching?"

"Yes, I think so. Currently, it's mostly just theoretical teaching. The courses are now arranged just like the 1950s, right after China was liberated. At that time, the universities were established using the Soviet system. Some techniques have changed, but the way the system is arranged remains the same. The textbooks are still similar to the 1950's textbooks. I think this must be changed. Our university students must be trained to increase their thinking skills and their ability to exercise those skills. Most students can do some assignments well, but when they go to work they can do nothing. I think the style will be changed, since we have already sent a lot of students abroad and in several years they will return with new techniques."

"The teaching techniques will be changed?"

"Very different. Nowadays in our university the main method of teaching is to give lectures. One quite good method of teaching is the seminar."

I am gratified to hear this since I have had to struggle to create effective seminars in the pre-departure program. He then explodes my fleeting moment of self-congratulation, "In China, the seminar is a lunatic method of teaching. If a professor said, 'let's go outside to have a seminar, in the grass, in the sunshine,' people would think that this professor had gone mad. The head of the department, the old principal or president of the university, would not permit that."

Thinking of many hours spent in summer seminars and field classes in America, I laugh and quip, "I would be in real trouble then!"

He continues, "Seminars are really quite good, exciting—an interesting method of teaching. But we can't do that now. The traditional, the old way of teaching is to have thirty, forty, maybe one hundred students just sit there, and the teacher stands next to the blackboard and talks, talks, talks. Some students fall asleep on the desk, others read novels, still others talk secretly. If they haven't anything to do, they just write something on the desk, you can see a lot of pictures on the desk. They are bored. Tired of listening to the lessons, they must find something to do, so they write words. This is the drawback of the old teaching method. We should reform the teaching method."

"I think the teaching methods in Western countries are better; we can learn from that. We can stimulate the student's creativity, his imagination. He must think about the problem, find the problem, solve the problem. But, in China, most teachers just give old knowledge . . . a waste of time. We want to find new knowledge. To create more useful knowledge. We want to face the challenge of the future."

"So, do you envision improvement in primary schools and universities, in both the cities and the countryside?"

He reflects, "Yes, across the board."

"Will the education in the countryside be the same as the system in the cities?"

"Currently, I think 30 or 40 percent of the young people who live in the countryside have an educational level much lower than the town-dwelling person. This is not a good thing. I think we need more professional schools [schools with vocational, not academic curricula] in the countryside, not normal secondary schools, where people can learn a trade. A double education system needs to reflect the double economy of agriculture and industry. I don't think education is an isolated problem. Sometimes education is determined by the economic base structure."

"They reinforce each other?"

"Yes, it is a difficult pattern to break, but it is very important for China."

He is saying something important about China, pointing to a fundamental break between the peasant-based agrarian economy and the rapidly growing urban industrial realm. The two domains may require different approaches in educational planning and pedagogy. Wang's personal knowledge of the countryside dates back to his *fang xia* experience more than a decade before; he has spent most of his life in cities.

I ask him to speculate on society at large. Could he go more deeply into the quality of life in this best future?

Wang speculates, "Some problems like the environmental problems will be solved. In thirty years we may have some methods to cure some kinds of cancer, or at least the patient will live longer."

He pauses. His vision is terse and one-dimensional, suggesting vague "technical" solutions rather than the flavor of future life. I feel as if I have just experienced another interview "serve and miss." After what seems like minutes I prompt him with some provocative scenarios other interviewees had postulated: "Some of your colleagues have painted a very bright future in which people are healthy, hard work is done by robots, there is no pollution, no unemployment, no starvation, no population problem. New energy sources will be used, and the people's work and living conditions will be better. By 2020 the productivity will be increased tenfold. People in China will have houses to live in, and everything will be better. What do you think?"

"There will be difficulties. For China, the best possible future will come with successfully controlling the birth rate. I hope this problem will be resolved in the next thirty years, but it will be difficult. In the countryside many people haven't accepted it. Because of economic conditions in the countryside people only want boys—in the Chinese language a girl is for people outside the family, she is 'out.'"

I understand that he is referring to the most fundamental rule of Chinese kin-ship—patrilineality. A son is a couple's valued heir and security; he will bring in a future daughter-in-law and continue the family. A daughter will marry another couple's heir and produce a child belonging outside their patrilineage. Preference for male children has been accentuated by the state mandated one-child policy. Now the birth of a daughter actually precludes the birth of a son and heir. Yet uncontr-olled population expansion—or even maintenance of a 1.1 billion level—would result in poverty and famine. Wang expresses the fundamental "two-mindedness" that Chinese intellectuals feel toward population control policies.

"I hope that will change in the next thirty years. Birth control isn't the best policy, but we have to do it. It is necessary."

"What else will life be like?"

Wang pauses,"I hope many people can travel or go to other countries. As you know, it is very difficult for Chinese people to travel abroad, for economical reasons and for other reasons. Now the people have little money; thus it is not possible to travel. So they live in their small groups, their small houses, and watch TV. I think their views are very narrow. They can't easily communicate with other people. I think in the best life style, people will improve relationships with other members of the society."

This desire for broadmindedness is consistent with *kaifang*. He goes on to discuss other implications for social change. "Ideas about family will change a lot. For example, now a lot of young people want to get married young, but they don't want to have children. They think children are a heavy burden. In the past the Chinese did not associate getting married with happiness. But now these things are changing. Lifestyles are beginning to change. In the city, people want to live more as individuals. Chinese have been living in an extended family—that is, three or more generations living together. But now instead of this situation, young people want to be more independent. They want more freedom. They don't want to be controlled by their parents. We can see fewer extended families, more nuclear families. An individualistic lifestyle. With this comes a higher rate of divorce."

"Social problems come with the social changes?" I ask this, realizing as the words come out that the very nature of my question is value laden, implying that divorce and independence necessarily produce "problems."

"Yes, the rate of divorce is going up in China now as people are getting richer and richer—freer to choose their own partners."

"What do you see for the best social future in the countryside?"

"I think, even in the countryside, the society of the future will be more individualistic. The peasants will have more rights to determine their own lives. We can also see more impact from urban areas—more civilization brought by industry. There is one very important factor that is changing the peasants' lives in rural areas—rural industry. The traditional agricultural economy kept them a closed society with no links with the city. But the development of rural industry gives them more contact with urban areas. They must get raw material from urban areas, and then the products must be sold to the urban people. So there is more interaction between rural and urban areas. Many peasants have never left the place where they were born and have lived their whole lives. But now the young peasants are moving from the rural area to an urban area."

Indeed, this migration has reached a massive scale. By 1986 nine million peasants had left the countryside (Tan and Li 1993, 355). That exodus has expanded exponentially. This shift had grave implications for China's urban infrastructure—housing, traffic, education and law enforcement.

"Are there any other ways in which the attitudes will be different in the best future?"

He responds with an unexpected, but frontier-like, elaboration of what *kaifang* means to him. "I think in 2020 more and more people are interested in adventure—in climbing mountains and conquering space. So their lives will be interesting. With higher productivity and improved education, people will face new challenges and new problems, and it will change their attitudes. They will enjoy life more. More and more people will be interested in politics and science. They will want to conquer space and the ocean frontiers. Political life will be much better. It will be more democratic. People will have more power to make their own decisions in the future. At least more of the people would realize that if they want to live a good life they must build a good society. So more of the people will work to contribute something to society. I hope our society will be more open—open not only to the world but also to ideas and open in the workplace. We can change, we can build a good world. This is the most optimistic future, but I think it may not be by 2020."

Wang has painted a bright future beyond 2020. But by adding the last phrase, I was left wondering. He had reached the limits of his optimism.

DEAD END

The "worst future" was a difficult section of the interview to conduct. Few people wanted to directly discuss the flaws of the system or consider what would happen if those defects worsened. Several forces inhibited the voicing of such pessimistic outcomes. The "social problems" approach in Western anthropology, sociology and political science is decidedly non-Chinese. One of the gravest consequences for the international social science research community in China after 1990 was the directive that Chinese social scientists avoid sensitive topics that dealt with Chinese social problems (Jacobson 1991, A1, A27). Such sensitive topics are *neibu*, for internal Chinese consumption only. Topics were often avoided so as not to be construed as criticism. To discuss problems is to risk being considered a "rightist," someone who criticizes the orthodoxy of the "leftist" socialist path. Censure would also diminish China's "face," making the country seem weak. To make critical comments to a foreigner would compound the transgression. This is surely the shortest portion of the interview since few were willing to speak at length.

At the same time, there is an intellectual tradition of *youguo youmin*, worrying about the country and the people (see Link 1992, 5, 249). There is a sense that China should be a global model for conducting human affairs, and when it is not, intellectuals have a moral obligation to understand what is wrong and what should be done. Even if nonestablishment intellectuals are relatively powerless, they still feel a duty to "worry."

Thus, critical statements emerge. The ambiguous and often paradoxical status of the intellectual forms the basis of widespread dissatisfaction. Concomitant are the dissatisfactions with the nature of central planning, discontent over government priorities, and frustration over the lack of effective infrastructure. Some very real demographic problems plague China as well: population, resource shortages and impending pollution on a scale the West can scarcely imagine.

Wang clearly enjoyed speculating on potential Chinese successes. But as I mention "worst," he sighs ever so slightly and listens to my prompt.

"You have described the best future, in which many of the problems will be solved. I would like you now to imagine a future in which the problems will *not* be solved, the worst possible future. In that future China, what will science and technology be like? How will education fare? What kind of society will be produced? Can you describe this for me?"

"I think there are three forces that have an impact on science in China. The first one is politics, the second is economic policies and the third is tradition. The traditional forces are quite strong because we have a long history, an ancient feudal social system. The traditional forces are quite strong, but they are not negative."

Wang is referring to the Confucian educational tradition that has shaped his outlook positively, in spite of recent disrepute, and he continues: "The most important are political forces, for they can improve science and technology, or destroy them. For example, in the Cultural Revolution, science and technology remained at the same level for more than ten years. This would be tragic."

"In your previous scenario, you mentioned a number of problems that China will face. Can you tell more about their impact on the worst possible future?"

"The worst possibility is that the Chinese government cannot control population growth. As the population of China grows, the country will face civil problems. One problem will be the educational level. Another will be insufficient resources for the population. In the undesirable future, we won't pay enough attention to people in the countryside. They will become comparatively poor. About 80 percent of the people live in the rural areas. And that will cause problems in education and the standard of living. They may have enough grain, or enough money to buy color TVs, to improve their living standards in several respects, but if we do not improve their level of education and ability to mechanize they will be disadvantaged in modern culture."

"Does that mean that the urban/rural gap would prevent the whole country from developing?"

"Yes. Second, if we don't change our system of policies, the intellectuals will be disheartened . . . reluctant. About two to three years ago I saw a picture drawn on the wall.[4] It was called 'They are equal.' In it were drawn four typical Chinese. The first one is a PLA man (People's Liberation Army), very strong, handsome, and tall. They are fed by the government, the People, so they are very strong. Next to the soldier is a worker, not very strong and shorter, but under his foot there is something that increases his height—that is his bonus. That means that the workers can get a bonus. And next to the worker is a farmer, a peasant. He also is shorter than the worker but under his foot is 'rent land.' That means that every farmer can rent a plot of land from the government so that he can get a profit from his produce. And the last one is an intellectual. He is very thin and very short but has a very high cap. In China when we give someone a 'high cap'[5] it means we respect him but we don't give him anything, just homage. So this picture represents the situation for intellectuals. If this pattern continues, the consequences cannot be foreseen."

Wang goes on: "In the worst possibility young people may not be willing to go to the university, since they will see their parents living poorly just because they are scholars or teachers. So if this situation doesn't change, I think most young people won't go to the university. As a result, science and technology will not develop greatly, and the gap in science and technology between China and the developed countries will be widened. You can read about this in the *China Daily* [an English-language version of the *People's Daily*, the key official newspaper, one exported and read by foreigners]."

"So the status of intellectuals is declining?"

"In China, the teacher is the last class. It's very unhealthy. For example, when I moved to an institute to be a teacher in 1975, my father warned me not to be a teacher. Because when he was a teacher during the Cultural Revolution, he was tortured. So he warned me not to be a teacher. I don't want his prediction to be true, so I hope our government can take some action to change and improve the teacher's situation."

"Society is very complicated. China is a big country and has the largest population in the world. It is a big problem to know how to administer the country, how
to hold the country to the government's course. At this moment, the government
wants people to concentrate on economic construction. But since China has opened
to the outside world, people are getting more and more new ideas from other
countries. People are beginning to think and react as they would not have before.
The most difficult thing is how to direct the country to construct the Four
Modernizations."

"Why is this difficult?"

"Nowadays there is quite a strong feeling, in most of the citizens in the
countryside. They don't like the [Chinese Communist] party, but they are willing to
wait because they can still live with it. There is no vital reason to strike or
something like this. So things still appear to go okay, but that is only appearance.
Underneath something is going on. A sort of unhappiness . . . yes. So if something
really happened, maybe after a period of time things might get better, or maybe
worse."

He reflects, and then continues, "Maybe another Cultural Revolution, worse than
the last one. If there were another Cultural Revolution, universities would be closed.
There would be no students. Teachers wouldn't do research work, and there might
be fighting among people. If China has another Cultural Revolution, it will exclude
the foreign technology and become isolated. The worst is civil war. In thirty years
I wouldn't want to see more political conflict, I mean, like the Cultural Revolution.
Nowadays I think our government's better. I don't think it will happen again."

"So it's not likely to happen even in the worst future?"

"Yes, the majority of the people hated the Cultural Revolution very much and
want a better future. People create their own future. They won't let another Cultural
Revolution happen. I think the most probable situation is that China will get some
improvements, but not very much. But it can't get any worse."

Had I known that six months later hundreds of thousands would take to the
streets in protest, I would have marveled at the prophecy in his words. In any case,
the trend in the conversation makes us both uneasy, putting our body language "on
alert." Aware that we are treading on politically touchy ground I shift the conversation back to the "safe" topic of science and technology: "What would happen to
science and technology in this worst case? Some of your colleagues have predicted
that science would become stagnant. What do you think?"

"I don't think science itself would have problems, but there might be some
trouble for development. I think science is always improving. If automation is used
and the number of robots is increased, then a lot of people will be unemployed. So
we first must introduce some intermediate technology. We shouldn't develop too
quickly."

I consider what he has said. He reasserts the triumph of science, but clearly
understands there are social costs in any technological "fix."

He goes on a slightly different tack: "Some service work will be replaced by robots. The salespersons will be replaced by robots. When you shop, you will just look at a machine. I think this is not very friendly. Everyone will feel very lonely. I think your country has such phenomena—people just interacting with machines. I don't like that, I want the developed nations to teach us to avoid such problems."

In the last utterance he has outlined a negative consequence of technology—at least, he has defined it as negative. I can hardly tell him that one of the things I enjoy about America is the way automation has reduced the necessity of facing meaningless social encounters. I consider automatic teller machines to be a tranquil way to obtain cash, without encumbering myself with another social event. My attitude, embedded in individualism, separates tasks, such as getting cash, from the people who perform the task. My sphere of intimates, with whom I seek social relationships, is restricted. This specificity of purpose is contrary to a Chinese ethos that builds daily tasks around relationships. I have just encountered one of those twists in expected responses that highlights intercultural and interpersonal differences in values.

I prompt Wang on the future of education, and he discusses the two brain drains that plague Chinese academia—the flight abroad and the "money future" in which students are drawn into money-making pursuits. As long as the status of intellectuals is low, students will be discouraged. He points out the monetary disparity. Foreign professors make 50,000 American dollars a year, while his Chinese counterpart may make only 360 dollars, or 1800 yuan. Chinese taxi drivers may earn 6,000 yuan a year, and businessmen 60,000. As a result, some of his classmates and colleagues plan to abandon the academic life. Even recruiting students is becoming problematical. Some unpopular fields—education, agriculture, mining—can barely bring in new recruits. Wang is worried that China will be deprived of qualified and competent engineers or teachers.

I note that once again, his optimistic generality about the supremacy of the Confucian tradition of education eroded in the face of his lived reality. In his optimistic scenario, he postulated that the scholarly class was in no danger of extinction. In this scenario, he seemed less confident and deeply suspicious of a social trajectory that bases status on the possession of wealth.

"What will happen to those people who go into business? What will happen to the economy?"

"If this happens, I don't know. The economic situation may be very bad. Factory workers won't work, but just talk all the time. There would be no food to eat. No energy. These trade jobs don't produce anything, they just make money for themselves. They don't contribute to society, so eventually there will be no money for them to make. So society will become poorer and poorer until the whole country is worse off. As a result, I cannot say what will happen."

Wang is describing the "money future" in which the short-term pursuit of the profitable undermines the basic research and development effort that makes industry possible. This line of causation is a dead end—no student enthusiasm, no new scientists, no opportunities for engineering innovation, no new products. However, the disparity within China is of greater concern to him. For the reform policies lead to a bifurcation of those who can make money, and those who are locked into necessary but unprofitable lives.

He goes on, "Our biggest problem may be that the gap between the rich and the poor is getting wider. In the past the richest man in China has no more than 10,000 yuan. No man, no one twenty years ago, had more than 10,000 yuan in a savings account in the bank. In the city, my parents had several hundred yuan. Now some people have more than several hundred thousand yuan in the bank! On the other hand, in the countryside they barely have enough food and clothes. Even when China has resolved the food and clothes problem, a lot of people in the countryside cannot buy modern things. More and more people in the countryside can afford only a black and white TV. Only a few can buy color TV."

Wang feels this disparity can only lead to crime. People will not know what is right and will mock those who care about morality. He worries that crime will necessitate a police state that people will willingly tolerate since the alternative is chaos. Wang is concerned about the delicate balance between freedom and order, a debate familiar to Americans as well. Too much freedom without personal internalized constraints produces crimes that would provoke harsh governmental constraints. The police state, in his worldview, is not just the opposite of freedom; it is the consequence of freedoms combined with moral ignorance.

"What other factors will affect education and science in the worst future?"

He points out that the most critical locus of power is the state: "We have no control, so I think government policy is the most important factor. Only political considerations can affect the scientific development in the worst future. Something like 'monocracy,' not democracy. In a 'monocratic' society, people can only do little things for society. They work only for the leader. After the death of Deng Xiaoping, things will be difficult to predict. The tradition in China is a feudal system, and we don't have a democracy. So our national destiny depends on one person. This is the tragedy of our nation. Many Chinese people who live in the countryside don't realize the importance of stable and fair laws, not just an upright leader. This is a common problem. Now we have just started, so I think we will not have a very big change . . . because of cultural traditions. But if policies and people's ideas shift I think we'll get even more changes."[6]

I echo and clarify, "So there could be more change, but it depends on the policies and the attitudes of the people. Whether they are willing to accept change?"

"Yes, because this process needs a long time, longer than thirty years. Right now China has just started."

Repeatedly, the theme of law and personality politics was struck. As long as the social constraints of the society were based on policy, manufactured through individual leaders acting in their *guanxi* networks, the system would always be vulnerable to sudden changes. Only laws, external to personalities, would ensure that freedom, and perhaps rights and obligations, would be built into the system.

Once again this highlighted the importance of predictability. An unpredictable system is in itself something to be feared, a horror to be shunned. Scholars like Wang have suffered through enough unanticipated and radical shifts in policy to know the cost of unpredictability. Their concerns are well-grounded in the modern Chinese experience.

Moreover, my brilliant, rational, *weiqi* playing friend is also part of a global intellectual community in which predictability is highly valued. Rationality, reproducibility, and consistency of cause and effect are hallmarks of the scientific worldview. The messiness and capriciousness of political life are discordant with that belief system.

It took me a number of interviews to understand that the repeated phrase, "it can't be predicted" was not merely a description of the complexity of the situation, but a value judgment—indeed, a condemnation. The pessimistic scenarios clarified that the dislike of unpredictability stems in part from the *irrationality* of the change, not the change itself. *Now* traversing the open door to gain expertise has been declared to be a proper patriotic pursuit. But what if—and given the historical fact of the Cultural Revolution this is hardly implausible—Wang's association with Western technology were to became a liability? What if policy shifted and such a pragmatic association came to carry the stigma of spiritual pollution and counterrevolutionary contamination? Then years of hard work would be wasted. That is the unpredictability the scholars fear.

At a deeper level, unpredictability is a challenge to maintain *mianzi*, managing the presentation of face. Face is gained by successfully fulfilling social roles and receiving recognition for that achievement (Hwang 1987, 960). If scholars cannot predict how their roles will be conceptualized and evaluated by society, they cannot systematically work to gain face. Repeatedly, informants mentioned that they played the academic game for prestige, not wealth. Unpredictability undermines their ability to discern and fulfill the rules of that game.

BETTER, BUT NOT THE BEST

Wang is showing some signs of wear as I shift to the last scenario. The content of the probable scenario recaps the two previous ones, adding little in the way of new issues. Like an optometrist trying different lenses, the final scenario tests for consistency, determining which issues are really essential. The "most probable" scenario is centripetal; it pulls the radical ends of speculation toward the middle. The "best" and "worst" scenarios encourage conjecture and stimulate imagination. Concerns over invading space beings or accidental incest arising from sperm banks—two items from others' "worst" scenarios—are not likely to keep most scholars awake at night. The most likely scenario is the narrative in which the interviewee expects to live in the future. It has the most direct transferability from the present. The "most probable" scenario is the most accurate mirror for the interviewees' existing social reality.

"You have examined the future on that end of the spectrum of possibilities," I prompt, "and you have described the worst possible future. What do you think is likely to happen? Can you describe the probable future for science, technology, education and society in China in the year 2020?"

Wang reflects for a moment, leans forward and says, "The situation will be better than now but not the best, because thirty years is not very long. Maybe it will be 60–70 percent like the best it could be. I think China needs at least a century to develop a well-balanced social structure. In thirty years it will be on the path to improve the social structure."

Since my purpose in eliciting this scenario is to clarify the forces that are perceived to shape the "best" and "worst" possibilities, I ask "What are the positive factors that shape the future?"

"The first is work motivation brought by the market system and more competition. The second is more opportunity for individuals, for people, that is the result of this change. The third is to make use of more advanced technology in food and production in order to compete with other enterprises. The fourth, I think, is the democratic political system which will make more reasonable policy because the policymakers must take into consideration the people's wishes. Another key factor in scientific research is cooperation. But if scientists can get more chances to visit, do research or attend international conferences, then China can raise its academic research level. It is very necessary. As we exchange scholars with other countries for science and technology, we learn their advanced ideas—like human rights, something like democracy and so on. Such people can take a very important part in our country's science and technology. By that time they will be in charge of every aspect of science and technology, and the situation will get better."

He is, of course, talking about his own likely destiny, the one the open door policy makes possible. He makes this clear with his next comment, "We can see how these other countries have developed their science and technology, and we can take these ideas back and apply them to China's situation. I don't mean just copying but creating our own solutions. We can't just copy from others. After Liberation we copied things from the Soviet Union, but that did not work out. These are the forces that are good for the future."

Wang is arguing that it is necessary for China to create its own scientific and intellectual destiny. He understands such inventiveness to be an important service to the state, and to the reformulation of his own status in society.

"So policies on education and international scientific cooperation are important?"

"Yes, but domestic policy is more important than international policy because China must depend on itself. Anyway this situation is much better than it was ten years ago, and we have changed a lot. The government has changed a lot, the attitudes, the policy, the open door policy. A main problem is essentially the lack of systematic thought or a scientific approach to planning. If a policy is based on unscientific theories and natural rules, then the policies will be random, sometimes promoting development and sometimes preventing it. Planning is not rigorously done. It has been done on a trial-and-error basis. The best possible future hinges on trying to smooth out the planning system."

Wang lives in a centralized planned economy in which the locus of control is in the hands of the government. In the past, government policy has only reacted to changes in leadership or ideology. Wang is proposing something different: a government that can respond to feedback from the people.

"I think most probably we will develop faster in forty years. So far in Asia—Taiwan, South Korea, the Philippines—these are some small countries that developed very fast. And I think we also can learn from them, from their experience. To solve this kind of problem, democracy is very important. So I think the government should consider the people's desires, the people's demands. For example, give the people the freedom to speak their minds and to think about things that challenge authority. If the government will give more democracy to people and the people can work more creatively, maybe they can do more things and improve the general standard of living."

"You mentioned earlier that traditional values toward education may be important. Do you see other cultural traditions as powerful factors in the future?"

"There are a lot of traditional ideas in China that limit people's activity and thinking. For example, even now young peoples' marriages are decided by their parents. But I don't think in the future they will do this; they will choose their partners themselves, more freely."

He clearly thinks this is a positive development, but then he goes on with what he believes to be the darker side of individualism, "I hope people will be friendly and helpful. I meet many foreign professors and scientists who have told me that human relationships are not as friendly, as warm as you'd hope. In Japan relationships are not very good. People don't want to pay any attention to other people's lives. I don't know if this is an inevitable or avoidable trend. In China, if you go to some undeveloped areas, people are very friendly. Go to the East [Coast of China], and you see a difference in peoples' attitudes—not as friendly. Why? I don't know. I think their living conditions may be better, but their attitude may not be as good."

I ask him to outline the negative forces he foresees in the most likely future. He responds that indeed, some factors will be "painful," such as the obvious problems of overpopulation and pollution, and the increasing social demand on a limited educational system. He sees the current economic reforms as both generating and solving problems for intellectuals, threatening their status while providing entrepreneurial opportunities. The transition to a market economy will be a rough one. The increase in competitiveness will spread throughout all levels of society, even into the classrooms of young students competing to get into the "key" middle schools. Wang fears that childhood will be joyless. Competition will accelerate the gap between those who use education to get ahead and those for whom it has no meaning. Finally, he notes again that the lack of motivation to do basic research will have a far-ranging impact on industrial research and production.

"You mentioned the lack of motivation to do basic research as a factor, could you talk a bit more about this?"

Wang adds, "We also need basic research to do our best in theoretical sciences, because this is intrinsic to building applications. As you are aware, our country is one of the biggest in the world. We not only need applications of science but we also need theoretical science. So we should do both of them. Now research institutes get less and less money. Some critical research can get some money but not very much. The government demands that practical research projects should be sponsored by the manufacturing companies. These projects will develop very quickly."

"I think applied research is always useful, but some of it is not very advanced. Many projects are only doing repetitions. They aren't creating new applications, new practices; they are only doing 'you do it so I'm repeating it.' Application sciences are a waste of time, a waste of money."

He is referring to what we had joked about as "space heater research." In south China official policy is that no central indoor heating is provided. But this supposedly clement territory includes glacial Tibet! Consequently, companies try to design their own space heaters to sell to chilled urbanites. The companies are institutionally self-contained, if not in outright competition, and so they rarely communicate. As a result, large numbers of isolated engineers replicate identical—and mundane—research.

Wang then touches on a new and critical issue, adding, "Especially in China the exchange of information is not convenient. The people in the Chemistry Department need help from the Department of Physics, but teachers in the Physics Department don't want to cooperate with the teachers in the Chemistry Department, so the result is that both of them suffer from that lack of cooperation, that mental insulation. I don't understand why some people isolate themselves."

Both Wang's understanding of the scientific worldview and the reality of Chinese institutional constraints are at issue here. Wang values "openness" and "communalism." In the 1930s sociologist of science Robert K. Merton described those values as "normative" for the scientific community (1968, 610–612). Ideally, the knowledge products of individual scientists are the common heritage of all.[7] This statement about scientific epistemology touches the cognitive structure of scientific culture, but ignores rival values and social factors that are separate from "the scientific method." Secrecy, the strategic withholding of information, is a value that has deep roots in Chinese culture and has been graced with official sanction in moral education texts in the post–Tiananmen period (Hayhoe 1993, 39). The construction of market competition requires a certain degree of reticence; information given away cannot be sold. The social promotion of competitiveness inhibits the practice of such idealized values as communalism.

There are also structural factors that inhibit communication of scientific and technical information. As mentioned in the previous chapter, departmental and disciplinary lines are sharply drawn in Chinese higher education, a legacy of European university organization. Although American universities are formulated with more permeable boundaries, it is difficult to arrange a cooperative research project among an engineer, a health scientist, a sociologist and an anthropologist, for example. They share different academic cultures and languages. In addition, their deans may require each of these to jump through different institutional hoops. An administrator who supervises the health scientist may want grant money, while a dean of social science may want publications. The engineering dean will want corporate connections and visible products. The barriers to cooperation can become insurmountable even in the American context where such linkages are imaginable.

The structural barriers are obvious. Of greater interest is how Wang understands this process to work. To what cause does he attribute such isolation? I ask him to explain the cause of this bureaucratic segregation and inefficiency, and his answer is telling.

"Because usually the leadership in a research group is not strong enough to have firm control over every small group. Some leader says, 'you cooperate with them,' and the people under him don't obey."

"Is that because the leader is not powerful enough?"

"Yes, because the leader is not powerful enough. For example, teachers in different departments in the university do not cooperate well in their research groups."

His focus on leadership points to another intercultural difference. Cultures differ in the degree to which they assess the rights, privileges and obligations given to their leaders.[8] Americans are unlikely to readily give the responsibility for all social interaction within a group to a leader—we would be more likely to pursue a decentralized solution, perhaps reeducating individuals "to communicate more effectively." However, Wang's comment describes an implicit Chinese cultural fact. Power is in the hands of the leaders, and so is responsibility. Along with the privileges of leadership come obligations. What is at issue is the competence of leaders, not the intrinsic authority of leadership itself. This is an important distinction.

Wang goes on, "So many companies don't know where they can get information, where they can get help. So maybe this will affect science and technology. People in China do not cooperate very well. Almost all research in today's world is cooperation between different branches of science and technologists and engineers, but now they don't cooperate very well."

Once again, a feature of social organization highlights a difference between the conduct of research in China and the United States. University research is essential to America's "R and D," and it is highly intertwined with corporate support. American research often takes place in corporate laboratories in which interdisciplinary work groups must produce results. Chinese research is still largely housed in academic institutions, where the bureaucratic separation of departmental subjects is a supreme fact of life (Conroy 1989, 38–39, 47–51, 60). Cooperation is structurally built into American research, at least on the microlevel, while Chinese organization impedes collaboration.

"I think scientists, science and technology are very important in improving my country's situation, but you see that in China the most important thing is authority, the government. The situation must be changed because in China the government controls everything including your work unit, your research topics. So in this situation we can't work creatively. We can't work actively. We just work but we have little interest. And secondly, some competition system must be introduced, meaning if we do better we get higher pay, a higher standard of living."

I probe to clarify the reasoning behind this statement: "More incentive?"

"Yes, we must change a whole series of policies, such as scientists being able to choose their own work freely. But this will take some ability to develop."

"Are there other problems that bother you that might still be there in the most probable future?"

"The worst thing is corruption in the leaders. They are doing everything they can to make their own profits. They are destroying the country's economy. The good positions are occupied by the leaders' sons and daughters. The people hate this kind of thing. The leaders told us before, 'Don't be selfish,' and things like this. These principles are all destroyed, because of the deeds of those leaders. We talk most about this problem. People have very strong feelings toward this kind of thing. Now people are just confused."

These attitudes were echoed in the conversations of June 1989. One of the primary issues behind the protest was not that leadership was authoritarian, but that it was corrupt, hypocritical and ineffective.

"People don't want to work very hard," Wang said. "They ask, 'Why should I contribute? Do more? Why should I work hard and not take care of my family and children?' It makes the people disheartened. In the streets many people spit, and some people throw rubbish from their windows. People think more and more only of themselves instead of the country, a bad habit. These things are contradictory to our traditional Chinese customs."

I ask him to expand a statement that "maybe in the future Eastern and Western morality may be melded to produce a new morality."

He responds, "I can't imagine what it will be like. Family relationships I think will also change—between husbands and wives, parents and children. People are moving around, and society is more open than before. People will be influenced by Western cultures because we import so many films and TV programs every year. People see how people live in America, how they live in Britain. China's style of living will also be influenced by the Western style of living."

"Style or values?"

"Both. Most people will not take marriage very seriously. They will not see it as a bond to fasten people together. They're more free to divorce and marry. If one of the partners has met another man or a woman, I think they will easily divorce."

"People will be more independent of their families?"

"Yes, almost everyone will live on their own. So nobody will depend on another for a living, and it will be easier to divorce and there will be less argument before divorce, fewer quarrels. There will be less control of children by the parents, more independence."

"Will it work both ways? Will you be dependent on your child in your old age?"

"I want the relationship between me and my child to be the relationship between friends. We will show respect for each other, know each other, show concern for each other, but we will not try to control our children, as our fathers did."

His attitude is consistent with the value changes that have been detected in Wu's large scale multinational study of Chinese socialization. His study of Shanghai parents reveals that new values are emerging. Wu has noted that 77 percent of Shanghai parents disagreed with a statement that children should not talk back. Indeed, 75 percent thought parents should apologize to their children if they were wrong (Wu 1994). This represents an acknowledgment of the "rights" of a child that was not evident in traditional Chinese socialization beliefs.

Wang shifts his attention from the more intimate society to the body politic, saying, "If they ask the government to do something, the government should consider it. Then intellectuals can report, 'You are not right' or 'in these things you are wrong.'"

I clarify, "So it is the responsibility of the intellectuals to inform the government of their opinions?"

"Yes. As you know, the situation in China is decided by policy, not by law. If law gained more power in China, the situation would be better; more stability would be possible after the death of some of the leaders. But now it is decided by leaders, so after they go the whole situation will change. No one can predict such a change; it's too unstable."

He goes on to state, in what for him is strong language, what this instability has meant: "So I have to say society will be changed, but toward which direction, good or bad, always depends on our government policy. I should frankly tell you I'm not antigovernment, but I think this system has not really been well run. Since Liberation all these political movements have wasted a lot of time and also hurt people's feelings. Some people want to do good for their country, but are always involved with political things. Like my friend . . . he graduated in the 1950s and is an excellent engineer, but later there was the antiright movement. He became a leader, but he didn't want to hurt people. He said these people shouldn't be called 'right people,' but then later he was declared 'right.' So he was sent to the countryside for twenty years. In 1979 after the downfall of the Gang of Four, he was liberated and then became an engineer again. In China the biggest problem is not just science and technology; it is the system . . . all graduates, if they were not the sons or daughters of leaders, had to go to the countryside. At that time I wasted almost six years."

Wang feels his that formative years were held hostage to political decisions beyond his control, resulting in lost years of productivity, for both himself and China's scientific establishment. Scholars younger than Wang have grown up with that handicap and have inherited the duty to close the gap between China and the rest of the world. Yet their ambitions have been thwarted by mundane obstacles. As a consequence, they direct their scientific passions toward more personal goals.

5

The Mountain of Flowers and Fruit

Today he will make his name;
Tomorrow his destiny will triumph.
He is fated to live here;
As a King he will enter the Immortals' palace.

(Wu Cheng En, *Journey to the West*, 1:6)

In his youth the monkey who was to become Sun Wukong played carefree with the other monkeys. Having nothing else to do, his monkey friends become increasingly curious about the source of their water. They ran upstream to the top of their mountain and found a lovely waterfall cascading from a spring. One suggests that should any monkey be clever enough to find the source of the water-fall and return in one piece, he should become the king of the monkeys. The challenge is shouted three times. Of course, Sun volunteers. Behind the waterfall he finds a bridge, a house and a stone table bearing the inscription: "Happy Land of the Mountain of Flowers and Fruit, Cave Heaven of the Water Curtain." By leading the other monkeys to this newfound paradise, Sun becomes the king of the monkeys. The Monkey King's innocent high spirits do not last, however, and after a few hundred years as sovereign he becomes restless. He tells his subjects that although he is happy now, he worries about the future. With the specter of death in his mind the Monkey King sets off to found the secrets of immortality. He sails across the seas and traverses several frontiers, masquerading as a human. The young Monkey King has many longings that drive his restless spirit.

The young scholar Zhou, the engineer featured in this chapter, is also restless, trying to solve the puzzles that face him. While he is much like his elder colleague Wang in many of his opinions and concerns, the young Zhou speaks with a clearly different voice. The 1960s born cohort to which he belongs has been called "a swing group" (Gold 1991, 604). They were children in the Cultural Revolution, and their families and communities would have been affected by the chaos. The oldest may have been "sent down" to the countryside for a short period, the youngest would not have experienced this episode. They grew to consciousness as the class struggle rhetoric was replaced by the quest for the Four Modernizations. This group, less controlled by the state than Wang's cohort, felt more responsibility for "their own economic well-being" (Gold 1991, 606). They are skeptical of state rhetoric and are searching for some niche of their own.

Nonetheless, state policy shaped their options. Examinations were again in place in the universities. In a survey taken in Shanghai among graduated senior middle school students in 1982, 90 percent of the young men in key schools and 40 percent of all young men in ordinary schools wanted to attend university. Presaging the favoritism that was shown to applied science from 1983 onward, students' attitudes favored engineering, medicine and technical work (Lan and Zhang 1983–84, 164–165).

The university graduates of the 1980s are strongly affected by the economic reforms that are transforming higher education and research in China. Wang's age and status insulate him from the brunt of those changes, but younger men must pursue their dreams in the face of the realities of competition and economic reform. Private business is a serious option. Even state industries, in their case universities and technical institutes, have broken the iron rice bowl. They must accomplish their visions encumbered by the disadvantage of youth in a society that rewards seniority. They are idealistic about the destiny of the Chinese spirit but cynical about their own personal futures. The pragmatic tone of these younger scholars emerges in the voice of their spokesman, Zhou.

Zhou is a composite of younger men, ages 25 to 31, average age 27. Eight of the forty-nine in this set were single, although they expressed the willingness to be married. Indeed, some have since wed. Of the forty-one married men, all were married to women who would be considered intellectuals, even if the men themselves had come from worker or peasant backgrounds. Twenty-seven had children. The overwhelming majority, two-thirds, were engineers, with only a few scholars of biomedicine, chemistry, mathematics or physics. One lone social scientist fell into this category.

Most of these scholars come from northeast China; fewer lived in central, southeast and southwest China. Zhou is probably not from the northwest, since a mere 15 percent of the sample had lived there. Only 10 percent had lived in Beijing, and 12 percent in Shanghai, and these had done so primarily to obtain graduate education. Most had been educated in their local provincial capital. This age group made up the majority of the third round of interviews conducted six months after the shocks of Tiananmen.

The reserve that Wang displayed is not always apparent in Zhou. Zhou laughs more, and his anger is more visible. While Wang would sometimes wear the blue

Mao jacket that symbolized his generation, Zhou always wears Western-style sports jackets, dark slacks and fashionable leather shoes. He often talks about money, a favored Chinese topic of conversation, much like the weather in the West. But Zhou talks about it with an intensity that reflects the fact that, as a young struggling professional, he must hustle.

His age mates and friends are either newly married or still unmarried, and females are sometimes a topic of conversation. Usually, this banter would end when a woman entered the room, but as a slightly older foreigner, my presence does not have the same dampening effect. Some of Zhou's age mates are quite outspoken about the flaws of women, calling them flighty, weak, foolish and unintelligent. Like Wang, Zhou seems genuinely concerned about the prejudice against women, but more often he is unaware of it. He casually mentions that a female scientist has been denied entry into the job market, but he sees this action only as backlash against intellectuals, not as sexism.

Zhou is proud of his 2-year-old son and tells me he is amazed that I should feel the same about my daughter. He had thought only Chinese people understood the central importance of family. He has not met many foreigners, and I am somewhat of a revelation to him.

Throughout our many conversations we have explored our common ground. He is from the countryside, a Liaoning peasant village. He has used a scholarship as his ticket to urban life and relative material prosperity. He "plays taiqi" and is an avid science fiction fan. He even belongs to a amateur writing group and passes his mimeographed futuristic stories around to an audience of his peers.

He is bright and professionally ambitious. His English is not as polished as Wang's—as a child he had to learn Russian—but he makes up for this with his enthusiasm. He knows that computer skills and English proficiency are the wave of the future. He is acutely aware that the decision makers who stand above him in the hierarchy may know less than he, but have years of *guanxi* and seniority (see Odgen 1992, 9). His early professional successes have earned him the envy of his peers—an envy tinged with resentment.

He was a child during the Cultural Revolution, but he has grown up with shifting political winds and hours of weekly "political study" meetings. He is cynical about such efforts—"people just say what they have to, and no one really believes it." But that cynicism does not extend to his love for his country, which is sincere. He prizes his Chineseness.

THE DAO OF SOFTWARE

The circumstances of Zhou's interview, while much like Wang's, are different in one important respect. Zhou—a 27-year-old engineer—is being interviewed near the end of 1989, after the turmoil of "June Four," and the fate of the open door is very much in doubt. This fact lends a certain skittishness to the conversation. In the background section, I ask him about the details of his life. He tells me of his wife, who is a doctor in his work unit, and their 2-year-old son. Although he is also an engineer, Zhou's specialty is not as research oriented as Wang's; he designs the automation systems of chemical plants. To do this he must understand chemical plant function and design, computer-aided design (CAD) and automation engineering. His profession is similar to what we would call a systems analyst in the West, yet within his *danwei* his classification is much narrower than that.

He was born in the countryside near Dalian on China's northeast coast, where his parental family still lives. In his youth he was a mathematical whiz kid, but he describes himself as too practical to spend his life as "just a teacher." His parents, who were peasants, did not help him select his profession, but he had advice from his middle school mathematics teacher. He picked his undergraduate university largely through geographic preference and chance, only to discover he was not particularly fond of his undergraduate major. Like Wang, he graduated in 1982, but with a bachelor's degree in electrical engineering. Having discovered an interest in automation, he orchestrated a career shift as a postgraduate in Shanghai. He loved it there but was assigned to return to Shenyang, a highly industrialized city in Liaoning province, notorious for its pollution. Shanghai had become a center for higher education, expanding its degree and nondegree programs. About half of the people who use the Shanghai programs come from elsewhere. Most of those will return to their homes on graduation (Hayhoe 1988, 263, 283).

Zhou plans to complete a Ph.D. abroad. He will probably go to Britain, but he has a backup plan and a scholarship to Canada if that falls through. He is deeply troubled about his career potential if he doesn't go abroad. Young men do not usually have the *guanxi* to get assigned to interesting or lucrative projects. That privilege is customarily reserved for more senior scholars. (In the years following this interview, his hard work does begin to pay off as his expertise and drive make him more valuable in the new entrepreneurial environment.)

Zhou sometimes contemplates returning to the countryside to work in rural industry. It is an area of rapid economic expansion, some areas outstripping the more bureaucratically constrained cities. His standard of living would be higher—he could live in a large house and earn a much greater salary. But he would have to leave the urban life he has worked so hard to secure.

We begin to flesh out the projected scenarios with the now standard introductory question, phrased in "Chinlish." "In the best possible future, what do you think the situation will be for science and technology?"

Zhou answers: "First of all, I think China will make great progress in science during the next thirty years, in almost every field of science. I work a lot in computer science, and I consider this topic often. I think China will make great progress. We have now already started to realize our Four Modernizations program in industry, agriculture, defense, and science and technology. But the key is science and technology. At the present time our government is paying more attention to the development of science and technology. So if it develops as we hope, there will be a huge improvement. Let me give you an example. Now we are using coal as our main energy resource, but in thirty years we may change to solar and nuclear power—they are less polluting—and we may have only a minimum of industrial pollution. As you know, Shenyang, my hometown, is very polluted."

His "opening remarks" differ from Wang's. He does not even mention the Cultural Revolution, and speaks only of the current "Four Modernizations." His projected high-energy future is both optimistic and grounded in the personal hope that he will not always live in a polluted environment. So far, his statement is raw techno-optimism—a one-dimensional projection of material prosperity based on technology itself.

I wondered if he would elaborate: "So the key is science and technology?"

"All factors are connected. First of all we should consider the economic system. If the economic reforms of today are successful, then maybe the entire system will run more efficiently. If the government is stable, and the political environment is good, then science and technology will develop. If China still has an open door policy, China will, at least in some areas, keep up with some developed countries in the next thirty years."

Clearly, although technology is the driver of Zhou's positive vision, many variables may influence the final outcome. He goes on to point out that he believes necessity will stimulate innovation and efficiency in this new China. "The application of molecular biotechniques will be developed to a great extent and will be used in many fields such as agriculture, medicine and industry. New kinds of wheat and rice will be developed. Agricultural science should be emphasized in China." Zhou is arguing what should happen, not what will. Recall that agriculture is the least favored field, either in science or practice.

In just a few short minutes, Zhou has given me the outlines of his mental model. Need, economic efficiency, political stability and intercultural exchange will foster technological growth. These are acceptable answers, given current policy and the prevailing theories of technological change. Yet I sense he has more to say, so I prompt, "What factor is responsible for this improvement in science?"

"I think the philosophy of China is different from that of the West. China has a leading role in different fields so it must follow a different path. If China tries to follow the same way as developed countries, I think it cannot overtake them—but at most catch up with them. Medicine, space science and maybe some others. I think as scientific work becomes more and more complicated, we sink deeper into the nature of reality. At that point the philosophy of China is more appropriate for complex systems, more than the simple, practical, analytical philosophies of the West."

For the youth of China, much of the "essence" of Chinese culture was damaged by the political movements of their childhood, especially the Cultural Revolution which promoted hatred of the "olds," (old customs, old habits, old culture, old thinking) resulting in cultural self-mutilation. Unable to adopt the foreign Marxist ideology as a substitute, young people of Zhou's generation are striving to rediscover their cultural heritage. Their efforts resonate with those of young urban

Native Americans who are seeking their ancestral customs, philosophies and rituals. My Chinese sociological colleagues have written about the youth movements in China that are trying to recapture and revitalize the mystical philosophies of the traditional Han past—studying Daoism, traditional Chinese medicine and *qigong* (Wang and Gao 1989). This vision flows from the "entrepreneurial" youth of Shanghai and Guangzhou to university students, and from them to the intellectuals. Perry noted a widespread fascination with *qigong* among intellectuals in the late 1980s, one that seemed to be at odds with their otherwise Westernized values (Link 1992, 206–207). Certainly, it is an issue of cultural pride. But Zhou is suggesting more than that.

He continues, "In China there is a different philosophy—to consider everything about the whole problem. Often it is so difficult, sometimes the problem so complicated, that they cannot solve it. If science develops so that we can simulate or model the problem with the aid of computers, we can solve it. Then, Chinese philosophy may be useful."

He believes the West has provided the analytical models that can predict the cause and effect of simple systems, an essential feature of physical sciences. However, he is postulating that a more holistic approach may be necessary for managing complex systems. The epistemology of traditional practices is a virtual landscape, a nonmaterial reality, with inseparable subsystems that constantly affect one another. The logic of such a worldview is fundamentally different from the rationalist worldview that can segregate variables, pull them apart and test the impact of each one (see English-Lueck 1990a, 74–75). Extremely complex natural systems—ecosystems, societies, cultures—are less amenable to "analysis." In Zhou's view, the Chinese are innately good at such a strategy.

I want to know more. "So what you are saying is that the philosophical system of China is better for very complex problems? But as we get the technology to help us with complex problem solving, then China's philosophy can really flower? It can have a chance to express herself?"

"Yes, exactly. Generally speaking, I think the Chinese people are very capable; they can do the best things in the world."

Zhou is realistic about China's current position in the scientific and technical world. His assessment is that the Chinese national character is one of patience, competence and diligence, and that only the limitations of poverty have held China back. "I have a lot of classmates who have studied in America. They do quite well. If the conditions and the policies are okay for them, they can be successful."

"Is that why you anticipate the appearance of truly great Chinese scientists in the future?"

"Yes, I look forward to it. I think Chinese scientists can do it because they are very hard workers and they have the patience to persist with something. Generally speaking, the Chinese are especially intelligent, diligent and hard-working. They don't care much about money. I mean, of course they care *something* about money, but only if the money is insufficient to support everyday life. But generally speaking, even if the money, compared with other countries, is not too high, that is okay. They will still do their best."

Does his optimism extend to automation, his own field? I ask him about the role of computer hardware in China's best future. His answer again refers to the part Chinese epistemology might play in shaping the future of technology.

"Chinese are good at software. *Yi-jing* (*I-ching*) is a kind of software; Chinese have many things like that from Daoism—*bagua, qigong*—the potential power that is stored in the body. Quite different from the nervous system. They are so clever to understand these things—earth, fire, water, metal, wood—very complicated ideas."

Zhou is discussing the cosmology that is the basis of Chinese mysticism and Chinese medicine. In a cosmos divided into *yin* and *yang*, the five elemental forces harmonize and interact in thousands of permutations to create health, longevity and power, but thrown out of balance they create chaos and disease. Acupuncture, herbal medicine and yoga-like *qigong* exercises are designed to carefully balance the elements and energies to prolong life.

He adds a modern techno-twist: "Many ancient scientists, philosophers, and thinkers have complicated ideas. Even with my university training I can't understand them. Until now the Chinese haven't been very good at computer hardware. We have only produced microcomputers. Maybe five or six years ago, we made a supercomputer, but the compilation speed was not as fast as the Americans'. But once we imported many computers from America and Japan, we were successful in making software. We are better at software engineering. In the future, thirty years from now, our computer science companies will be more competitive if we have good software. We can import hardware from outside and export software to the Japanese. The Japanese think Chinese are better at software. China's government policy [favoring applied sciences] will provide the foundation for competition with foreign companies, especially in software."

Zhou's comments directly challenge one of the epistemological norms of Western science, universalism. This Mertonian value suggests that scientific culture is at odds with the ethnocentrism of the larger society. Merton suggests that scientists must not judge the value of knowledge by the status of the producer of that knowledge. Race, nationality and gender should be discounted.[1] Such linkages, he notes, are factors in social life but are in contradiction to science. However, such a separation of scientific culture and Chinese culture is problematic to Zhou, whose cultural status is ambiguous. Adopting Mertonian universalism would merely widen the breach between him and the cultural core. It is better to bind his Chinese identity to his scientific prowess. This recasts Chinese culture and sinicizes his alien expertise. His upcoming comments on mathematics are an example of this transformation. Mathematics was not a high-status brand of knowledge in the past, for it was not an intrinsic skill for Confucian morality and political administration. It is, however, indispensable for applied science and has become a valued marker of talent in Zhou's lifetime. Yet he talks as if this talent is part of the "national character," a concept to which he seems to subscribe.

I ask, "Are there any other fields in which Chinese science will excel?"

"Certainly. For example, most Chinese people are good at mathematics. This is a pure science, along with physics, they need the most imagination, so I think perhaps in these two fields Chinese people have potential. In ancient times China's mathematicians did very important work. Chinese people are a logical sort, and the study of mathematics doesn't need much equipment. It is very suitable for a developing country. You only need a pen or a book, so that even without advanced facilities, mathematicians can make a contribution. Since Beijing has given us the open door policy, we can get some advanced facilities [i.e., supercomputers], which will give us an even greater advantage in doing our work."

I know that Zhou was quite good in mathematics as a middle school student. He has told me that it is a high-status field academically. In China, to be good in mathematics is the highest indication of intelligence. It is, in his estimation, an utterly impractical subject. It provides few avenues for employment outside of teaching, and it does not lend itself to lucrative private contract work. Zhou reconciles his pragmatism with his nationalist pride by pointing out that the government does recognize that mathematics is useful to the "applied sciences."

In spite of his mysticism, Zhou's heart is clearly in engineering. His mindset has a parallel in American engineering cultures, in the materialist "fix it" approach that views the world as a series of technical problems to be solved. In the American ethos, this rationality is coupled with a mystique. Americans believe themselves to have the "right stuff" or "know-how" imbued with a tinkering spirit that is believed to provide the crucial edge over Japanese competitors. This American attitude is roughly equivalent to Zhou's mystical belief in the special qualities of the Chinese people.

Concurring with Wang and the wisdom of the popular media, Zhou evokes genetics as a future Chinese success story: "We can expect great progress in genetics." However, as he expresses his esteem for the Chinese ethos, he adds a twist that Wang had not implied: "Chinese are good at that subject. Chinese scientists are used to studying human beings and the self, trying to unleash the potential power in the body."

Zhou continues to explain his intriguing point of view—one that combines a revival of traditional beliefs with a faith in twenty-first century technology: "The gene is the scientific way of releasing potential power, just as *qigong* is the traditional way of releasing potential power and finding how the body works. It will be a successful science. Biomedical engineering will be developed. Perhaps in thirty years some babies of high intelligence will be made by man, selecting talents through genetic engineering. In the future, both biology and genetics will be developed. That is true. But only as an applied field, not as a basic science. That's my hope."

Skalnik, in discussing strategies for outwitting the state, notes that the imposition of modernization might foment a round of "retraditionalization" in China (1989, 15). Zhou has found a way to partake of that retraditionalization without undoing his own, clearly technological, future. This cultural synthesis is necessary for safeguarding his own niche. It is a pragmatic choice.

His determined stance on applied technology is at odds with that of some of his colleagues who, like Wang, are in basic research. I summarize their point of view and ask him to comment. "Some of your colleagues have told me that they often discuss the relationship of science to technology. They feel that China now pays less attention to basic research than applied fields. If this situation continues longer, they fear that in the future there will be some problems—there will be no basis for further development. They say they are horrified by the decline of basic research."

"As far as I can tell, in our country's universities, there is too much theory and too little practical technology. So what we need is more practical technology and fewer theoretical subjects. Engineering will be the best field. Now the government gives more financial support to engineering. The director of my work unit deals with many factories, and they are all interested in getting new methods, new products and so on. So I think the engineer will be the most productive in the future."

As the acid test of his optimism, I ask him a key question: "Do you think science would be a good career in thirty years? Would you tell your son to be a scientist?"

"Maybe an engineer. Frankly, engineers make more money than scientists, so that would be more logical."

He goes on to speculate about the scientific landscape of China's best future. Zhou believes that "In general, some new fields will be developed, especially optical fibers, superconductors and some space technology."

He believes these new fields would not be hampered by the legacy of the Cultural Revolution when China isolated itself from the scientific world for ten years. Fields such as internal combustion engines, telecommunications and power plant automation relied on decades of steady global development. During the Cultural Revolution, Chinese progress in these fields came to a virtual halt, resulting in a persisting disadvantage. Newer fields—such as genetic manipulation and materials engineering—did not begin to grow until after the end of the Cultural Revolution. These fields offer a level playing field to young Chinese scientists competing for global recognition.

I ask him once again to elaborate on the development of computer automation in China. He answers, "Maybe by 2020, the computer can be widely used just as it is today in developed countries, such as the United States and other countries. Computers can be widely used in many fields, especially in engineering and management and maybe even in daily life. Applications will be available to common people. Now it is only accessible for study or government use."

He waxes speculative, reminding me of his bent toward science fiction: "In the future maybe we humans can invent something that will give everybody the ability to operate computers. Sometimes we imagine making equipment—a plug—a biological socket, that can connect the computing block to a human being. This interface will give them that ability to do things they couldn't before." He adds, as a practical proviso, that computers are not self-aware. He realizes that the linguistic problems of computer-human communication are difficult to surmount. Even if they could be surmounted, there would be many other practical barriers, making the plug-in interface a possible, but unlikely, occurrence.

Zhou approaches computers in a way that Wang did not. Zhou can imagine the penetration of technology into daily life, not just in the isolated realm of research. In addition, his speculations go further than Wang's; his imagination ranges further afield. Zhou is more comfortable with technology, much as American youth navigate more happily than their elders in a sea of computers, VCRs and cellular phones. Zhou is much more enthusiastic about the Chinese space program than Wang, and he views automation as a boon.

I ask Zhou: "Considering the advances in these new fields, how will China stand in relation to the rest of the world in science and technology?"

"It will be difficult to surpass the developed countries, but the gap will be narrower. It will take at least fifty to a hundred years to catch up. Even in the history of Chinese science, Chinese people were better in theoretical fields than at technology. Our technology is inferior. By 2020 we can't catch up with America's level. America has a strong industrial and educational foundation that we lack. Our government has tried to show the world that China is very strong, by emphasizing—pumping money into—some fields that will show quick results, such as astronomy or atomic weapons research. Great progress is possible in high technology, only because the government addresses these issues."

A strong international image demands this policy direction.[2] Highly publicized projects—the Beijing proton accelerator, the Yangtze Gorges Dam—reflect cultural pride more than they do technological planning (see Link 1992, 207–208; Pye 1988, 100). A strictly rational planning system would build infrastructure as its highest priority. Of course, such a system exists only in the imaginations of rationalists. Zhou is aware of the reality.

"Practically speaking, in daily life, industry is really very weak. It hasn't much of an impact since that type of science isn't being developed. Some special fields might catch up, can catch up to the West. But thirty years is too short a time, even in the best future. There are two factors. First, everything must go well. Second, even if everything goes fine, we still lack a strong foundation. We only have a strong basis in some special fields."

Zhou's language and formulation of the issue reflect the "racetrack" metaphor of modernization. The "advanced countries"—the United States, Europe and Japan—are in the lead, while the rest of the world trails behind on the track. In such a model, front-runners are inevitable, and China, as a late starter, lags perpetually behind. In this model the ten-year interruption of the Cultural Revolution is particularly disastrous. This metaphor also underlies the observation in the interviews that, while China may make progress, the well-fed West will progress yet faster. The racetrack model dominates both the general academic discourse on modernization and the informants' individual impressions of China's scientific standing.

The general distrust of intellectuals that formerly permeated the popular attitude toward scientific expertise in China has given way to the atmosphere of a spectator sport. In the media, science is no longer depicted as merely something borrowed from foreigners. The Chinese government has used both the popular press and the educational system to emphasize the antiquity of a Chinese tradition of science and technology (Orleans 1980). Scientific accomplishment is portrayed as a research Olympics, praising Chinese achievement, but always in competition with "the advanced countries."

Yet there is another emic model of reality at work. While China is disadvantaged by the grim limitations of a "developing" country, in its own estimation, it has the best players. Zhou paints a detailed picture of the Chinese national character—stalwart, intelligent and mystically intuitive. While in the short run China is bound to lose, her strategies are those of the long-distance runner who knows that in time, she can endure and win. The optimism, simultaneously mystical and technological, is for the long haul. The debate is over whether they will catch up in one, two or more generations.

I ask him about this time frame, and he considers: "My friends in research think it may take fifty years to develop the kind of equipment we need. We lack the money. The pressure comes from supervisors—they define the direction, give the goals, but most of the supervisors are political appointees, not scientists. Most leaders are not scientists or engineers and they don't know what is possible. My friends say, if conditions are optimal we would need thirty-five years to reach the world level, but just in some fields. Generally speaking, we would need seventy to a hundred years. Recently, a friend, a provincial official, said that if we had enough money and enough thermal engineers, we could get usable atomic power in fifty years. I asked him about the current situation, he said, 'I can't imagine . . . this is not a not normal situation, I just can't predict the process.'"

The "not normal situation," of course, refers to the "specter of Tiananmen." The clear, if unspoken, implication is that stable political support is necessary to long-term research and development. Without that stability, the "playing field" will be strewn with hurdles.

Zhou makes his argument more specific. Political instability is counter to scientific and technical progress, largely because it intermittently and unpredictably slams the open door shut. Without global communication, China cannot hope to be a serious scientific contender. "Think about Japan's development of science and technology. It knows how to learn advanced technology from other countries. But the Chinese don't know how to do that. After the student movement, I fear that the open door shall be a little bit closed, not too open."

Zhou gives me an uneasy look; he has nearly committed the unpardonable sin of directly mentioning the aftermath of Tiananmen. He continues, "I think the open policy should not be changed. We should learn advanced science and technology from other countries. Doing research on our own is a waste of time and money. We should keep the door open. Compared to ten years ago, today science and technology is developing well in China. Then there were no TVs, tape recorders, washing machines; now every young couple [in the city] has this, even refrigerators. Why has China developed in last ten years? Because we have learned things from other countries. If we stay closed, we will learn nothing. Just as people should help each other, countries should help each other."

Zhou applies this intercultural exchange to a new topic, education: "I think in the future we will combine the Western and Chinese system to develop a new system of education. Western education pays more attention to the individual. Now the Chinese system concentrates on fundamental knowledge and overlooks creativity."

When I ask Zhou to expand on these educational changes, he concurs with Wang's point of view, adding twists of his own. Chinese education favors passivity, not creativity. By focusing on memorization—which Zhou scornfully concedes may be suitable to history, but not "logical subjects"—the students' problem-solving abilities remain undeveloped. Teachers should be less narrowly focused and should have a better grasp of their fields. Curricula should be updated, not teaching "things that are useless for the future, theories that are so old they are not useful." Zhou recommends such drastic changes as internships to break up the boredom of classroom study.

He believes that students should choose their own subject of study, since "At the present time, many students who graduate from university can't find a job, because what they were assigned to study is not needed by the society. I don't think that is very well planned."

Zhou adds that American students "must think about their subject. This is the best way to teach technology and science. Several years ago, education experts experimented with this program in some key schools and universities. Gradually there have been changes. For example, in our university the president told us, 'In your university, your primary task is to study, not knowledge, but how to solve problems, how to work.'"

"Do you think this is what happened to you, that you learned how to work effectively in your education?"

He reinterprets my question in a way I had not anticipated. I had thought he might reflect on his own "innovative education," but instead he discusses the engineer's problem in making the school-to-work transition. He points out that when conditions are good, as when young people go abroad to study, they can accomplish a great deal. But only a few can have such opportunities, so the remainder stay mired in unsatisfactory conditions.

But that will not completely mar the best future, for Zhou believes that another variable will intervene. Young scholars will persevere in spite of the odds. Zhou agrees with Wang that the Chinese tradition of education will help the country in its future. "Chinese culture has a deep tradition of education, so many, many people in China know that education is the most important thing. So, I think the whole of China will have continuous study, especially self-study. Because of improved communication techniques, perhaps even in ten years, anyone will be able to sit down in his own room to study using television. That will make it easy to do self-study. Educational progress may be easier to do here than in other countries because it is in our cultural background."

When I ask Zhou to go back and elaborate on the "conditions" that impede young intellectuals, he gives me a surprisingly personal response: "At the moment my brother-in-law is a lecturer in a university. In his family he has a mother, a wife and a child—all living together. They live in 10-meter-square room. At the moment four people share a room with only one desk, and you have to rotate. During the day or during the evening, his 9-year-old daughter will have to study, and during the night he must study from nine o'clock until midnight or one A.M. when he goes to bed. The next morning he has to get up at six. Teaching, he feels very busy sometimes, very tired. I think his teaching quality will be affected by his lack of sleep. He is driven by the lack of money, calculating how much money should go on food, how much for clothes or utensils. So he spends a lot of time and talent on this, rather than on his work. But he can't do otherwise, or he can't make ends meet. In the future housing will be improved, with each person getting at least 10 square meters. People like my brother-in-law will have a place to study, to prepare lessons."

Zhou places this vignette in a larger context: "This is very difficult. Money plays a more important role in society now. We have to live out our intellectual status in the real world. If we get on the train we can only eat some food if we carry it on, but some other people, like the self-employed businessman, can pay twenty or thirty times more money to buy some fresh food. Then their reputation is enhanced in front of the other passengers." Clearly embarrassed by this humiliating situation, Zhou adds, "I think my country will make much progress if we give more financial encouragement to the intellectuals. It's important because in modern society, money gives you prestige. I think the problem now is that our country wants to give more reputation to the intellectual but not give much money. So the basis of the reputation is only imaginary. We, in fact, haven't much reputation."

Nonetheless, Zhou is a believer in education. He is very conscious of his rank, which is based solely on his education, not on his peasant heritage. One of his chief desires for the "best" future is that there will be more access to education in the best future. He notes: "Many people want to go to university. Most will want to get a job. In the countryside, some peasants want to go to live in the cities. One way is to pass the university entrance examination." This view is in line with a nineties trend in which disadvantaged groups—rural people, women, minorities—seriously pursue academic tracks to bypass their liabilities (Hayhoe 1994).

"The city and countryside are very different. Educational conditions are very much better in the city. Students in the cities' middle schools will have the first pick of universities. I was brought up in a village, and the conditions were not very good. Facilities were poor, and some teachers were not responsible. After all, they didn't want to go to the village after they graduated. This should be changed. Farmers *are* interested in education."

He adds, in direct contradiction to Wang, "All the people in one village raise money for education.[3] In this way, education will change for the better. I know the educational system in the countryside. It is useful for preparing for higher education, but not for acquiring skills. You can just memorize knowledge, but you don't know what to do with that knowledge. In the future this situation will still exist." Unlike Wang, Zhou does not believe that the educational system of China will change to accommodate the realities of the countryside. He does not postulate a vocational education track, but instead projects his own experience that secondary school can be a springboard to formal higher education.

Yet this doesn't mean there is no place for the highly educated in the rural sector. Because of the "spark" plan that promotes appropriate, intermediate technology, rural industry has become a real presence. In the countryside the leaders of these enterprises lack the expertise to be efficient. Zhou's experience has been that such peasants are happy to have the opportunity to develop *guanxi* with engineers and would like to lure them to the countryside. (In the years immediately following this interview, Zhou has become even more certain that rural industry is important.)

The peasants know that even if they get their children to study science, the children don't want to come back to their hometown. Zhou is a case in point. Peasants, however, can offer housing, prestige and money to young frustrated engineers—perhaps 20,000 yuan, ten to twenty times a professor's salary! Although the countryside doesn't have amenities to offer, it is tempting to a young intellectual who feels trapped in a dead-end job as a junior engineer, assigned to a work unit for life. If rural living conditions improve, Zhou points out, then maybe this will be a future trend. He himself considered it before he had his chance to go abroad. He says that students younger than he are less passive and might grab this chance at independence.

Having hinted at Zhou's view of Chinese society in the "best" future, we finally approach it directly. I ask, "What impact do you think science and technology will have on Chinese society in the best future? Describe the way of life . . . the standard of living."

"Our situation won't change much, for at least ten more years. There won't be much difference between urban Chinese and [overseas Chinese], particularly for high officials. In thirty years, I think there will be change, especially for families in the countryside. Housing is no problem in the countryside. Most Chinese farmers have a big house; some families have five rooms. Recently, some farmers have purchased televisions and are getting wealthy. TV will be popular in the countryside. The most progress will be made in the countryside, along the East Coast. Tibet or Xinjiang won't change much. In the mountainous areas, minorities won't change much."

He projects a social future in which "a couple can live apart from their parents. Nowadays more and more couples live apart from their parents. But I think that the couple and their parents will still love each other. And I think that morality will be slightly changed, but not too greatly. Attitudes may change regarding marriage and divorce, but the relationship between the generations will be the same."

By phrasing his predictions this way Zhou highlights another cultural difference. The basic American social dyad is the married couple—husband and wife. American morality is defined by that relationship. Marital stability—often associated with sexual chastity and fidelity—is intertwined with morality in American popular discourse. Yet, whenever I would ask the Chinese about their families, their first association was their parents and siblings—not their spouse and child. In China, the bond between parent and child was the more significant social connection.[4] Hence, it is not surprising that Zhou defines morality as a continuation of his father-son bond, rather than in terms of an enduring marital relationship.

"I think the living style will become more Western, because younger people, in China are interested in Western lifestyles. This trend will increase through the generations. For example, marital relations, sexuality, food and many other things will be influenced by the West."

"How will this affect society at large? Some of your colleagues have suggested that relationships between people will be casual, not as intimate as today. You might know a lot of people, but you might not know them very well. What do you think of this idea?"

In contradiction to Wang, Zhou thinks that China's social chill is an artifact of the Cultural Revolution, not a product of modernization. He hopes his generation will be immune to the suspiciousness that has come to characterize China's interpersonal ecology. "I think people, especially young people, will get even closer to each other. Now people are afraid to get closer to other people. This may be because some people suffered from the Cultural Revolution ten years ago. People didn't like to make friends, they were reserved. They suffered a lot from the Cultural Revolution. During the Cultural Revolution, people who were once friends became enemies. So older people are especially afraid to make contact with other people."

"People in their forties?"

"Yes, but young people don't care about the past history—they have a long life ahead of them. They want to have closer relationships. I think that in thirty years people will become honest and sincere. They will have closer relationships, because they won't be afraid of each other, so the whole society will be friendlier."

"I think the best future should be both modern and moral. By morality I mean every person does work ethically—especially doctors, train conductors, officials." He does not mean that these people are thieves or liars, but that they are breaking their tacit social contract. All these people work with the public, even for the public. By being surly, passive-aggressive or actively selfish, they fail to meet their obligations to the greater whole.

Zhou continues, decrying the tendency toward selfishness and passivity: "They work for the society, the country, not for themselves. Of course, they also get money, but now there are too many people who work all day for themselves and get money from the country as well. Everyone should be responsible at work and be self-motivated. These days no one wants to work very hard. In the next century there may be much progress. . . . But I am afraid this will not happen."

KUNGFU, CRIME AND CONFIDENCE LOST

Zhou's pessimistic scenario echoes the issues brought up by Wang, but this interview is even more difficult. Zhou is speaking in late December 1989. The tensions wrought by Tiananmen linger and color his pessimistic scenario. Whereas Wang had earlier rejected the likelihood of a return of the Cultural Revolution, Zhou is keenly aware that political winds might shift unpredictably.

After introducing the concept of the worst scenario, I ask Zhou to visualize a future in which the problems he has discussed in the best scenario do not fade away, but persist.

He responds, "Hard to imagine, I always like to think about the best future." Nonetheless, he goes on to elaborate on the demographic barriers to development in China. At the root is the huge population. Zhou points out that there will be a widening gap between a large, illiterate, rural population and a small population of educated urbanites. He adds, "And there will be epidemics. Isn't there something in Shanghai like that?"

I ask if he is referring to a hepatitis B epidemic mentioned in the *China Daily*.

"Yes. Another problem is pollution. In our country, as far as I'm concerned, we are not paying much attention to the environment.[5] Perhaps this is the situation in all developing countries. They just want to develop, not consider the consequences of development. This makes environmental conditions worse, especially in our country, since we have so many people. If the environment deteriorates, then people may develop diseases. I would not want to see urban people always coughing from the pollution. In thirty years, many cities in China, especially the industrial cities, will be even much more polluted than today. As we discussed before, Shenyang, where I live, is the second most seriously polluted city in the world. Shenyang may take first place in thirty years, or even less! This must harm the people's health and produce a shorter life span. Of course you already know that air pollution, industrial pollution, is one of the causes of cancer and many other serious diseases. If this situation happens, the gap will widen with the developed countries. Perhaps our country's science and technology will only stay at today's level."

"It sounds as if you think that science and technology won't develop much in the worst possible future? In the worst future there will still be modern technology?"

"Yes, I think so, because the development of science is the natural human tendency. In spite of everything, technology and science will develop and become better in the future."

Scientism again. Zhou concurs with his colleagues in describing science—and to a lesser degree technology—as a force in itself. In this worldview, science progresses along an independent path, regardless of the circumstances in any particular place or situation. If China is not in the lead, or drops out of the race entirely, some other nation will pick up the baton.

"So, what kind of problems will science and technology face in the worst future?"

"There are two potential directions for modern technology. I think the best one is that technology will be used for society, for the people. The other contrasts with this—that modern technology will be used to harm people, to be used only for selfish purposes. In the future, the most undesirable thing would be that scientific discoveries would be misused. A good example is war in space. Another is nuclear weapons. If scientists work on nuclear fission or fusion, we just want to produce electricity. But the people who develop them don't want to use these discoveries to make a war. But of course scientists and researchers cannot control what will happen."

Again, realpolitik—the locus of power—is the important issue. The government leaders make policy; policy directs decisions and regulations; scholars must function within those constraints.

I ask him to elaborate, "Can you think of other examples of the improper development of science and technology?"

"I worry about some computer applications. Maybe only a few people know how to control robots—only a few researchers make the programs. We have just imported robots from Japan in our institute. If you don't know how to use them properly, the work is very dangerous and the operations are complicated. Only two people know how to operate it. The others just stand around and look, saying 'ahh'!"

The future Zhou is describing is sometimes called the "technocratic elite" scenario (Bodley 1985, 223). This negative projection sees the ordinary individual as disenfranchised by his ignorance of technology. Those who understand and control technology and industry form the new elite. I admit a moment of dislocation—should not Zhou, the brilliant young engineer, feel he is part of that elite? Clearly, he does not. His expertise is not central to that particular technology, and, in any case, he does not identify with the forces that wield the power. He places himself in the role of those who try to look wise and say, "Ahh."

In an inevitable reaction to the technocratic elite projection, Zhou also suggests a social rejection of technology. Like the nineteenth century Luddites who smashed the looms of the Industrial Revolution, future Chinese workers might lash out against machines and those who design them. "Some robots may replace human beings. If this use is not well managed, there will be too many unemployed people. They will commit crimes against society or turn against science. They want jobs. But because most of the jobs would be taken by advanced technology, they will rebel against technology."

He elaborates that as a result of unemployment, "The unemployed workers will commit crimes in the society, destroy and vandalize equipment, or demolish the universities. Also the students and teachers in the universities or scientists will be killed, beaten or frightened by the unemployed. I think this would be very bad."

"China will have heavy social problems. As you know, China has a policy that each couple has only one child. Every parent spoils the child because they have only one child. When these children grow up in the future, they will become criminals. This problem is happening now. This is very serious. No one has a brother or a sister, and maybe that will make him become immoral." Zhou is expressing a popular sentiment, a "moral panic" that single children cannot be properly socialized (Wu 1994). The explanation for this moral decay is the potential spoiling of the child by the four grandparents and two parents pouring attention, food and money into one child—the 4–2–1 syndrome. I had been a bit dismayed to see a family spend nearly an adult's monthly income—150 yuan—on a trendy American-made transformer toy. There were plenty of less expensive Chinese toys, including transforming robots—but they were not the current fad. So families scrimped to buy the "young emperor" his heart's desire—feeding a selfishness and materialism not conducive to communitarian self-sacrifice.

"Television also leads to crime. TV programs, Hollywood movies and Chinese kungfu (*gongfu*) will affect people's minds, especially children. Yesterday, my brother sent me a letter that a 13-year-old child raped a 22-year-old girl. Very strange. My brother said he learned it from TV. If children develop and the parent and society cannot lead them correctly, they will commit crimes." Zhou could have been a Midwestern American parent bemoaning Hollywood's sex and violence.[6]

Zhou continues to describe a pessimistic future fraught with crime: "I can imagine the worst future with immorality on the rise. If there are more people who use technology to deceive, that would be very terrible."

He goes on to describe American white-collar crime—computer fraud and sabotage. He states, "Now, in China, there are only a few instances of this kind of modern crime, but I think in the future it will be more frequent. Modern technology can help people live more comfortably, but it can also help some people to commit crimes, very secretly and very effectively. Society will have more criminals. This is a natural condition of society. On one side there will be very high technology. Some will be richer. Some people, not really poor but with nothing to do, will find stimulation through crime."

In the past ten years China's highest crime rate was 8.9/10,000 while the U.S. rate was as high as 515.9/10,000 (Tan and Li 1993, 353). In spite of the low crime rate, the public perceives crime as a serious problem (Tan and Li 1993, 352). Preventative measures such as bars in apartment windows, glass shards on compound walls and increased neighborhood vigilance are evident (see Jankowiak 1993, 117–119) and suggests an increased concern with theft. Zhou believes that growing class distinctions will contribute to that disorder.

He pauses and reflects: "Yes, there will be more crime. Now I think thirty years from now there will be more differences in wealth between rich and poor people. The poor people will get poorer, and the rich people will get richer. Some poor people who can't get education won't be able to stand up to this pressure. So they will want to hurt the society, and so there will be more crime."

"Will this be everywhere in China, or primarily in the cities?"

"I think the cities will be affected more seriously than in the countryside. In the cities where people are gathered together, the criminals can easily shoplift, or steal."

As long as money is the basis of prestige, the moral fabric is endangered. The "money future" has grave social consequences in Zhou's mind. He points out, "One thing is that most people just want to earn money, the more the better. I think it will cause a chain of problems. One of these is the way people treat each other. We won't be able to trust each other. I will give you an example. Maybe in the future everyone will act very impolitely, and the whole feeling of community will break down. They will not treat each other nicely, politely. They will just be trying to get the most money from each other—selfish, very selfish. I feel very disappointed when I see the way people in the streets get on the train, on the bus or, in the canteen, how the students get their food. It's terrible! It's very crowded!"

He has pinpointed an area of culture shock to many Westerner sojourners—the free-for-all scramble for scarce resources, from train seats to rice soup. Wang and his peers had told me they found this antisocial behavior shocking and embarrassing; and now Zhou concurs.

The emphasis on money poses special conflicts to intellectuals who are low on a hierarchy determined by prosperity. Zhou notes that "Chinese government officials and many people don't consider knowledge a high priority. Nowadays some people think it is useless to go to the university. In fact, most professors' salaries are lower than barbers' or shoe menders'."[7]

Zhou reinforces his point with a "contemporary urban myth." "I know a famous professor who wants to do research on the logical problems in artificial intelligence. I think the subject is very interesting and important, but when he applied for funds to continue his research from the State Education Commission, he got only 10,000 yuan, just about 3,000 [U.S.] dollars. I can't understand this matter! If a famous professor cannot apply for enough money to really do research, then younger scientists can do nothing. I understand China may not have a lot of money to give researchers. Money is invested in matters it thinks are urgent. So this is the problem. China is a centralized country. I often wonder about some policies, about the Chinese government. I have heard of an example from a neurosurgeon in a medical university. He did operations for a whole night and got 1.6 yuan!"

I mentally cringe. A moderately fancy hair ribbon for my daughter costs at least 5 yuan. Zhou continues, "Well, you'd think he'd rather go to the free market and sell eggs or something; they make many times more than that. The maximum income of a doctor is not as good as a barber. I think this is very unfortunate."

"So students are not interested in pursuing their teachers' careers, for they think they will be poor. If this situation continues, it means that production, income, will drop in the near future, in 2000. Many students don't want to go to the university to teach or do research. They want to go into trading and make more money!"

It is true that the universities are experiencing student dropout—once an unthinkable phenomenon. In 1988, 6000 undergraduates and 2000 graduates discontinued their programs (Du 1992, 86). Those who persist face blows to their morale.

Zhou adds for emphasis, "For example, I have a classmate, a good, intelligent classmate. After he graduated, he worked in the university for two years but never got a house. He was married for six years and had a child. Finally he gave up teaching and went to Shenzhen to trade and now he has 5,000 yuan a month at least. He has a beautiful house for his wife and child. Before this, his wife quarreled with him about housing. I have no house either. I married over three years ago, and have a little child, and my flat is very cold in winter, and hot in summer. When my wife was pregnant, she would ache from the wind. If I did not have this chance to go abroad, I might exchange my job and do other things."

"These things have a negative impact on education. Higher degree, less money. I have no chance to do other things for money. The government won't let us do other things. If we want to do other things, we must give up our jobs. If we all give up our jobs, then China will have no teachers or scientists. Many scientists, professors and teachers worry about the student's lack of interest. The 'Do Nothings' have little interest in science. They only seek a way to earn more money. That's very dangerous. When they graduate from college, they won't be able be help China be competitive. But I want you to know that I was not so pessimistic before, only recently." He adds another oblique reference to Tiananmen. Almost in response to his own politically suspect thought, he adds, "I do believe that the socialist system is the only way to save China."

I ask cautiously, not wanting to compromise Zhou by leading him into politically dangerous territory, "What factors have made you so pessimistic?"

"In our unit, we have almost half-stopped. We have tried to do business with some American and British companies, very big projects, joint ventures, very busy. This year [1989] foreign companies stopped investment, so our unit hasn't very much work to do. To me this future looks very dark."

Many foreign corporations had pulled their investments in the bleak time following Tiananmen. To someone who has pinned his future on the open door, this withdrawal is numbingly depressing. He continues, "I would not like to see our political system change over and over again. Most people will make an effort to avoid political quarrels, like the Cultural Revolution. I don't want to see our people fight, either between countries or within our country. A civil conflict would be the worst possibility. I am a little worried about the democratic movements—in China and East Europe. In China civil war may be the result; many people worry about that. If this happened, it would continue several years. That would be the worst situation—even more so than now."

I do not want to pressure him to continue on this issue. I myself had felt the fear that accompanied the mere thought of civil war—*and I could leave*. I knew that such a nightmare would be a terrifying possibility to Zhou. Most Americans cannot appreciate the grimness of that vision. Our Civil War was over a century past, and the sheer scale of a Chinese internal conflict is beyond our imagination. With the specter of June Four so recently in all our memories, this topic is far too delicate. Zhou adds, "If there are political movements involved, it will destroy technology."

Like the American antiwar movement of the 1960s, China's political protests originate in the Chinese equivalents of Berkeley—places like Beida (Beijing

University) and Qinghua (China's MIT). So I ask him if the political movements would mean problems in education. He says, "Maybe some students like to get involved in such political activities and would abandon their studies."

I ask whether that is likely or only possible. His answer struck me: "Students always get involved in political movements; maybe that will happen. The worst case probably won't happen, because the people and the government will make sure it doesn't happen. We have already suffered this experience, so we will try to avoid that bitter ordeal again."

Time to change the subject. "Other than crime," I ask, "what other social problems might result from the changes brought about by science and technology? Will the family or friendships be changed?"

Again, Zhou returns to a core problem—the shift from extended to nuclear families with the concomitant shift toward individualism. "People are more independent. They don't want to rely on anybody. They also don't want to spend so much time on family. There may be some social problems. Because of the family planning policy, by 2020 the percentage of older people will increase in society. I will be 57. Maybe I will belong to this group of older people. But older people have only very few people to depend on. We have a custom that younger people are responsible for the older generation. In 2020 everyone would have had only one child. But some will have no son, no one to depend on. The older people will feel very lonely. This will cause a burden to our government. The elderly will have some medical and physical troubles, so the government will have to spend much money on this."

I ask Zhou to summarize. "In general, how would you sum up the worst future? How likely is it to happen?"

Zhou emphasizes that, in his view, the worst problems will be psychological, rather than economic or social. "The gap between China and the developed countries will broaden. People are losing confidence. If the situation is not solved, and solved well, I think the people will lose their faith in the government, and in themselves. I think this is the worst possibility, but I don't think that will happen in thirty years." He believes China will manage the situation.

BEYOND THE SLUMP

We have now found ourselves sliding into the "most probable" scenario, leaving the realm of pessimistic speculation and considering only the most likely future. Like Wang, Zhou's realistic future is optimistic, but the years of waiting weigh more heavily on Zhou.

"The most likely future is a mixture of the best and the worst. I think the most likely will be 80 percent like the best future and 20 percent like the worst future. It's not likely for China to overtake the developed countries in 2020. Maybe in some fields it is possible. And also most likely in that time the advantages of the Chinese philosophy will be known to more and more people. More and more people will come to realize that this philosophy will be useful again. And also the economic and market system will become mature in our country, and the system of incentives will be enacted."

"So you will be on the path of the best future?"

"Yes, we are more likely to achieve the desirable situation."

I probe, "Not the undesirable future?"

"Maybe, just now, we are on the undesirable [path]."

"The undesirable future is now, the continuation of now?"

"Now and continuing into the near future, maybe ten years. As you know the 'old proper men' will just go away, and the situation will change." China's party and military are dominated by elderly men in their eighties and nineties. In the decade before the millennium they will probably die.

"The situation can change when everyone realizes the value of the individual—that everyone can count. In the near future I don't think China's education situation is good, but I think this is just a slump. In five or ten years education will be developed. More and more people will realize the importance of education. Of course, it is a big society with a lot of inertia. It won't change too much."

I ask Zhou to discuss the significant factors that will enhance science, technology and education in the most likely future. Like Wang, he hopes for cooperation among diverse disciplines to achieve common goals. He also hopes that the open door policy will continue. International cooperation will protect China from isolation. The students, returning from abroad, will change the ideas and attitudes of "ordinary people." Some of these changes will alter traditional Chinese attitudes, promoting the "value of individuality" and the esteem of science as a profession—a key element of modernization.

When I ask what factors might lead to rapid scientific change, Zhou responds philosophically: "In my opinion crisis, need and desire will promote scientific advancement. For example, military needs can foster new weapons. Scientists will try to solve any threat to humans. Desire is another element. People will want to travel in space, explore other planets. The desire will drive science and promote progress."

He shifts to a more sociological consideration. "I also think a certain amount of unemployment is necessary, because this promotes competition in workers." Like Wang, Zhou values equity—the notion that rewards should be in proportion to effort. This principle was undermined in the days of the "iron rice bowl" when work—even if meaningless and insignificant—was guaranteed by the state. Zhou adds, "If everybody gets work, like ten years ago, when our government guaranteed that anybody could have work, workers didn't worry about their job. The workers could do nothing at work, and managers couldn't do anything about it. So I think a certain unemployment is necessary for competition. It will stimulate the workers to work harder. And also the managers will be more powerful than at the present, for they will not be controlled by government. They will have the right to fire workers. They will be more responsible than now."

He seems to be describing an urban phenomenon, so I ask, "You are from the countryside—what do you think will happen there?"

"Everything can change. Generally speaking, the people in the countryside were quite poor in the past, and people in the countryside wanted to emigrate to the cities. But nowadays there is a complete change, and they are quite rich. If we investigated a small village, the average salary would be three times my salary. Many people have color televisions and important people even think they can buy a car, a private car! I really can't imagine it. At first there were a lot of rumors—there must be criminals running the rural industry, getting the money illegally. After I really investigated this matter I found that this is wrong. Generally speaking they are doing things legally. But compared with government industries, they are more flexible. In a government factory some leaders just care about their own positions and promotions. They don't care much about the factory, because it doesn't matter to them."

Zhou discusses the drawbacks of this "iron rice bowl" mentality as it applies to education. He adds that those who manage to enter the university "have a relaxed time, taking only a little time to study. . . . The teacher makes the students lazy [by spoon-feeding them]." After a pause, he considers another aspect of "spoon-feeding" and the resulting impact on science, "There is another big problem in science—we don't have much curiosity to invent or improve. We can imitate a product, but it is not necessary to invent it by ourselves. We are in a different stage than Western countries. The West has been industrialized, but Chinese society is a mixture. Scientists know that they can get technology from Western countries. Maybe this attitude limits progress. This is a difficult conflict to resolve."

"I had a very talented friend who had just graduated from the university. He took a 100,000 yuan to develop a research project but this successful process was never applied to any industrial plants. Some people just did research, others were in operations, and still others designed. It was not a unified process. If I developed a new technique, applying it would be very difficult. In the government there are different departments—research is controlled by the research department, and applications are controlled by the industrial department."

The bureaucracies that control Chinese scientific planning are structural forces that also inhibit its cohesion. Research may be under the control of a number of high-level state bureaucracies—the State Education Commission, the State Planning Commission, the State Economic Commission and the State Science and Technology Commission. There are also planning arms at the provincial and local level. Below this level are the ministries—eight would oversee industrial technology in the ministries of machine building. A technology that cross-cuts categories, such as computers might be housed in several such ministries (see Volti 1982, 98–101), fragmenting technological planning and processing.

Communication and diffusion within this system depend on the Chinese Academy of Sciences or professional organizations such as the Chinese Association of Science and Technology (Volti 1982, 102), organizations whose effectiveness diminishes when intellectuals are under duress.

Wang had mourned the lack of cooperation in university-based research. Zhou reiterates the lack of connection between planning, process and production in industrial research as well. He adds, "We could use new materials to make some special machines, especially in designing tools. Tools are essential in manufacturing machines. But it is quite difficult to use new materials in China, because there are so many conditions that can't be fulfilled."

This was a common complaint: "conditions that can't be fulfilled." It might refer to the unavailability of critical parts or the lack of ability of human technical teams to repair or construct the new equipment. One agronomist used the phrase to indicate that even the most modern farms were not clean enough to support sensitive breeding stock. In other words, cutting edge technology requires an infrastructure that simply is not yet present in China. Zhou notes, "If we try to use some new materials to manufacture lathes, we may know some new material is very good for this purpose. But we can't manufacture it because the foundation of our industry is so low. We need some of the new technology of the West. If we continue to open to the outside, we will develop faster."

I ask, trying to understand if the issue is educational or industrial: "Is it a problem of lacking knowledge, or of lacking the skills to use this knowledge practically?"

"The quality for most of the products made in our factories is very poor. I don't think this is because of the technical design; rather, I think this is because the workers are not operating properly. The main problems are production process and sometimes poor materials, but mainly the process."

"Of construction?"

"Yes, construction and assembly—putting the components together. Many old factory leaders are peasants, a few workers, very few are intellectuals. Now that China has adopted an open door policy to introduce techniques from foreign countries, we import equipment, but no one can use it. It's a waste. We can't use it well. If it breaks down, [we] have to invite technicians from abroad to repair it, and the costs are very high. Many machines or pieces of equipment are put together in China, but the components are imported from other countries. If we import the same machine from other countries, it works properly and lasts for many years, but the same components that we put together have many problems. Sometimes machines refuse to work or work just for a few days, and then they are out of order. I think the process is very important for producing products. I think if most people are well educated and take the process seriously, they will not just rely on the equipment or tools, they will rely on their own minds. This will help to improve the quality."

He then told me a highly appropriate satirical—and typical—joke about Chinese space flight that was currently floating about the science fiction crowd of which he was a member. Emphasizing the improbability of the scenario, he quips, "China builds a rocket . . . and it works!"

After that remark, he replies more seriously, "The larger population must have basic knowledge and better skills to do science. This would be helpful. Middle school students lack general popular science materials. Even university teaching materials are out of date—thirty to forty years old. It is difficult to learn new material. In my university we did not know enough astronomy to discuss a general class article. We did not have the background in popular science—Einstein's relativity theory and cosmology. If you don't understand a term, you can turn to a dictionary, but you would still need a broad science background [just to understand the definition]. What a pity. And we are university graduates! What about ordinary people? There is a long way to go."

"At present, people don't know what science is. If people are ignorant, they won't want to invest in developing science and technology. Society is not changing that fast. Such changes do not depend on the party; they depend on the people. People resist if you try to change some ideas. People are also influenced by propaganda and by traditions. Sometimes the government tries to do some good things, but it is difficult to get understanding from the common people. For example, the government tried to raise intellectuals' salaries—in the primary and middle school. But the workers didn't understand it. They think teachers have an easier, less valuable job. So, they objected. If the workers oppose the leaders, it will be difficult [to create positive change]. I think the leaders ought to gradually start to improve this situation. Now intellectuals officially make more than workers, and the workers have bonuses, but the intellectuals don't. A lecturer receives around 95 yuan each month. But other workers, with a basic salary of 50 or 60 yuan, can receive as much as 200 to 300 yuan each month! So their real living standard is much higher than ours. I think that if the government really takes us seriously our salary will be much higher and our living standard will be improved."

For Zhou, the status of intellectuals is the most concrete feature of the probable future that most concerns him. He adds, "Intellectuals are not afraid of hardships, but are concerned that it is not fair for them to get so little. All society should be fair. If people work hard they should be paid more. Some private businessman just sell. Although the teacher doesn't seem to work hard, he must read books all day long. The people in China do not seem to understand."

In the interviews, three distinct concepts of justice are repeatedly set at odds with each other—need, equality and equity.[8] In the need model, the resources are allocated to the most critical parts of society. This socialist ideal is expressed in policies designed to contain the damage caused by agricultural shortages or unemployment. In the equality model, resources are shared equally. Zhou, in his disgust with the corruption and special privilege allotted government officials demonstrates his value for equality. He believes that "all should be [treated] equal." Finally, a third model remains, equity—the concept that rewards should come in proportion to effort. This is the view of justice that Zhou sees as violated by the low status accorded intellectuals. Their work is not valued and compensated as they believe it should be. The intellectuals' repeated use of sobriquets like "egg sellers" and "people who just use some trick to make money" expresses their concern that there are those who contribute less to China than they do, but are better rewarded.

"I can take myself as an example," Zhou says. "In my *danwei*, many young people wanted to do some research work. But we have no chance, no opportunities. I am lucky. I have worked there only three years and the head of my department likes me very much because I work very hard. So he lets me go to an institute to get further training and lets me begin to work."

"Many other of my classmates just teach students, year after year. After teaching they have time in which they could do something. They want to do some research work at this time, but they can't. When they become old, they must attend to many other problems. They won't have the energy to do research work at that time, so their best time is lost. Yes, they could do research, they can put in their own time, but they can't earn money doing research work. When their results are published, it is of no use. There is no reward, so why should they do it?"

I have no answer to this rhetorical question. Zhou has, in fact, probably been able to sidestep this stumbling block through hard work and *guanxi*, but he is clearly angry that his fate is the exception, not the rule. He goes on, increasingly irritated.

"With this new thing you can see . . . we can't talk very easily. We are different. You can leave China. This is the system. We can think about it, but we can't talk about it." The barrier between *waiguoren* and *neiren* has just snapped into place. I didn't think I had done anything specific to elicit it—besides being a foreigner—but as his frustrations build, they flow toward me, and then pass.

"Of course, no matter what the condition, there will be progress. It's true. The question is how much progress can we get and how much progress should we get? Chinese scientists have had some mistaken attitudes. Chinese scientists put up with everything from government and from society. They are too patient. They don't want to confront the society. I think maybe this is a dangerous thing. Maybe in the future young scientists will become stronger than we are."

His disappointment is tangible. I wonder whether to end the interview here, or let him continue to talk. He spontaneously continues, "If our country wants to stand in the ranks of developed countries, we need to invest a lot of money in education. Sometimes I think deeply on this problem."

He goes on to relate the widespread parable cited in Chapter 2. "Just two years ago, there was a harsh article in the newspaper. It talked about students' choices. The students are being asked to move into the three roads—one is the gold road [trade], one is the black road [education, with the Western image of the graduates' robes], and the red road [the official party member]." These choices are unique to Zhou's generation. Wang really had no "gold path" and the "red path" of a young ambitious functionary is quite different from the revolutionary veterans that created the party structure in decades past.

"But the beliefs of the new generation are quite different from the old generation. Nowadays, few young people believe in any religion. They don't believe in capitalism or socialism. They make their own judgments, based on their own criteria, for what is right and what is wrong. They have their own ideas about which system is good for China, socialism or capitalism—quite different from their fathers or grandfathers. Because our system is now very strict, they don't say anything, but they have their own ideas. Maybe in thirty years, when they are in power, they will do things according to their philosophy. That will bring change. And I think that the young people in Taiwan have the same idea. I think in thirty years, young people now will reject the enmity that their fathers or grandfathers feel. They will treat others quite differently. And they will find their own way to run the country. They will make their own choices about what social system will be proper for the country. There will be great confusion for a short time. I think maybe many people, young and old, have already seen this kind of thing happening. They get together to talk about it, but not in public."

Zhou is stating the desired destiny of his generation—his prospects for himself, his peers and his child. He is both enthusiastic and wary. He has found a powerful inspiration in his own Han heritage, and wants that tradition—not a Marxist or capitalist utopia—to be combined with technology to be the template for the future. Li, his female colleague, has a different combination of tradition and modernity in mind.

6

Golden Coins, Red Phoenixes

To the left are docile dragons,
To the right are tame tigers.
Iron oxen plowing are a common sight,
Golden coins are always sown as seeds.
Hidden birds sing beautifully,
Red phoenixes stand in the sun.

(Wu Cheng En, *Journey to the West*, 1:34–35)

When Sun Wukong, the Monkey King, returns from the cave of the immortals, he discovers that the Demon King of Confusion has been bullying his little monkeys in his absence. He flies to that spirit's domain described so elegantly in verse. Dressed in a red gown, yellow silk sash and black boots, apparently unarmed, Sun challenges the Demon for mistreating his children and grandchildren. The Demon mocks him for appearing small and weak. But the Monkey King's Daoist training allows him to suddenly change size and to transform each of his eighty-four thousand hairs into anything he wants. He creates a small army of little monkeys to surround and defeat his adversary. Victorious, he rescues the captured and abused monkeys and returns to the Mountain of Flowers and Fruit. There he celebrates, announcing to his subjects that he has earned a surname—Sun, and with it, an enduring place in the geography of Chinese kinship. Now his monkey subjects also bear that name and are united in a single family.

By founding a family, Sun Wukong establishes their place in Confucian tradition. Throughout the vicissitudes of Chinese history, the central importance of the patrilineal family has survived. In present-day China, it is the women who are the primary caretakers of that tradition and the stability it implies. Providing that stability has become more difficult to modern women intellectuals as those traditions are increasingly challenged by Westernization.

Furthermore, just as women in the United States have had to face fluctuations in cultural expectations regarding female employment and gender equality, Chinese women have experienced shifts and modulations in prevailing attitudes. The women interviewed here have lived through struggles for parity and recognition in addition to the historical upheavals experienced by their male counterparts.

In the early part of this century, the activists of the May Fourth Movement of 1919 focused on the low status of women as a symbol of Confucian failings. This feminist legacy was inherited by the Chinese Communist party from its inception in 1921. When the party began to court the peasants in earnest in the 1930s, however, women's issues were placed in the background (see Gilmartin 1993).

At Liberation, the movement for women's equality experienced a resurgence. The Marriage Law of 1950 abolished the barter of women, concubinage, polygyny and prevention of the remarriage of widows. The new government established the Women's Federation to protect women's interests. But alas, those reforms conflicted with the redistribution of land to male peasants, and implementation of the spirit of the Marriage Law proved difficult. During the 1950s, collectivized dining halls and kindergartens became widespread, releasing women from some domestic chores and funneling them into the agrarian workforce. Many of these new reforms collapsed during the chaos of the Great Leap Forward, but collectivization was also resisted by women themselves.

The Cultural Revolution witnessed a feminist media campaign that promoted such slogans as "Women hold up half the sky," and depicted images of noble young women in heroic realist art. The entrance of young women into the Red Guards provided unprecedented mobility. Few Chinese women had ever enjoyed the freedom to leap on trains, travel across China to Beijing and join the struggle to create a new socialist paradise. But these women, like their male comrades, were restricted to the battle against class differences, to fight specifically against gender inequality was condemned as reactionary and bourgeois. As the chaos of the period intensified, fellow Guards, peasants and soldiers treated female Red Guards as prey. Young urban women "sent down to the countryside" were particularly vulnerable to physical and sexual abuse.

The end of the Cultural Revolution and the new economic reforms brought distinct challenges. The "relocated" urban women who could not find suitable husbands in the rural sector found themselves, once past the age of 30, in the ranks of the unmarriageable. The new policies decentralized rural production back into individual households. This gave rise to new prosperity for some and encouraged others to put women back into the role of domestic worker.

The new Marriage Law of 1980 emphasized divorce and the right of male choice. The one-child policy placed an additional burden of inferiority on women who bore daughters, resulting in an increase in marital abuse and female infanticide.[1]

During the 1980s, women were once again becoming "domesticated," changing

the parameters of relationships in home, school and work. While women's participation in education had improved in the New China, there were caveats. The
percentage of women in higher education had risen from 19 percent in 1949 to 33
percent by 1988—nearly comparable with the United States (Hooper 1991, 354). A
third of the people listed as being in science and technology (admittedly that may
include many *zhuanke* low-level technicians) were women (Rhoodie 1989, 424).
Others, however, noted that the percentage of women participating in higher education was actually falling during the 1980s after its dramatic rise after Liberation
(Whyte and Parish 1984).

To enter university, women had to have higher examination scores than men to
be admitted (Odgen 1992, 315; Rhoodie 1989, 419). Educated women were clus-
tered in the "normal schools" and in low-prestige institutions. Only 10 percent of the
students in the prestigious Beida science program were women (Hooper 1991, 356).
Postgraduate training was a scare resource, and women felt they had little chance to
pursue it. In a mid-1980s survey by the State Science and Technology Commission's Human Resources Research Institute 42.7 percent of the technically trained
women responded that they believed they had no chance at all, or less chance than
men, to study further (Rhoodie 1989, 420-421). The selection of candidates to study
abroad corroborates this bias. In Hayhoe's work on women studying abroad, it
appears that the lower status of women gave them fewer such opportunities. In
addition, women were included late in overseas study programs (1990, 296). The
lack of postgraduate degrees, now a fixed standard for academic promotion, can
lock women permanently into the lower ranks of academia (Hayhoe 1994).

The most visible barriers for women emerged in the school-to-work transition. In
late 1988 new regulations "protected" women by extending maternity leaves and
barring them from employment in "unsuitable jobs" (Ma 1989, 68). One of the most
vivid examples of sex discrimination occurred in Tianjin. In 1984 only 3 percent of
the city's new hires were female, although the protest of the Women's Federation
eventually forced an increase to 20 percent. Many units simply refused to hire
women, who were widely held to be inferior and problematic (Honig and Hershatter
1988, 245). At Shanghai's Fudan University, a third of the prospective employers
stipulated "men only" (Rhoodie 1989, 420). Hiring a man makes better economic
sense to employers because it is assumed that costly child care responsibilities are
the realm of the mother, not the father.

In the late 1980s, the official policy was that women had special "strengths" in
"domestic mothering" that they were advised to draw on as economic competition
intensified. Contemporary official edicts reveal a wealth of value statements
regarding gender. Post–Mao officials promoted an ideal of domestic work for women based on "distinctive female characteristics," namely, nurturing, domesticity
and thrift (see Hooper 1991, 363). Chinese Communist party General Secretary
Jiang Zemin (Anonymous 1989e, n.p.) encouraged women to be "industrious and
thrifty and contribute to family planning." By promoting a broad concept of female
mothering roles, officials compensate for the lack of public social services. Thus,

the state creates conditions that foster traditional gender attitudes (Robinson 1985, 35).

American women thirty-five years ago heard similar rhetoric (Odgen 1992, 314). The 1961 Kennedy Commission on the Status of Women was asked to examine the social and legal position of women and make recommendations that would promote equality. When issued in 1963, the document recommended equal access to education and proposed the passage of equal pay legislation. The report also sanctioned the primary role of "mothers and homemakers and society's stake in strong family life" (Goldberg 1991, 197).

The social changes wrought by the economic reform policy itself place new constraints on the status of intellectual women. The decade of reforms has elevated the power of money far above the remaining Confucian vestiges of scholarly prestige. Even *guanxi*, the ability to make things happen through connections, now increasingly relies on financial power and mobility—two items generally unavailable to women.

This milieu is the setting for the interviews with the women scientists. The problems they encounter clearly place a strain on their visions of the best future, producing bright but vague hopes and sometimes bitter forays into personal pessimism. Their tragic tone echoes that of popular literature as illustrated by the classic story, *At Middle Age* by Shen Rong. This story describes the bitter lives of Lu Wenting, an ophthalmologist whose selfless devotion to others imperils her health and her life, and the sensitive Yafen, who must abandon her friends to go abroad to learn "advanced" medicine for China. Like their fictional counterparts, the women scientists interviewed here must try to balance a series of impossible alternatives.

The fictional composite Li is the vehicle for the visions expressed by the nineteen women scientists I interviewed. While the number seems low, it is a high proportion of the women at my institute who struggled to go abroad. Few of the women I knew declined to be interviewed; most were pleased to be asked. Although the women, too, were part of cohorts that had been differentially affected by the educational and political shifts in their lifetimes, their gender stood out as the dominant social fact of their lives. Young or middle-aged, women were overwhelmingly conscious that their womanhood made them a separate category of intellectual.

Their ages ranged from 23 to 42. Fifteen women were married—to intellectual men, of course—and nine had children. The four single women and the nonmothers all expressed the desire to marry and have children.

Nearly two-thirds of the women were from Beijing, which like Shanghai, is a nexus of higher educational institutions. The next highest number were from China's wealthy southeast region, followed by the northeast. Only one-tenth of the women came from other areas. Few women had changed residences as often as the men of Wang's sample.

While Wang's sample was concentrated in the first set of interviews and Zhou's in the later set, the women's interviews were evenly divided between the first and second/third periods. One woman was interviewed twice, and her experience will be the model for Li by setting the initial interview with the fictional Li around the same time as Wang, with a quick followup in June 1989.

Li is 31. She juggles many roles—mother, wife, daughter, biochemist, medical researcher and teacher. She is meticulously groomed, always wearing a scarf, skirt, jacket or sweater—classically stylish, but not trendy. She even managed to seem comfortable in her sensible low-heeled pumps. She was always prepared for classes, her homework was never late and unlike some other students, she actually did the recommended reading!

She is eternally responsible. She does not enjoy being a teacher, but she is determined to do her best. She reads educational texts and is interested in developing multimedia classroom aids using computers and television. Her shyness makes teaching particularly burdensome for her, since it requires such sustained public assertiveness. Yet Li is quite capable of privately expressing her outrage if one of Zhou's peers makes snide remarks about the "foolishness" or "weakness" of women. She is one of the few people who, in conversations, expresses the opinion that the Han attitude toward Tibetans or Manchurians is discriminatory, and she scoffs at the rationalizations that the official efforts to reeducate them into a Han mold are "good for them." Li is keenly aware of her social environment. She remembers her minority childhood neighbor; she knows which friend is struggling academically, who is lonely and who can make her laugh.

Li puts in long hours at work, in addition to her "second shift" at home. She spends at least three to four hours a day shopping and cooking, an hour and a half more than her "soft-eared" husband.[2] Sunday is the catch-up day when the week's washing, cleaning and sundry shopping must be scheduled, in careful synchrony with the hours of running water and electricity. This is also her day to spend time with her husband and daughter. They work and attend preschool the other six days.

At least four hours a week Li must attend the weekly political study meeting. She finds this activity oppressively boring, but it does provide a chance to work on her continuous string of knitting projects. She sees little point in even feigning interest. Both her father and husband were "sent down" to the destitute ethnic borderlands in northwest China during the Cultural Revolution. She was raised by an aunt who could keep her in Nanjing city. She does not consider herself "political."

Each day, six days a week, she must work—teaching or researching. She forgoes the daily *xiuxi*, the midday siesta that is her Chinese constitutional right. Instead, she uses the time to study English in order to improve her chances of going abroad for further education. If she does not use the open door, she will have few opportunities to pursue a doctorate or advance in her academic hierarchy. Nonetheless, her English skills lag behind those of her colleagues. She will seldom speak out in language classes, although she eagerly participates in small groups. I welcome the chance to interview her. She takes the process very seriously. Wang brought elements of wry irony to his interview, and Zhou cracked satirical jokes, but Li approaches the interview with an air of sobriety.

KEEPING HUMAN NATURE

Li's interview takes place a week after Wang's. She tells me about her family—describing first her parental family and then her husband and child. I had originally designed the interview with background questions about the marital family preceding questions about the parental family—a clear American bias. Li was born in Nanjing and was educated in Beijing. Her father was an intellectual and had been "sent down" to northwest China when she was a young girl. Very few women intellectuals are the children of peasants; overwhelmingly, they are the daughters of intellectual families (Hayhoe 1994). He was a chemist and helped her choose her profession, medical biochemistry, as one "suitable" for a woman. I try to find out what she meant by that, but she only repeats her statement, although she implies that the meticulous dreariness of laboratory biochemistry is a key component of that "suitability." The same logic places women in laboratory work in America as well.

Li now lives in Beijing with her husband and lively daughter. We share stories about our daughters who are the same age—3 years old. Li's husband is much like Wang, an older scholarly man who takes his paternal duties very seriously and helps her with the housework. The time he once spent abroad pursuing his education was a difficult period for her.

She has earned a master's degree and would like to get a doctorate, but such a pursuit would require her to move away from her husband and child. Certainly, that separation would be traumatic under any circumstances. But I find myself wondering whether her worries about parting from her family go deeper. Changing residences is not a simple matter in China. Is she afraid that, like so many intellectual couples, if she officially changes her residence and leaves for another city, she might continue to be separated from her husband for years?[3] Peculiarly, he runs less of a risk of long-term separation from her family if she goes to San Francisco rather than Shanghai. So she hopes to go abroad and earn her doctorate, acquire up-to-date skills and return to help her country.

I begin the scenarios by asking her to describe what she thinks will happen in the best possible future for Chinese science and technology. She opens with, "I think maybe [science and technology] might succeed and we can accomplish what we want to do. Research conditions will be very good, and people will respect intellectuals and science. The government will pay more attention to scientists. They really will, not just talk about it. I think in thirty years science and technology must improve."

Once again, the idea is expressed that before progress can be made government must redress the slights given intellectuals. Li adds a note about the role of the open door: "Nowadays many young people are interested in science and technology and they study and work hard. Many have gone abroad to study, to America and other Western countries. I think these people are our country's hope, and they will certainly contribute a great deal to our country. I think most of them will surely come back, and then they will be the mainstay of our country. If they can have better opportunities to apply their knowledge and abilities, they will make China develop quickly. I think Chinese people, especially university students, are intelligent and hard working. They aren't afraid of hardship."

Li points out that the investment of time and effort internationally educated scholars make—her investment—must be allowed to come to maturity. The returning scholars must be allowed to come home and practice their newfound skills. She says: "It depends, if the government cannot give the students good facilities and chances to apply their knowledge and talents then the future may not be the best, but only middling"—or to use a phrase she taught me, *ma ma hu hu* (horse-horse-tiger-tiger), only so-so. Promises are fine, but actions are better.

Those students who do return, largely those sponsored by the state, face the most profound barriers in implementing their newfound skills and furthering their own careers (see Hayhoe 1991, 136). Unless they are quite innovative and entrepreneurial, they will return to their old work units to be again indoctrinated in lengthy political study meetings. They will be poorly paid and undervalued. Their newly acquired skills may languish in unsuitable jobs and environments. In 1984 it was estimated that 70 percent were underutilized in this fashion (Du 1992, 106). In the late 1980s, efforts were made to enhance their effectiveness by increasing their opportunities to choose their own jobs, but ties and obligations to their *danwei* inhibited such mobility. Socially, although they were admired as those who have been to the promised land, they also faced bureaucratic hostility and the envy of their coworkers (Link 1992, 245).

When I ask Li how China's science and technology will compare to the rest of the world in the best future she tells me that in high-level theory she thinks her country will be "among the top-ranked countries in science and technology." Like her colleagues, she notes that may not be true in industrial applications since the rest of the world "will continue developing. The gap will get smaller, but there will still be some distance to go."

I ask Li about her vision of China's leading sciences thirty years hence. Her litany of successes is congruent with that of her male colleagues, but even more broadly writ. "Computer science, mechanical engineering, and agriculture—these three are important for China. China is an agricultural country. Mechanical engineering is the basis of industry. Computer science is critical for science and technology."

She goes on to cite the familiar fields of theoretical mathematics, genetics and robotics as potential successes. In this she is hardly unique. Since her field—biochemistry and cell engineering—actually skirts one of these exalted fields, I wonder what she will say. Other interviewees have praised those other fields, only to denigrate their own. This self-effacement may stem from the Chinese value of modesty, but it may also reflect a greater knowledge of what is possible. It is easier to imagine someone else's laboratory as productive and trouble-free, but such optimism is more difficult in the face of the inevitable frustrations of one's own daily experience. Li is optimistic about her field's potential, she believes that biochemical research offers the best hope for curing diseases. However, she is more cautious about the lived reality. "Some of the research has now reached an advanced level, but in my opinion, a lot of the research work is still backward, due to the lack of expensive, advanced instruments. In my job the instruments are very important. If I want to identify a molecular structure, it is a very complicated job. It takes a long time and needs many kinds of instruments. This is difficult to do even under the best conditions in advanced countries."

Li's comments about computers and robotics also reveal a different slant. She takes these technologies out of the rarified atmosphere of research and puts them into homes, factories and schools. She notes that "The best thing I think would be for computers to do many things, to be used in various ways. In China the ladies' work is quite hard. They do a lot of work in the institute or factory and when they go home they have yet more housework. So the best future for them is for robots to do it for them. All of us like robots very much." Li is projecting the positive attitude Chinese women display for domestic consumer machinery onto a new level.[4] None of her male colleagues made that leap.

Li points out the efficiency of computers in production and argues in favor of automation: "I think the computer will be used very widely—in automatic control in factories—to do dangerous and boring work. Eventually, robots will be common. Maybe not very complex robots, just some robotic arm doing some very boring work—picking something up and moving it again and again. If we used our own eyes to do fine work, we would get tired easily and make errors. But if we send a robot to do this [same work], it will be very precise, and we could even say there would be no mistakes. So the quality [of products] would be very good, much better. I think it is very possible. The first computer was made forty years ago, and it developed very quickly. Thirty years from now, it is very hard to imagine what will develop. But computers can be used in schools."

We have talked in the past about Li's interests in education and her desire to learn a variety of pedagogical techniques. I am curious as to how she envisions the "best" future for Chinese education. She seems much more conscious than her colleagues that she is an educator *and* a researcher, not just a researcher with a teaching "day job." The themes she values have already been expressed in her colleagues' interviews. She believes that education should be respected and funded. Basic education should extend to the most remote parts of China. Like Zhou, she suggests that rich countries can help her poor one in their technical education efforts, but the key is to get the government to invest money in education. Without educational investment there will be no science, and without science production cannot flourish.

Her attitudes about university education also recap issues brought out in the other interviews. While one of her female colleagues thinks there will be little change, Li is optimistic, believing that almost every person will have the chance to study at the university level. She adds that in the future there will be more universities, perhaps doubling the present number, and new methods of funding—not just public universities, but private ones as well.

She points out that television "open universities" are considered an optimal cheap way of providing higher education, especially to workers and farmers who can study only part-time. She says that "Although there are many technical problems in communication and television, I think we may have great potential in using them as information technology. In the future you will be able to look up any information you want to look at on the television. If you want to borrow a book, learn about a specific place or know the weather forecast, you could get all this information from your TV."

At the time of the interview, television education was the significant form of adult education. A total of 2,700 classes were being broadcast from Central TV University in Beijing, amounting to 60 percent of the total television university system. Another 40 percent were broadcast from provincial level colleges (Du 1992, 35). Although degrees from such institutions were substantially less prestigious, the curriculum and output were impressive (see Lull 1991, 79–80; Wang and Coletta 1991, 153–154). Classes were primarily technical ones in science, technology, management and agriculture. The TV university had trained 1.05 million accredited graduates, 40 percent of the total number of tertiary graduates in post–Mao education. TV students also accounted for 90 percent of all the graduates from adult learning institutions (Du 1992, 36).

Li's special interest in university education is in computer-assisted education, which she hopes will allow students to study efficiently without being "spoon-fed." She adds, "The students will study very actively. As you know, there is a knowledge explosion. Students must study a lot of information, but if they only can memorize what the teachers give them, I think that is not enough. They should use their brains. That is how they develop interests in their fields."

She is an advocate of continuing education, providing adult education to people who are not in the traditional age range of university students. She believes that students who failed their entrance examinations initially might, after working for a few years, relish the challenge of higher education and return to school. She posits that choice and life-long commitment to learning are necessary elements for a healthy educational system.

I find many parallels with my experience in American education. In the United States the trend is toward active learning, making the learner participate in class processes by using projects, discussions and, if available, multimedia. Having taught in the public California state system, I knew that returning students are an increasingly important part of the late-twentieth-century educational landscape. These older students enliven classes with their wide-ranging life experience and display the highest levels of motivation. Their presence also has fueled the trend toward practical education. Students in general, and reentry students in particular, want their newfound knowledge to be usable. In my anthropology classes, a detailed investigation of kinship charts will evoke agitated impatience. But when I show the students the link between their own nomadic mobility and the decreasing size of their families, or the way in which the diffuseness of American kinship allows them to call on an ex-mother-in-law's step-daughter to babysit, they are captivated. Li wants this sort of educational atmosphere to appear, not just to make students happy, but to enhance the learning process and improve China.

In Li's view, practical education must be emphasized at every level. Expounding on this notion, she says, "Because our country needs more scientists to contribute to the construction of our country in a short time, researchers must use more practical methods for solving the problems of the people's living standard. For example, in our university, some new departments have been established in food science and agricultural economics. The students who graduate from these departments will be very useful to our country."

Li is most idealistic when she talks about the education of China's future children. She says, "Almost all the children will go to school and get an education, especially in the rural areas, in the more remote regions, for example in the northwest, in Xinjiang and Ningxia." I can't help but wonder whether these were the "northwestern" provinces where her husband and father were "rusticated" during the Cultural Revolution. She seems unusually knowledgeable and sympathetic. She clearly has a greater concern for minority issues than many of her colleagues: "It's hard for minority people because minority children get fewer opportunities to go into university. For some people the living standard is not very high, especially in rural areas. Some children must earn a living and then they lose their chance for an education. So I think that as living standards rise, the children from the poor families will be able to enter schools and universities."

By now, Li's worldview is apparent. She has a "social problem" orientation. Unlike Zhou, who will go off on enthusiastic digressions on the beauty of a human–computer interface or space travel, Li's attitudes toward technology, research and education are firmly situated in society. She is not a "tinkerer" who plays with ideas or gadgets for their own sake. Li is too responsible. Her opinions are filtered through her conscience and judged—what does this technology or that educational method do to solve human social issues?

Li demonstrates this worldview further as she expounds on technology in the *best* future: "Beneficial technology can still be harmful." She worries about the gap between the cities and the countryside. At the same time that the peasants' desire for sons increases population, automation will make unskilled labor superfluous. Those "extra" workers must then find employment in factories or service industries, which will be difficult with such a high population. Trying to feed this population with high-yield automated farming might be deleterious to the environment, causing "floods . . . drought." The context for her mental simulations is intensely social. For Li nothing happens outside of a human environment.

Her chief concern is population. She points out, "There will still be a large gap between China and the U.S. and Japan because the population problem cannot be solved very quickly. It will still be a problem in thirty years. Think about housing. In the future, if the population is reduced then, of course, there will be more houses." For Li "population" refers to living neighborhoods, not merely impersonal numbers.

"So if the population is controlled, you foresee a wealthier standard of living in the best future?"

She responds by describing that standard of living: "Yes, and I think most of the people in China will have cars. Every family will have a phone and a color television. In the near future telephones will be very popular in Chinese families. Maybe that's a kind of impact by science and technology. Also other aspects of the family life may change, like the living conditions—the house and the cooking facilities, like microwave cooking."

"Will other technologies be important in the home?"

"Yes, the pace will be fast. Many appliances and the computer will enter the home. Families will actually feel the impact of technology in the home. I can barely imagine this. What I can visualize is like what America is now."

"You mentioned television; what impact do you think it will have in the best future?"

She again responds with a situated assessment, looking at television in the context of the home. "In my opinion, I don't think television is very good to people. Watching TV is a waste of time if you watch violence and boy-girl love stories. Then young people don't pay much attention to their studies."

In contrast to her earlier, positive view of television teaching, Li assesses the daily use of television quite differently. It is not the technology itself she is analyzing, but the human context in which it is put to use. Television is a relatively recent innovation in China.[5] It remains largely unconnected with family or social life. Li's associates in the media complain about the poor quality of programming available in China.

Li adds, "If all the members of a family are sitting there watching TV, they will have no time to communicate with each other, to express their feelings." This view of acceptable forms of communication is based on a pre-television model. In time, in societies in which television was a central feature of socialization, the medium itself became a forum for communication and expression. As in America, future Chinese family discussions would revolve around favorite programs and react to the virtual reality displayed on the screen.

"Will there be other changes in the society—in the best future?" Since Li's last statement seems far from optimistic, I feel I need to redirect the flow of the interview.

She replies, "This will be a comfortable life. The quality of food will be very high, much higher than at present, and people's life expectancy will be increased. The killer diseases will be wiped out as medicine develops. Generally speaking, people will live better than they do now. Maybe people will travel more easily. Work efficiency will be improved, and more people will have leisure time."

Li now makes a most telling social commentary: "Advanced technology should make people more efficient and effective, but I think people should keep their nature. Technology has advantages for communication; we can see the people on the screen, but I think we should remember people's nature. We should talk to people, not just screen-to-screen but face-to-face." The valuing of personal relationships over efficient, but nonpersonal interactions is an important feature of Chinese psychology.[6] Without that intimate sense of connection, social interactions are considered to be sterile and unsatisfactory. Li, far more than Wang or Zhou, is expressing a value associated with collectivism. She clearly *expresses* a rhetoric that values belonging and the concomitant nurturing of her relationships. She does so primarily when talking about the social arena, her attitudes become more ambivalent when talking about work. Her beliefs about her gender and her own career history indicate that she is not as collectivistic as her discourse would indicate.

"I don't like competition," she goes on. "Maybe competition will be more prevalent than now. In some ways it is reasonable that any society has to compete to make some progress. If we all share identical conditions, people won't [be motivated to] work hard to attain their goals. I myself like cooperation. I think that is better. If there is more cooperation, people will not lose their human nature. Competition makes people more crude . . . cruel." Li goes on to tell about a movie she has just seen in which high-tech industrial competition leads to cruelty and death. That is a vision she does not want in her "best" scenario. Perhaps competition is a necessary evil for motivating hard work, but she wants to make it clear that she sees it as an evil.

Li notes wistfully, "and I hope they will treat men and women equally."

I jump on this issue instantly: "One of your colleagues told me she believes men and women are already equal. Do you agree with her?"

"No, because after graduation most units don't want women to come to their units to work. Often people think that women's abilities are lower than men's—at least sometimes. But I think we can do the same things as the men." I want to know more about the difficulties of the school-to-work transition, but she drops the subject.

I ask the final question, designed to gauge her level of optimism: "Overall, how would you describe Chinese society in the best future?"

Li pauses thoughtfully. After a moment she continues: "In the best future, I think China will succeed. She can be successful and her scientists will be respected—by other countries' scientists and by the Chinese people. But I don't think China will get so successful." Li's optimistic assessment is guarded. She can clearly articulate the goal she shares with Wang and Zhou. In her own mind, however, China's success is plausible, but not probable.

DOUBTING YOUTH, SELFISH CHILDREN

Even more than her male counterparts, Li is uncomfortable describing a "worst" scenario. Yet, hers is rich with social details. While her concerns about science and education are similar to her colleagues, hers is a distinctly pessimistic social future.

"In the best scenario, you discussed problems that would be solved in the best future. In the worst scenario, the problems might get even worse. Would you discuss this situation?"

"In that future, we won't have had much progress. We may just stay at this level or just a little higher."

"What would keep the situation from changing for the better?"

"I think there are many influences—the world situation, policies, our ability to interact with other countries' science and technology." Li is referring to the "open door." Like her colleagues, she sees China's participation in the larger world as crucial to an optimistic future.

Like Wang and Zhou, Li is very aware of population as a critical limiting factor. She believes that increasing population will keep even expanding educational facilities out of the reach of the many. This problem will be worse in the country-side. Only increasing agricultural technology can reverse the cycle of low educational motivation and expanding population. But now, access to education is limited, in a downward spiral inhibiting the growth of science and technology.

Li elaborates, "This is not just a thing of science and technology, maybe we won't have enough money, enough food, so that soon we would have starvation, and poverty will create huge social problems. No person, no country, will be able to help us, since we have so many people. We can only help ourselves. But if we don't do well, then maybe many people will die! It's a pity!"

She goes on to describe a situation that sounds suspiciously like the United States, a society in which technology has raised the standard of living but created a new set of problems—high-technology warfare, environmental pollution and unemployment. Li reiterates that television, at least in the home, leads to time wasted and skills unpracticed, and goes on to say that relying on technology, such as calculators, will diminish children's intellectual abilities. She is also concerned that chronic illness may increase as the built-in exercise supplied by a nonautomotive, bicycling way of life is replaced by more convenient transportation modes.

Again, Li returns to the central importance of relationships: "At that time most people will use advanced equipment in education, unlike today. Maybe it will have changed to just equipment alone. And you won't need to talk face-to-face to the teacher, and so the teacher and student relationship will be lost." Li considers the potential loss of this fundamental Confucian teacher–student relationship to be a tragedy. The intertwining networks of classmates, teachers and kin allow information to flow, back doors to open. The strength of the social bonds of the intellectuals' interpersonal community is a vital component in her ability to flourish. Impersonality is threatening.

Li adds practically, "If students have unusual questions they won't get the answer immediately because almost all of this equipment is designed to be used for a mass audience and for remedial problems." In other words, the advantages of widespread, cheap, multimedia learning would be offset by the narrow range of discourse possible in programmed education. As any American 7 year old can tell you, once you have played the fun computer learning game, it is the same game over and over again. While Li may be judging the technology too harshly, she is speaking from her experience.

"I am most concerned with the education problem. Only a small percent of the government's funding goes to education. I think it's too little, for without a good education system we can't develop very quickly, especially in the long run. I think the worst possibility would be that science and technology will be criticized, just as they were in the Cultural Revolution. They criticized a lot of science—such as Einstein's theory. They won't respect scientists."

I ask Li if she thinks the "worst" future would be like that time. She does not think so—but only because scientists would have fled to other safer and more lucrative professions! Such a possibility would leave science and technology "the same as the present—no development except in some fields. I think computers will be developed for many fields, because the government is focusing on that problem. But medicine and other sciences, especially fundamental sciences, will be ignored."

So far, Li stands firmly in Wang's camp, knowing that applied sciences ultimately depend on basic research. In spite of her stated concerns for the educational institutions that house research, she supports the prevailing view. There will always be scientific "progress"; only the degree will vary.

Despite her basic optimism regarding scientific progress, Li is less optimistic about the fate of the people who work in science. She says, "I'm afraid that in the worst future few people will want to do such work. I have mentioned that the research worker, the scientist and the teacher have very low salaries. They won't want to continue to work if the policy does not change. Students don't want to go to school. And the parents don't want their children to go to school. Young people won't want to waste time getting higher degrees. I think this is a complex problem. We cannot merely criticize these young people, and I think this problem is bound up with policy."

Li points at the responsible party—the leaders. The policymakers are *responsible*, in the sense of a parent who is expected to be accountable for his child. Policymakers are genuinely mandated to solve China's problems. But the complex blend of Marxism, capitalism and Chinese culture amid shifting international currents does not easily provide simple solutions. Li continues: "Many Chinese people worry about this question, we don't have a correct policy at present to create educational and economic reforms, because we have no model to follow. We are encountering many new conditions but we haven't any existing policy to follow, so the society is very confused."

Li now shifts her focus from the policymakers to the people, saying: "Currently some people are making mistakes, by focusing only on money. I think this is not a good phenomenon, especially for teachers and researchers. We cannot improve our level of science if everyone is concerned only with his own welfare and not the country's. For example, in the university, some teachers are not focusing on teaching or research, but on some method of making money, such as opening a training class for special people. In a short time, a teacher can make some money, but this teacher isn't responding to his students' needs or doing his research." Li feels these intellectuals are failing to honor their implicit Confucian social contract with their students—and with the whole society.

"There are two serious problems: one is the economic policy, another is attitude. So many people only want to find a way to earn a lot of money. Like having a business—but not doing genuine work." Li utters the Confucian bias against mercantile prowess.

Li sees the result of current policies as a double brain drain—into business and overseas. "So I mean, young people resign from factories or small offices and then go to Shenzhen [a "free trading" zone of experimental capitalism adjacent to Hong Kong] and earn much more there. In addition, many young students want to go abroad. You can see the problem. If the best stay abroad, our country can be built by only very poor level people."

She adds that this brain drain into business will be worse in the countryside, for "in the countryside the farmers can earn more money than before. So their parents think that education is not important, only money is important. This increases illiteracy."

Li returns to an important woman's issue: "Another trend is that the parents don't make girls go to school because they think that education does not matter. They want their daughters to learn such popular skills as sewing and embroidery. And in the countryside, when a girl marries the parents can get a large sum of money from her husband. So these farmers believe it is unnecessary to make the girl go to school. In this way, there are more and more illiterates."

An estimated 70 to 80 percent of China's illiterates are women, so her worries are hardly exaggerated (Jiang 1993, 18; Rhoodie 1989, 419). I ask her, "Is this a trend that will continue?"

"Yes. Many young people are not idealistic." Li equates idealism with the motivation to learn, I discover. Indeed, her placement of the loss of idealism in the pessimistic scenario is further confirmation that Li herself is an idealist by her own definition.

She continues, "Many doubt, 'how can we realize the modernizations?' I worry about the spirit of the young people now. Many young people have no vision for our society and our country. If the government system doesn't change a lot, I think it will continue like this."

The young people to whom she refers are the 1970s cohort, her students in the late 1980s and early 1990s. They are weary of politics and are moved primarily by materialism (Gold 1991, 610; Link 1992, 242). Their study patterns suffered as a consequence. Absenteeism was 35 percent at Wuhan University, and increasingly the attitude was to be content with mediocre performance, since excellence went unrewarded (Du 1992, 86).

Li adds a tone of moral panic, wrought by the one-child future, to her existing worries about youth: "And I think it might even get worse because a lot of the workers in the future will be single children. They won't know how to cooperate with each other. This will also be a problem in the future, and if this attitude does not change, there is no practical way to solve this problem. Maybe it will be a terrible thing in the future."

"What might help?"

"I think the main problem is always policy. Our policy now is not very steady."

She adds a poetic touch of millennial optimism, "But even if there is a complete social collapse out of that, she [China] will come back."

"Like a phoenix?" I ask, using the transcultural metaphor of the mythical bird, reborn from its own funeral pyre.

"Yes . . . " she replies, humoring me. "I don't think education will be affected as much as science and technology because we have a good tradition of respecting the people who are educated, so even if the society collapsed some people would still try to learn."

I echo her thought: "The people themselves will keep education going?"

Li's worldview has a built-in limitation on the possibilities for disaster. As long as the Confucian educational traditions—replete with respectful relationships—remain intact, the worst future will be checked. As Li responds with an affirmative nod to my clarification, we begin to discuss her "most probable" visions.

CALIBRATING HALF THE SKY

When I ask Li to think about the most likely future, she responds, "I'm not sure, but I imagine the future should be better."

After a long pause, I ask her, "One of your colleagues has said that she believes your society won't be much better than today, since the education level and morale are so low. What do you think?"

"In thirty years, in China, we can do better—maybe catch up with America in the 1960s. Because our country is so big and has so many people, many problems are hard to solve. Maybe half of the people in the countryside can be educated at that time. Maybe, in fifty or sixty years, the Four Modernizations will be realized."

"So in thirty years you will be halfway there?"

"Yes. I think I'm an optimist, the positive [factors] in the future will overcome the worst things. I think the future will be bright."

Li thinks that educating future leaders in a more open learning environment would make a difference. "These factory leaders must learn some languages, such as Japanese, so that the factory managers can follow their model." Again, her comments emphasize the burden and responsibility of leadership.

I ask, "You discussed many problems in education in your last scenario. Do you think they will be solved in the most probable scenario?"

"I worry so much, especially about teenagers, who do not like to study. My students are always playing cards, Mahjongg, and wanting to go dancing. They hate to study; they think it is not useful for their careers. After four years of study, they will be sent to some factory or school to do something they don't like. So they feel disappointed, and now, you know, government policy about teachers is not very favorable. Before, most people thought education was important, but now they think money is important. I don't know what to say to those teenagers. So I always say to my students, 'You should learn very hard even though society is not so good to the intellectuals.' I can't make a very strong statement, because I, myself, still have some problems with the belief. You know we do not believe in God, we believe in nothing . . . and sometimes I feel so disappointed."

Li and I had spent time before this interview discussing her desire for some kind of moral anchor, a framework for her idealism. She feels a great void. The little injustices she has experienced only add to her feelings of alienation.

"Sometimes I have produced the same as someone else, and maybe I am better than he, but he get opportunities that I cannot—just because of our relationships. In China relationships are so important." Li is not speaking here about her emotional ties, but about her *guanxi*, her ability to create the "back doors" that will allow her to overcome the inherent obstacles of the system. My impression is that she is a master of *guanxi*, yet she is frustrated with her ability to make enough ties. Li had already told me how concentrating on her field and learning English had interfered with her ability to give the dinners and make the contacts so necessary to enhance her *guanxi*. This lack has hurt her in her efforts to improve her career and go abroad.

She is disturbed by the values implicit in official policies. She relates an appropriate illustration, another urban myth, similar to those told by Wang and Zhou. "For three years a professor and his colleagues did a research project in an institute. The quality was very high, and he received many awards from the government. He got some scholarship money since he helped China. Each person got 30 yuan. So I think that's funny, because you know 30 yuan is almost nothing! An ordinary salesman of eggs will make maybe 30 yuan per day. So a lot of people feel disheartened, and even though the government encouraged scientists and technologists to do high-level research, this situation is distressing. I think thirty years from now the situation may be changed, maybe not. It's hard to say."

Realistically, Li adds: "A lot of the system will stay the same. For example, in my institute, if the leader doesn't like someone, they won't work well [together]. The leaders can't accept [new] qualified workers, because the institute is already full of people. Even if some are not very qualified, they have to stay there."

She is referring to the paradoxical glut of academics. While China desperately needs an expanded educated workforce, university lecturers are in excess. In Beida the teacher–student ratio is 1:5 (Hayhoe 1994). In a northwestern university the ratio changed from 1:3 to 1:6.9 as student numbers expanded (Du 1992, 22). Informants complained that they did not have meaningful and effective ways to teach, research and write, because there were so many lecturers stumbling over one another, each with varying degrees of competence. While they had to work long hours, they could not do so efficiently or with the promise of appropriate reward.

She adds, "I don't think China will change a lot. I have worked ten years, more than ten years, and I don't think my institute has changed much."

I want her to clarify what she means: "So thirty years is not such a long time?"

"Not a long time."

"Do you think there will be any changes in lifestyle in that time, maybe not so much at work, but in society?"

"I'm worried about my daughter. I think she will be in a very difficult society. I think perhaps I will send my daughter abroad; it's very difficult. I'm worried about it now."

Li explains what worries her most about the future. "We now have close relationships between people, especially outside the family—in our unit, with our neighbors. In the future maybe the relationships between the people will change. Right now we don't have much privacy. For example, if I have some question for my family or my family has one about me, we can exchange ideas, or we will gather people together to get some good advice. This is very important in China." What an American might consider annoyingly meddlesome is clearly positive to Li.

She continues, "But in that time I think not as many people will be there to help you. Relationships will be more distant, unlike this time when they are close, kind and friendly."

Li's positive evaluation of neighborhood life matches the glowing comments made to Jankowiak in his study of Huhhot in northwestern China. Good neighbors ought to be "honest, polite, kind, unselfish, and willing to help others during a personal crisis" (1993, 104). Mutuality, being involved with your neighbors, is a vital component of neighborliness as described to him. This stated ideal was sometimes in sharp contrast with lived experience (1993, 105). It is not surprising that Li paints such an ideal picture in the abstract.

Li's description of the worst future also castigated isolation, and she uses the probable scenario to again express her concern that relationships may one day become too casual. She adds, "If [people] have too many things to do—sports, travel or things like that—maybe they will have no time to help you, to think of you. Now these people have less to do. They have time to hear what you are saying and think about your problem and give you suggestions. In the future maybe there will be some organization to help you. But now there is no organization to help you solve your family or personal problems. So we help each other."

This chilling forecast of the institutionalization of friendships calls to my attention a heretofore hidden American bias that respect for privacy—"minding one's own business"—is a virtue. Li's response reveals that she values its opposite—human-heartedness. She dislikes and fears the social isolation that accompanies a busy life. She continues, "The relationship between people will change and will be similar to the West"—a situation Li clearly considers to be negative.

After discussing the usually mentioned barriers to positive change—population, pollution and policy—I bring up a topic that we have only skirted before: gender equality.

"Are women and men equal?" Li echoes my question. "I don't think so, especially in China. But it's not easy [to change]. Even though almost all women work, in the family or society they still haven't equal rights with men. I always want to be equal, but people say I am a 'woman who fights for woman's rights.' Maybe they feel that is dangerous—but I think it is okay." In apparent contrast to her deference to traditional opinion, Li is outspoken on this particular issue. Having defined equality as proper, she is duty bound to defend it.

"In China, traditional ideas are very firmly held. Traditionally, [people] think girls are less useful than boys, so they only allow boys to go to school. They don't allow the girls to go to school. It's not fair."

"Will this change?"

"Yes. I think our government will find some method to improve the situation. They can pass a law to make the education of young children compulsory—for both little boys and little girls. If the parents don't allow their little girls to go to school, they must be punished. I think they could make a law, but some officials don't pay attention to this situation."

I am reminded that when I pose social problems to my students in America, they also propose passing laws to solve them. Then I ask them how many of them obey the traffic laws and speed limits. After sheepish grins, they come to see that culture cannot be so easily legislated. Laws are confirmations of norms or attempts to change those norms, but they do not guarantee compliance or harmony. Even in China, jaywalking is commonplace.

Li continues: "Especially in rural areas some leaders are only concerned about their privileges. They aren't concerned about the children. So I think the situation should be changed, should be improved in the future. This depends on efforts from the whole society. In the city this is not a problem. For example, for two years I employed a girl, just 18 years old, to help me wash clothes and clean house. My husband went overseas, and I was very busy, so I hired a girl from the countryside, from the rural area. She didn't know any Chinese characters. She didn't know how to write and couldn't read any letters. She asked me to help her, and so I asked her if many girls in her hometown did not get an education. She said, 'Most of the girls did not go to school because their parents didn't want them to go to school.'"

According to the "custom" that has been revised and revived only in the last decade, men give large sums of cash as a betrothal present to their future parents-in-law in order to marry.[7] Li explains that these young rural women are thus forced to subsidize their brothers: "The parents just paid attention to the boys, not the girls. They want the girls to earn their own living, to make more money for the boys. When the young men want to get married [the men and their parents] will need a lot of money, so they want the girls [sisters and daughters] to earn that money. I think it's a great pity. We have lived in China almost forty years after Liberation—so many parents are so short-sighted they just want to earn more money. They don't mind that their children can't read! I think this girl was not happy."

Li's concerns are borne out by the trends. During the 1980s yet more women dropped out of primary and middle school (Lavely et al. 1990, 61–62; Zheng 1989). This was true especially in the countryside, where daughters were taught handicrafts to earn money, as well as to improve their chances to attract large betrothal gifts. "What about educated women, in the city, like yourself?"

"The women in China doing the same work as the men can get the same pay, but it's more difficult for a woman to get opportunities to work—even for students who have graduated from the university."

"It is harder for a woman to find a unit?"

"Yes. When they graduate from the university, they find it hard to get a job. Many units are concerned that a woman will get married, have her child and then she will pay more attention to family and less attention to work. They think that women have more problems than men—this is the traditional opinion. Our unit is concerned that women will have more problems after they get married. So sometimes they won't give the same chances to women."

Zhou once told me an off-hand anecdote that corroborates Li's comment. His wife's sister got her B.S. in mathematics. She worked in a unit for three years and then returned to the university for three years to get her master's degree in theoretical mathematics. She found it very hard to find work again. She could teach, but she could not really apply her talents in any meaningful way. She was running into the Chinese version of the "glass ceiling." She was on the team, but she was not allowed to play to her full capacity.

"Will this be different in thirty years?"

"I think maybe in the future this problem will be solved, because now so many people feel strongly about these issues and maybe half the workforce is women. If women are not given a chance, then too many workers will be lost. In my institute many female researchers do excellent work. In the past, people might not have had the chance to know women's potential ability. As women achieve more and more, people will realize these things. I think at that time more and more women will work. Even now most women have a job. I think in the future more women will have important jobs in the society. They will be self-confident and get more education in order to improve themselves and their social position. Maybe the family role will be changed. Wives and husbands will be equal. Women will have important jobs in leadership positions."

Her strength of spirit is impressive. Her projection of attitudinal change will have to surmount a tide of powerful popular opinion. Chinese men believe themselves smarter than women, especially older women, who are believed to become unfocused with age (Wolf 1985, 130). This belief was often apparent in casual conversation among my male students. The Confucian concept of honorable men and inferior women is far from dead.

The saying that an educated woman is bound to cause trouble is still current (Hooper 1991, 356). Wang once mentioned that it was very difficult for educated women to find husbands. This was partly due to their age—nearly 30 by the time they finished postgraduate work! The other reason is that women are expected to marry a man of higher or equal status, but never lower. Since there are not many unmarried men in China who have at least a master's degree, this leaves the pool of marriageable men quite small (Honig and Hershatter 1988, 98–99).

I ended, echoing her last statement, "Then there will be more women in positions of influence and power with better educations?"

"Yes. But I think thirty years is not long enough."

POSTSCRIPT

On that tentative note, we parted. When I interviewed Li again, it was as part of the ill-fated set in the summer of 1989, shortly after the turmoil of June Four. Having arranged in May to do another "practice" interview, we thus met again in early June 1989.

Li is shaken. She had previously told me how the people loved the PLA (People's Liberation Army)—the same army that had just marched through Beijing into Tiananmen Square. If her idealism had been endangered before, now it was nearly extinct. This is what she had to say in that June, in her "*best*" vision of the future.

"If the government provides a good policy, we will have a good future. I don't think this is possible. As you know my father was a scientist during the 1950s. But because the policy was not good and in the past it hurt the feelings of the scientists very much." By now I knew the Chinlish phrase "to hurt the feelings" was used to describe not bruised sensitivities, but humiliation and serious loss of face.

"I think maybe this is impossible," Li continued. "I don't think anything can go well. If they don't change the policy, maybe it will become worse and worse. As you know, China has four big problems. The first is a large population, and no matter who is running the country they can't respond to so large a population. The resources are simply not enough for such a population—that is the second. The third is the people's moral nature. It is not good."

She goes on to explain the current controversy about the envy generated by newfound wealth in China. In anthropology this predicament is referred to as "the concept of limited good."[8] Although undoubtedly this association is overstated, the idea that "there is only so much good to go around" is most marked among peasant groups. Thus, if Mr. Chen lives to be 65, it is only because someone else died at 55. If the neighbor runs a carpentry shop at night and makes furniture for sale, his extra wealth means that someone else has less, and thus provokes jealousy. Li wonders how economic reforms can thrive in the face of this attitude.

She repeats the pivotal issues of her argument; "The first is population, the second is resources, the third is personality, and the fourth, the last one, is our country's own system. Now China studies [economics] from the West, but the systems are very different. All the property [in China] belongs to the people. But how do you change the basis of economic life? Everyone is changing to private enterprise. But what should be given to individuals?" She clearly sees this as an insoluble dilemma.

"No leader can dominate this kind of country so I'm not criticizing the government. I think no one can be a good leader in this kind of environment. To criticize someone is very easy, but who has a better policy system? No one does."

Her pessimistic future at this time is even more pronounced. "Since 1977, I think the Chinese people have been acting strangely. They aren't studying the good aspects of foreign cultures, only the bad things. It's terrible. Some people like democracy, and they want to live in freedom, but desire only the sexual freedoms and the bad parts of freedom." I wonder if what she means by sexual freedom is profligate behavior, or merely ideas like Zhou's onetime comment that couples should remain childless and just enjoy each other. Certainly she is referring to the social disorder, competition and envy she had discussed in her earlier (1988) interview.

She continues, "I think foreign people have very many good traits, but the Chinese people don't study those and since last Sunday (June Four) the relationships between people have been weakened. Before the [Cultural?] Revolution people liked to help each other, but now this temperament is fading. People don't take care of each other. They are too selfish.

"Some people say that foreigners don't take care of each other. They don't take care of their neighbors and they don't know each other. Now in China the moral fiber of people has become weak, and some people have said that you [the foreigners?] are contributing to this occurrence."

I am uncomfortable now with my role as *waiguoren*—token foreigner—but that is what I am. I know that the impact of my culture has not been kind to Li. Along with Westernization and individualism come the forces that undermine a relationship-oriented worldview. Of course she is disturbed by rioting youth and troops out of control. But there is a broader context for her distress.

Competition and materialism break the ties of academic, neighborly and familial *guanxi*. As long as social relationships remained intact, women could navigate successfully through life. If *guanxi* is replaced with a purely impersonal monetary interaction, women are disadvantaged. A woman can no longer make ends meet by cultivating a relationship with the neighborhood butcher. She finds it increasingly hard to use her status as an educated woman to connect that butcher with the medical specialist he needs. Yet these are the very activities and connections that help scientists, particularly women scientists, bypass the liabilities of poverty. As money looms larger as the basis of status, Li finds that she is barred from social advancement. Without money, she is increasingly powerless.

Techno-*guanxi*—cultivating relationships with burgeoning industries—is an important new source of social mobility for scientists and engineers. It allows ambitious young technologists to earn extra money as consultants. That avenue is largely barred to women who—as in America—are not perceived as "field people" but merely as support staff. Li's strategy for creating a successful social environment in which to advance is no longer effective.

Moreover, as the "money future" takes hold, with its underlying value of materialism, the latent Confucian value of honoring the scholar is under attack. The values that affirm Li's identity are shifting. It is not surprising that she sees the fabric of the future as lonely, chaotic and dangerous.

She goes on: "I like people to have a good morality, to help each other. I think the Chinese young people have no aim; they don't know what they ought to do. Some students in our university were in the demonstrations, but they didn't know why. They just joined the demonstrations. I asked students why they joined the demonstrations. They didn't know. They wanted to release themselves, to release their frustrations."

Her final note was somber indeed, as Li gave a postscript to her "probable" scenario, "I'm not so optimistic as before. We love our country, but our government doesn't like us. And now in Beijing, especially in the universities and units, they want to clean out the people whose opinions upset them—and some hooligans." "Hooligans" was the official designation given to the rioters, branding them as uncouth criminals. Li notes, "They lump these people [intellectuals and hooligans] together. They will clean out the Chinese Communist party. It is a disaster for the intellectuals, because many of the people they want to clean out are intellectuals."

Vulnerable, weary, standing in the midst of chaos, she adds, "I don't know, I can only eat and sleep and teach."

But Li does much more than that. Li—like Zhou and Wang—has learned to negotiate with the state to create her own place. I know from my academic participant-observations that even when she appears beaten, she does persevere. She has managed, against many odds, to practice her academic craft. She has a close-knit group of friends and family that give her life meaning and value. When aggravated by her peers, she stands up and makes her opinions known. She cannot face down the tigers and dragons that govern her *danwei* or her country—but realistically, who among us can? Like the Monkey King, facing the Demon of Confusion, she initially appears weak and unarmed. But she can create a way to transform her apparently inevitable defeat into success.

7

Transformations of the Disciple

Great are the powers of the seventy-two transformations;
Greatest of all is the art of improvisation.

(Wu 1984b:39)

The Monkey King's uncanny abilities are his greatest asset. Yet, repeatedly these gifts lead him into trouble. With utter self-confidence in his own genius, he challenges the Emperor of Heaven, only to be defeated and subdued by the Buddha. He is brought into the service of the Tang Priest, where he uses his skill in battle, and his power to change his form, to defeat the endless series of antagonists that plague the quest. Sun Wukong's talent makes him an invaluable asset to the journeying monk. His imagination and willingness to take risks is often needed as an antidote to the Tang Priest's diffidence and narrow literal-mindedness, but Sun's superior insight can be a bane to his master.

In one story the Tang Priest is deceived by the treacherous White Bone Dragon Spirit who assumes a series of human forms to entice the Priest to be her next meal. Sun, with his extrasensory mystical perception, sees through these deceptions and attempts to kill the seemingly innocent incarnations—to the horror of the Priest. On his third try, the Monkey King finally "murders" the demon, and she reverts to her skeletal form (Wu 1984a, 492).

In a fury, the Tang Priest punishes the Monkey King, using a spell to tighten the gold headband that keeps him in line with excruciating pain. Even though it is clear that he is right about the demon, the Priest decides he is evil and dismisses him from his service. Constrained by dogma, the Tang Priest does not always act in his own best interest. Even though he is humiliated and deeply hurt, the Monkey King is ultimately loyal to the mission and his master. Sun decides to return to the Tang Priest, who, as usual, is in need of help. The Monkey King rescues the Priest from yet another deceptive demon, for, not bound by the Priest's limitations, he is able to perceive reality as it is.

In this final chapter I return to those three central issues that have fueled this study. In the last four chapters, we have explored the social niches occupied by nonestablishment intellectuals in the last fifty years. This proved to be a demanding task, as shifts in policy and educational/scientific organizations buffeted intellectuals to and fro. Those convulsions directly shaped the self-perceptions of the scholars. They knew that their education should have afforded them great social esteem, but that was often not the reality. Their marginality, however, did not make them feel less Chinese; instead, they adapted to their changed circumstances by creating new definitions of Chineseness. That process is the focus of this last chapter. Finally, we can consider what consequences a reforged intellectual identity might have on a future Han ethos.

The stories presented in this chapter are different from the previous ones. Chapters 4, 5 and 6 present the central, common views of the data sets from which Wang, Zhou and Li were derived. The fictional voices seemed to speak coherently, but each one, after all, represents dozens of different interviews. Coherent primary "voices" may be able to articulate collective opinions, values and visions, but individual daily solutions are many and varied. Like Sun Wukong, who could transform each of his hairs into separate monkeys, each of our three main characters will now be transformed into many separate beings. In particular, the choices made by individuals reveal the systemic constraints and potential avenues of action intellectuals may take.

SOCIAL TRAPS, STRATEGIC TRICKS

China's intellectuals are heirs to a divided legacy. In imperial times intellectuals were the elite, and, at least in the perceptions of modern scholars, innately respected. Despite the ravages of decades of contrary rhetoric, intellectuals demonstrate that they still desire that prestige. These ghostly echoes of an earlier social structure set the stage for their struggles to redeem their status.

Modern intellectuals reflect a cultural desire, once steeped in Confucian tradition, to enhance their *social position*. This lust for *rank* has been transformed to motivate individuals to pursue the "black path." Education is an avenue of social mobility within the state structure, particularly for the large group of scholars who fled the countryside in the early 1980s. One young man expresses it this way:

I know my mother thinks attending college will help me to gain higher position in society. The Chinese people look up to officials. Intellectuals have official grades.[1] When I graduated from school after a year-long practicum, I would be twenty-second grade. The president of a company is thirteenth, twelfth, even eleventh grade. So we become officials, even though we are intellectuals. Somehow, that is their [the parents'] idea. College teachers are sixteenth to eighteenth grade. My parents think if I get an education I will have a high position in society—a very traditional idea.

The potential for social mobility, whether up a hierarchy of ranks or simply from the rural to urban sector, is a very real motivation. For a child of peasants, or a remnant of the Cultural Revolutionary effort to "send down" intellectuals, education might provide the ticket to prestige. However, to go down this path means compliance—compliance with the will and procedures of the state, "today's truth."

As we have seen in previous chapters, to be educated, in the Chinese ethos, also means to be concerned with the welfare of the state. "Worrying about people and country" is the right and duty of an intellectual. At times the immediate requirements of "today's truth" and procedure will be at odds with the long-term vision of what is good for China's scholars and China itself. That contradiction sets up a myriad array of social traps in daily life.

Social traps reflect the inherent pitfalls in planning or decision making in which short-term rewards dominate the perception of long-term losses.[2] All decisions, from the level of the individual to the government, tend to favor immediate gains over long-term ones and personal over abstract benefits. Given the dynamics of a planned society such as China, understanding this feature of decision making is crucial to comprehending scientific and educational policy.

Social traps also underpin some of the seeming contradictions expressed in the individual interviews. For example, one scholar denounces the selfish abuse of policy by those who go abroad without returning benefits to China, yet she, personally, wants to send her son overseas to escape the confines of the Chinese system. The sentiment is similar to that of American parents who devoutly support public education, yet, reluctantly in the face of a hostile reality, feel it best to send their own children to private schools. Such contradictions reflect the divergent perceptions of the distant, abstract cost and the intimate, immediate gain.

On a larger scale, social traps describe the bind that is so painful to the far-sighted scholars. The brain-drain "money future" reflects values that ignore the long-term social benefits provided by education. By promoting such slogans as "To be rich is glorious," the society may accelerate rapid economic growth, but this growth will be self-limiting as long as investments in the intellectual infrastructure of the society are ignored. Eventually, long-term growth depends on research and development.

A young engineer relates a self-inflicted individualized social trap:

While I was a student, I had some practical work at a work site, and I talked with the [working] engineers. They were really puzzled why I didn't study hard. They said, "We need to study, but we have no chance. You have this chance, but you don't study hard. Why?" I replied, "I don't know what I will be doing after graduation, and I have so many courses. Which courses shall I study hard? I can't study all courses equally hard." I needed to select some and concentrate on it, but as a university student I don't know which courses are useful and what will work well after my graduation. So, I treated every course the same . . . just pass the examination, this was my goal.

Clearly, his pragmatism had become his enemy, a social trap in which the pain of study had become a barrier to developing expertise.

One teacher has succumbed to the pressures of "appearing" to be a good teacher even though this damages his effectiveness. The pressures are similar to those facing teachers in an American university. He relates:

I am a teacher. I know the students. If one student fails the exam, what should I do? I will let him pass. If you don't let him pass, the next time he will give you trouble. Then, you must give him another examination and he will hate you. It is not my responsibility to be subject to this accounting. If there are a hundred students in the class and I let ninety-nine pass the exam, my unit leader says, "your teaching is very good. So you are a good teacher" If a teacher lets nearly all of the students pass the examination, he is a "good teacher," so he gets praise from both sides, the leaders and the students. If only eighty students pass the examination, the leader says, Why are the scores so poor? You can't work well, so you are not a good teacher." The students will say "Oh, this teacher is too hard. He won't let most of us pass the examination." So what should I do? Of course, I let them pass.

This teacher has allowed himself to be overwhelmed by the inertia built into the educational system. Here, the concept of "social fence" applies. A social fence is a situation in which an action that is immediately undesirable, but necessary to the long-term good, is avoided. The short-term cost is thus evaded, but a new barrier to social well-being has been constructed. The individual cost is too overwhelming to risk taking action. This fence is the foundation of the conformity that is so often observed in Chinese society. Acting on one's convictions in contradiction to the system is too personally costly.

Politics and the need to preserve appearances augment this self-restraint. This leads to situations in which the need—and ultimate inability—to second-guess social responses leads to paralysis, as in the following convoluted example. A class, whose associates had just seen an interesting English language film also wanted to see that same film, but was unsure how to introduce its request. As they discussed the possibility of asking to see the film, a social dilemma appeared. An engineer explains:

We really wanted to see the film. But no one said anything to the office. Some were concerned that if we said we wanted to see the film that, maybe, the office would think that we don't want to study very hard, but just relax. So some people don't want to say that they want the film. After some discussion, they elected me to say something to the office. And I went to the office to say "play the film." But really, in practice, no one would say anything to the office. Even I began to think that these people don't want to work hard. They only want to watch the film. This is the situation that is happening in our whole society now. Some people have good ideas that could be applied to society by the government. If people asked me for suggestions, I might have some thoughts. Maybe we would consider ideas contrary to the government. But then they might think I am against the government. So I will shut my mouth and not say anything.

I asked him to clarify himself, "You do not say anything and nothing gets done?" As he confirmed this, I perceived the enormous psychological reinforcements that buttress external barriers. The shortage of equipment, clean rooms, research funding and exchange currency for foreign conferences, and the difficulty in getting materials for teaching and research are quite real. So is the enormous drain of living on the economic edge in the land of political ambiguity. Yet the self-imposed constraints of duty, conformity and ennui give the barriers to success an added subtlety that only reinforces those practical difficulties. Nonetheless, as a group, nonestablishment intellectuals are finding ways to breach the barricades and gain greater control over their lives. "The center governs, the people trick." This is what I was told by my informants.

Social traps, luckily, are not indestructible. There are ways to "trick" the system. One way requires outside intervention, just as the "Higher Power" of Twelve Step groups, such as Alcoholic Anonymous, give the chemically dependent person leverage to escape that particular trap. For the scholars, participation in global international science can be such a lever, by offering recognition and support that come from a source beyond Chinese society.

A second, overlapping method of escape from a social trap is to change the system of rewards and costs. For example, in China, the teeth that form the population trap are the forces that promote population growth—patrilineality, high mortality, traditional labor techniques and a need for social security in old age. Immediate social and economic gains mask the cost of overused resources. China has tried to effect "ways out" of the trap by changing the dynamics—improving child health and educational care, providing old age pensions when possible, and instituting penalties for additional children and rewards for reduced family size.

Such structural solutions are not immediately obvious for the dilemmas facing intellectuals. One solution, as discussed by Wang in Chapter 4, is to restructure scientific and technological work so that it too can be part of the profit-oriented reforms. This would certainly change the nature of science in China. Sweeping large-scale social engineering can only provide the environment for change. Individuals must find their own "ways out," evading obstacles or transforming them to stepping stones.

These transformations are done at the microlevel; each life decision, justification and reflection is a move in a larger game. Each act is a placement of a stone in a game of go—weiqi—played with the state. In weiqi, a player can make an active decision and gain control of the direction of the game (sente), leaving the opponent to play a defensive match (gote). The state has sente and controls the game, but the nonestablishment intellectuals can still make their moves in gote. They place their stones in response to the moves made by the dominant player, protecting their gains and awaiting an opening.

In the following stories this means making educational and professional choices that can maximize the individual's goals, while complying to the state's mandates. These choices define the niche in which intellectuals must function.

The choice of one's own discipline illustrates the constraints and malleability of the system. As we shall soon see, this decision is rarely just a matter of individual choice. The state will support or cut scientific fields as it strives to manage the planned economy. In the United States the "unseen hand" of market economics has a similar impact as fields are perceived as relevant or profitable to a student's career. This same situation is beginning to arise in the socialist market economy of China.

The lack of real personal choice in education was one of the key sources of dissatisfaction for the students who protested in June 1989. Choosing a major is a luxury in a planned system where a shortage or surplus of certain specialists can upset the desired industrial goals. However, there are different levels of choice.

First, there is the choice of undergraduate major—which is the most constrained and subject to caprice. A student may pick general fields and list preferences for specific universities, but the final assignment is determined by state policy and test scores. Some departments will have many openings and require little competition by the students. On the other hand, the cream of each year's middle school graduates favor the more popular disciplines, increasing competition for those slots. The ability to enter a favored program will depend partially on how well one scores on the entrance examination. Students with higher scores can go on to Qinghua or Berkeley in the United States; those with lower scores end up at less rigorous provincial schools. No one of these factors is supreme; all play a part.

The stories scholars tell of major assignments are often tales of close calls and near misses. One relates:

Electrical engineering was the best field I could choose, although I wanted to choose some other field, like electronic computers. But in China many students want to go into such subjects, and there is a competition for those spots based on scores. My score was just in the high middle. So the ones with the higher scores will go into electronic computers, and the ones with lower ones will go to electrical engineering. And some other students who score even lower than me will go into civil engineering or hydraulic engineering.

One scholar had passed the entrance examination and wanted to go to the prestigious Qinghua. He had been a childhood star in a provincial middle school. Since he had studied Russian, and not English, his scores were shy of the needed mark, and he did not get his wish.

Other factors that influence Chinese choices are similar to the social and cultural forces that act on American students. Family and friends lend their influence and advice for good career choices. A scholar points out:

Generally speaking people didn't like to study [during the Cultural Revolution]. In that time studying didn't mean a good thing. But my parents, my father, was working in the middle school.

The legacy of learning in his family sphere fostered his choices. Note that even in the "worst" visions of the future, it is believed that learning will not disappear entirely, but will be subsumed into family traditions that persist in spite of larger cultural patterns. The scholars' experience of the Cultural Revolution makes this possibility plausible.

Motivations for becoming intellectuals are molded by family opinion. The family is a central setting for making life decisions, especially for the younger set of scholars. The following stories illustrate how this decision making operates within scholastic families.

When I entered the university, I was very young, 16, without any experience about majors or universities. My family helped make that decision. They considered my attitude. My father is also in the field of automation. Father graduated from college in Japan. My brother is a lecturer in computer science. All of this affected my decision. My parents asked me, "What field do you want to study?" I said, "similar to you."

This pattern is also demonstrated in several statements made by women, with an important difference. The locus of power is more distinct. While the men reported *consulting* with their parents about their career choices, the women expressed a slightly different tone. One points out:

My father chose this field for me. When I was in high school I liked chemistry and physics. When I took part in the entrance exam for the university my physics score was not so pretty. So my father convinced me there is a better potential for me to go to the university and learn chemical engineering.

Another states that she likes the subject but that it was chosen by her parents, because they thought it was good for a girl. She adds, "I found I liked it." People adjusted to state-assigned or parent-chosen majors in a fashion reminiscent of "arranged marriages." It may be true that they did not choose their intellectual life partners, but after they were committed, luckily, many found they enjoyed it.

The role of family input is highlighted by the number of people who were troubled by the lack of it. Such people envied those who could rely on family advice to make a decision—either by emulating a sibling or parent, or consulting a parent as the ultimate authority. When such role models were not present, the youths in question turned to popular opinion or whim.

One scholar ended up in his field by accident. He wanted to stay in his hometown, and there was an opening in a department that would allow him to stay nearby. He was the first in his family to go to the university, and thus could expect no advice from that quarter. The theme of familial ignorance cropped up often enough to be considered a pattern. In the 1980s and immediately before, many of the emerging scholars were the first in their family to be university graduates. That phenomenon created a social gap within families that upset the traditional pattern of young people accepting advice from their elders.

Consider the following remark,

Many high school students don't know their future very clearly, especially if they are from the countryside. I am the oldest son, my father and mother don't know too much about that [education]. I took the examination. I wanted to go to Shanghai or Suzhou, and I was good at chemistry in high school. It is a very old specialty.

A woman adds,

No, my parents are workers. They have no opportunity to go to university, so they really don't know what specialty suits me and what specialty is best. So I chose my specialty by myself, most students think electronic engineering is a good subject to study. And when I took the exam I got a very high score so I could choose the best department, so I chose electronic engineering.

Others are not so fortunate. They can only adjust to their assignment. This can be seen in the following assessments:

In China we have little opportunity—little right—to choose our specialty. It is what our government decides what we should do or study. Maybe five years ago I graduated from university and they said "You should do super hard materials." So I did it.

Again, I was reminded of arranged marriage so I asked him if he was satisfied with his field. He responded, "Yes, I think that I like it." This is the baseline response. He was told what to do and he did it. Fortunately it worked for him.

Not everyone shares his positive outlook. Intellectuals express their dissatisfaction in such comments as:

It is difficult to change to another specialty. The first three years, I think my specialty isn't very interesting. I can't change it. Many Chinese students have this situation. I like it, but I don't enjoy it.

This dissatisfaction is expressed by people who were assigned majors in disharmony with their desires, who had chosen poorly, who missed the mark by a handful of points or who lacked the connections to succeed. For some, the dissatisfaction in itself is a constraint; for others, it is a motivation to strive.

Some limitations are clearly self-inflicted. In one poignant story, an unhappy scholar reveals:

When I took part in the entrance examination for university, I selected my options by copying someone else. I was only 15. I had no idea. When they asked me to select a university [I thought], "don't go too far from home." I only selected universities near my hometown. I handed them in to my teacher. Someone else applied to those universities, so I copied his application. A terrible thing to carry my whole life. By 1983 I wanted to become something else.

But "becoming something else" is a difficult feat in the Chinese educational system, so he remains on a path that does not suit him.

By the time students enter graduate school, they know whether their undergraduate assignment will meet their personal goals. An individual's choice becomes less constrained in graduate school, and some scholars may use that opportunity to wriggle closer to their desired goals. "Picking" a research topic in one's work unit presents another opportunity for those who would transform their assigned occupation.

One scientist wanted to pursue his interest in the biophysics of animals, but positions—and therefore exams to fill them—for postgraduate work into that field were not forthcoming. While pursuing studies in plant biology, he was able to take courses nearer his interests. Eventually his chosen field, sensory systems, was deemed useful enough by the State Education Commission for him to be allowed to pursue it abroad. By that time, he was in a position to move into that research niche. Only by such careful "nudging" at each choice point was he able to achieve his professional and personal goal of doing work that interested him.

The constraints of the official system are compounded by the reality of "connections." Test scores may become irrelevant when *guanxi* creates special openings for competitors:

I tried to pass the university exam to get into a particular master's program. They have a quota to go abroad to study. I passed but hadn't any *guanxi* with the university. They just take students from their own university, or some with *guanxi*. I scored high, higher than those taken by the university!

After June Four, I interviewed someone who remembered the dangers of picking the wrong research topic. He originally had a degree in mathematics, but had been told to turn to social science by his departmental leaders at the request of the government. He notes, "In the Cultural Revolution many economists were sent down to the countryside, and the economics major was canceled. So this major is a dangerous subject." Now, deeply disturbed by the student demonstrations, this scholar suspected it may not be safe at this point to study economics and society. Perhaps it had been a "disaster" to change to this subject. He wanted to make a contribution to China, but wondered whether there was any point to it. Mathematical skills were important to reconstruct new economic theory, but what would happen if the political winds shifted again?

As long as China remained solely a centralized political economy, choices at the beginning and the end of a student's career were controlled by the state. Freshman major and job assignment would be derived from a detailed plan mandated by the central government (Du 1992, 84). This job assignment system was cumbersome and often led to inappropriate appointments. The number of bureaucratic hoops magnified errors as graduates assigned to bureaus would be passed to companies, then factories, and so on—each making its own decisions. The decisions were made by individuals, often party officials, in both the students' former department and in the new *danwei*. All jobs are not equal, a posting to a technical institute in a distant small city is infinitely inferior to a posting to a joint venture in Shanghai.

Maintaining a "good" political reputation and establishing *guanxi* with key officials are essential. Once assigned, an engineer has little chance to move to another system. The officials in the *danwei* have little incentive to keep new engineers happy, their attention is directed to their superiors. These two social facts combine to leave the newly assigned expert feeling trapped (see Link 1992, 61-63).

In the last few years, the system has become more accommodating to new graduates. The Reforms of 1993 suggest greater flexibility in job choice for the majority of candidates who are not seeking a job in the increasingly narrow realm of state-owned enterprises (Hayhoe 1994). Company/graduate choice leads enterprises to select more appropriate candidates and gives job seekers more flexibility. Of course, this flexibility works against women, minorities and individuals in unpopular disciplines and leads to gaps in the educational and industrial infrastructure (see Ogden 1992, 316). Moreover, the new flexibility does little for the older intellectuals interviewed for this book. They are left with the legacy of the older system, no matter what changes emerge for new graduates.

The context for choice is different in China than it would be in the United States. The relationship of an individual to the state is fundamentally different from an American's link to his government. In China, although this is slowly changing, the state is a primary employer, especially of intellectuals. In the United States, however imperfect, laws supply an external check on the relationship between labor and private employer. Such a legal system is not in place for Chinese workers whose "watchdog" is also "the boss." This creates a social atmosphere in which conformity and compliance are heavily rewarded, while dissent is not. "Choice" becomes a slippery concept in such a interpersonal environment. "Free" decisions are made in a tightly constrained social landscape.

The uneasy relationship between state and worker is complicated by the parental nature of the state's attitude. The state conceives of itself as a stern but loving parent, who corrects the flaws of errant individuals who cannot help themselves. The state is benign but tolerates no nonsense. I encountered this attitude when my daughter's Chinese preschool teacher sent her home after having cut her hair. Clearly, I did not recognize "proper" hair length, and it was her duty to correct my error.[3] The state identifies the "best interest" of the dependent and acts accordingly. Given the government's parental attitude, making a dissenting "choice" becomes more difficult. Students do have choices, but they are supposed to be in line with governmental concerns.

CO-OPTING THE MONEY FUTURE

Economic forces in the late-twentieth-century China—a new entrepreneurism, the blurring of rural and urban industry and the co-option of Western research, engineering and business practices—permit intellectuals to forge a different strategy from the one outlined above. Nonestablishment intellectuals can employ yet another tactic for outwitting the state—sidestepping political power to establish an alternative form of legitimacy. This strategy is to "avoid" the state (see Skalnik 1989, 11), eluding its power whenever possible. The intellectuals can use the policies of the state—the market economy and the open door—to establish a separate symbolic sphere that avoids political entanglement. That strategy, the basis of a new identity, rests on several key structural changes—the creation of entrepreneurial intellectuals, the blurring of rural and urban industry and the co-option of Western knowledge as the basis of professional identity.

Intellectuals have assembled an impressive array of strategies in creating alternative paths to success. In this section we will consider the means intellectuals have found for reshaping their own identities. While these means are a direct function of state policy, intellectuals have been enormously creative in transforming collective policy to their own ends. The economic forces that create the hated "money future" also allow them freedom to expand the scope of their work. Rather than relying on the government to institute a complete change for scholars, economic reforms create a niche for them to find success themselves, to make their own transformations.

The intellectuals, like the folk on the inner frontier before them, are culture brokers. Their role is necessary to the state, but their very proximity to alien cultures makes them liminal, subject to suspicion. To overcome that suspicion the nonestablishment intellectuals must forge a new identity giving themselves the legitimacy to function effectively. The change in state discourse concerning "entrepreneurs" and "experts" gives them the opportunity to revise their own status. Once their status is rehabilitated the intellectuals have an even stronger platform to build their collective *mianzi* and *guanxi*, face and connections. Only individuals with the demonstrable ability to mobilize resources and offer help can play the *guanxi* game successfully (see Hwang 1987, 953). Expertise provides the currency and financial autonomy creates a medium for mobilizing those resources.

By separating from the state as much as possible, using the new market opportunities to create an alternative to working for the state, intellectuals gain a marginal autonomy. Research is increasingly allotted to nonofficial or semiofficial research institutes that have only nominal ties with the state (Bonin and Chevrier 1991, 379–380). These may vary in size and official standing from nationally preeminent university-contained research institutes to small rural industries, with support from one of the provincial associations of science and technology. Such efforts represent a use of the gold path that provides some limited freedom from state control.

Younger intellectuals can utilize another economic feature that is emerging in the new, entrepreneurial China, the blurring of rural and urban space brought about by industrializing the countryside. Once wholly urban, intellectuals are beginning to penetrate the urban-rural barrier.

The eroding barriers between rural and urban offer opportunities. This may not hold true for the deep countryside, but entrepreneurial work may abound in coastal provinces or along the Yangzte. Given that older scholars may have connections from their rustification and younger scholars may be the educated kin of the peasantry, potential ties exist to be exploited. One man relates a story of engineering entrepreneurship:

I have a friend that has a small enterprise spreading technology to the countryside. At first he just invited some graduate students to do research for [the rural industries]. They do that in their spare time. This enterprise made a lot of money, helped his friends, the scholars, and the countryside. They have even been recognized by their provincial association of science and technology, a signal that the officials accepted them. Many intellectuals want to earn income in their spare time but also want to be primarily scholars. They think of themselves as middle class, more elegant, and are very proud of it.

When I returned to China in 1994, I found that this trend had accelerated.

In the past, Chinese and sinologists alike believed that the countryside held the "real Chinese," that is, the peasants. Their authenticity was contrasted to the Westernized urbanites associated with university graduates. Rustification during the cultural revolution and the new economic alliances of scientific entrepreneurs and rural industry have altered that distinction. The penetration of the intellectuals into the rural bastion redefines the relationship of city to countryside, throwing into question the whole notion of rural authenticity and paving the way for a more "modern" definition of Chinese identity.

Most importantly, intellectuals are mastering an instrumental approach to Western cultural beliefs and practices and are bringing that knowledge into a Chinese context. Nonestablishment intellectuals couple Chinese and foreign cultural information by using the open door to go either abroad or to gain foreign skills at home that enhance one's marketability.

For many scholars, study abroad creates a new pathway for success—it provides an opportunity to redefine their status and, for a time, avoid the state. As we saw in the interview chapters, the enhanced status of an overseas education is dangled as a carrot to encourage students both to go abroad and to return. This issue has been vastly complicated by the "specter of Tiananmen." The amount of *kaifang*—opening—available to returning students was ambiguous in 1988, problematical in 1989 and still troublesome in the 1990s.[4]

Some of the scholars I interviewed saw going abroad as the means of obtaining hard-to-get doctorates in their given field. Others expressed joy over the possible perks—increased pay, better housing, greater chance to change residence. Foreign study provides a rare opportunity that requires both language acquisition (a brilliant scholar who spoke no English would be an unlikely candidate) and professional expertise. It is highly competitive. These conditions are forging an individualism that will play a role in the new Chinese identity.

CHINESE IDENTITY FOR THE TWENTY-FIRST CENTURY

The practical vehicles of the "open door" and "entrepreneurism" are intertwined with cognitive tools. Intellectuals must first forge some sort of new cultural identity in which they reduce the cultural ambiguity they have experienced in the last forty-five years. They have done this by increasingly intertwining their own individual interests with the state's, creating a clearer discourse of individualism. They reinterpret Chinese traditional philosophy to incorporate Western forms of knowledge, à la the Dao of software (see Zhao 1995, 1153). Significantly, they are comfortable with using the knowledge of the West to serve their own purposes, forging a cultural bridge between China and "the other."

In action and speech, intellectuals have revealed significant areas of change in their conception of their identity. Increasingly, they enact individualism, couched in collectivistic language. Chinese intellectuals can invoke cherished ideals to support their individualist actions. They can muster pragmatic arguments suggesting that supporting intellectuals fosters "Modernization." They can also point to more traditional notions—such as obligation to family and respect for scholarship—to defend their individualistic bids for survival. Using a collective ideal to further individual goals is a trait of individualism.

Although Americans are on the extreme end of the individualism/collectivism continuum, they too justify their behavior in terms of "community good." This can be seen in the California town that is divided between those who oppose economic and real growth and those who support it. Each side invokes "community," but their definitions of the word differ. One side uses it to mean environmental health and rural seclusion, while the other points to the sanctity of business and private property. In both groups, individuals are actively pursuing their own self-interest, privacy and profit, respectively. All frame their justifications in terms of the collective (Madsen 1991). In a parallel way, the intellectuals are invoking collective ideals to support their bids for upward mobility.

Note the combination of *idealism and self-interest* in the case of one chemical engineer. He says,

To tell the truth, when I was in secondary school I got some information about the industrial situation of our country. At that time I realized that the chemical industry of our country was relatively backward. The chemical industry is a most important industry, especially in developing countries. This industry can use very simple raw materials to make some very important products. It can make a lot of money. So when I was in secondary school, I spent a lot of time on chemistry. And at that time I decided to do further study on chemical engineering. So when I entered university, I selected chemical engineering as my specialty.

He was able to capitalize on the "government's call" by choosing a field that was both strategically important and personally satisfying.

Other intellectuals may be motivated to seek out a field because of its potential for breakthrough discoveries, such as biochemistry or polymer science. Both of these subjects were cited in the "optimistic" scenarios as disciplines with "a good future." Some scientists agreed on a personal level, saying that, for them, "it is a promising field of science." Those scientists could combine the mandate for modernization with their own *career ambitions*.

Underpinning this shift in social identity is a new set of values—those associated with individualism. The desire for social mobility, concern for the *nuclear* family and yearning for individual success are not features of collectivism. While such individualistic sentiments cannot be articulated too loudly—that would be contrary to the rhetoric of collective socialism—these attitudes are intrinsic to creating an identity that rests on technical expertise, not political power. Collectivistic discourse must be expressed when "worrying about the country." But in the realm of career, individualistic practices can be quietly enacted.

By creatively using the new market system to their advantage, scholars can find ways to create competition, an inherently individualistic notion, and evade the inertia of the system. For example, as one man points out:

In my wife's middle school, two years ago, they hired some teachers who don't like their jobs. They wanted to leave their teaching positions. Teachers can't leave their jobs! They are trained, and their living expenses are paid by the government. The amount of money is fixed. The school wanted to reduce the number of staff. They assigned some to go outside to work to make money for the school. The better teachers were assigned to teach. They can make higher salaries than before.

By assigning some teachers to bring in "extra" income from outside work, the best teachers can be rewarded with higher pay.

FROM TRADITIONAL TO GLOBAL CHINESE

Scientists, engineers and scholars are revitalizing and updating traditional Chinese medical and metaphysical beliefs. Intellectuals, especially younger ones, are redefining traditional belief to justify their own scientific pursuits. Just as Zhou recast software writing and genetic engineering as Daoist activities, the co-option of tradition has been used in many parts of the world to give the marginal legitimacy. By valorizing Traditional Chinese Medicine, or the Daoist legacy of complex synthesis, young scholars make themselves more clearly defenders of Chineseness. It is difficult to marginalize intellectuals as spiritually polluted if they are the defenders of China's ancient traditions as well as Western knowledge.

Chineseness has been determined by a variety of variables in the past. In imperial times, connection to the land marked the distinction between Han and their more nomadic ethnic neighbors. A body of knowledge, Confucian and Daoist, defined the elite metaphysical cognitive realm. This Chinese identity, despite the permeability evidenced by historic contacts, was inwardly focused. In rhetoric, if not in economic fact, the Chinese worldview was self-contained. These aspects of identity have changed in the late twentieth century. These changes have been made manifest by the intellectuals discussed in this book. These are innovations in identity that can spread beyond their strata to the rest of China.

The intellectuals are reshaping their niche by coupling *pragmatic competency* with their *traditional mantle of respect*. Overseas Chinese have accomplished a similar merger—juxtaposing their wealth and global expertise with a knowledge of Chineseness that evaded the distortions of the Cultural Revolution. These global ethnic Chinese have played an increasing role in shaping the discourse on Chinese identity in the 1990s. At once forces of change and stability, descendants of the Chinese diaspora bring new modernized versions of Chineseness into the cultural repertoire.

Most importantly, the attitude the scholars displayed toward their Western expertise was highly instrumental. They would use their expertise in Western modes of knowledge to serve their own needs. Those needs incorporate individualistic ambitions for self and immediate family and loftier goals related to China's modernization. Intellectuals can then use the official discourse connected to the collective goal to enhance their status as a group. The state is not confronted, but acknowledged, and used. By emphasizing skills and expertise, the nonestablishment intellectuals create an alternative discourse to ideological purity, the red path. They use the needs of the state to enhance the legitimacy they gain from their own expertise. They can use their intermittent nemesis—their expertise—to give themselves, and their nation, an advantage.

Chinese intellectuals have created ways to enact individualism and combine Chinese spiritual tradition with secular Western knowledge. By reshaping their own identity, they have made the "black path" a template of modernization that will reshape the Chinese future.

Epilogue

Chinese scientists now must struggle to read and publish in English. But in 50 years the scientific world will need to learn Chinese.

(Sunny Chen in Jeffrey Mervis and June Kinoshita,
"Science in China: A Great Leap Forward," 1131)

Years have passed since the interviews were gathered. Some of the people interviewed have written from abroad. I saw others when I returned to China for several short trips during my 1994 Fulbright sojourn to Hong Kong. During that year, I was also able to connect with sinologists who had updated information on Chinese intellectuals. In 1995 *Science* issued a special journal on "Science in China: A Great Leap Forward," discussing the most recent policies and statistics. The educational system of China is being remolded at lightning speed. Universities are at the verge of becoming agencies of mass education, driven by a market economy. The lack of state financial support has forced educators to become creatively entrepreneurial. Although this trend has deep problems for industry and academy, it has fueled the creation of a separate sphere. The explosion of rural industry, predicted by Zhou, has driven a 20 percent growth rate in some regions, providing unparalleled opportunities for those intellectuals willing and able to move to the action.

The intellectuals themselves still "worry about China." Inflation is high and corruption is persistent. The culture of noncooperation still impedes scientific cooperation (Kinoshita 1995a, 1139, 1995b, 1149; Plafker 1995, 1151). Yet the bitter tone of 1990 has been replaced by an optimism for themselves. China and the United States have signed a new scientific agreement to replace the one that lapsed after Tiananmen (Mervis 1995a, 1144). The rate for returning students is reaching a new high as Chinese scholars abroad perceive fresh opportunities in their homeland (Kinoshita 1995c, 1142; Mervis 1995b, 1134, 1136).

As a group, they are more comfortable with their own identity. I was repeatedly told that the intellectuals are part of a "new middle class," not rich, but not destitute. Many have succeeded in using their expertise to bypass the quagmires of seniority and ideological dogmatism. As individuals they are successful and look forward to future achievements. Their impact on global knowledge is increasing. These nonestablishment intellectuals have gone on to do much more than simply "eat, sleep and teach." They have created a new, more global way of being Chinese.

Notes

CHAPTER 1

1. For critical literary discussions of the *Journey to the West* and its symbolic elements, see the Yu's introduction to his translation, especially pages 36-55 (1977). See Bantley for an exploration of Buddhist allegory (1989, 522-523), and Plaks for a discussion of Neo-Confucian imagery (1987). Dudbridge discusses the allegorical image of the Mind Monkey (1970, 175), and Wang examines the character of Sun Wukong as part of the trickster and stone folklores of China (1992, 223-242).

2. Two former foreign experts have created works of fiction that feature Monkey King. Vizenor (1987) reinvents him as a Western character in *Griever, An American Monkey King in China*. Salzman (1991) brings Sun Wukong himself into an American setting in *The Laughing Sutra*.

3. Clear methodological guides to the mechanics of conducting and analyzing interviews include Ely et al. (1991, 57-69); Fetterman (1989); Pelto and Pelto (1978, 67-102); Spradley (1979, 55-106); Werner and Schoepfle (1987, 314-343). Moerman discusses the ethnographic analysis of conversation, using transcript data, that can easily lend itself to interview analysis (1988, 48-100).

4. The literary device of presenting Chinese narratives, or "voices" is relatively common. Zhang and Sang (1986, 1987) present street vignettes of ordinary folk in the style of Studs Terkel. Chin (1988) relates children's thoughts, while Hooper (1985) relays youth narratives. Honig and Hershatter (1988) present women's voices.

CHAPTER 2

1. For a summary of the historical changes that have affected Chinese universities, see Cleverley (1985), Pepper (1990) and Hu (1987). Shive (1993 personal communication) was also helpful in conceptualizing the stratigraphy of Chinese universities. Tu (1979, 1985) provides an excellent discussion of Confucian values. Thurston, among many others, discusses the impact of the Cultural Revolution (1988). A translated essay from the *World economic*

Herald has the appropriate tone to describe contemporary university trends and life (Anonymous 1990), as do the essays by Ruth Hayhoe (1988, 1990, 1993). Hayhoe's 1987 article, "China's Higher Curricular Reform in Historical Perspective," is invaluable.

2. *Danwei* is often loosely translated as "company," but a *danwei* encompasses far more than that, except perhaps in a "company town." The work unit is nearer in feeling to a military unit, but one assigned for life. It was originally designed as a revolutionary device to replace kinship as the center of communal life: it now provides an institution in which family resides.

3. Bond (1991), Bond and Hwang (1986), Gudykunst and Ting-Toomey (1988, 58–59), Hofstede (1984, 151), Hsu (1981), Segall and his co-authors (1990, 218) and Yang (1986) discuss the Chinese psychology as "essentially" collectivistic.

4. Schwartz (1990), Brislin and Bhawuk (1992), Hui and Triandis (1986) provide stimulating discussions of the concept of situational individualism, suggesting that cultural contexts may be individualistic or collectivistic. But it is an overgeneralization to charac-terize whole cultures.

5. The various facets of Chinese anthropology have been discussed, from the insider's point of view, in Fei (1981) and more recently, Ruan (1993). Also see Harrell (1991), McGough (1979), Rossi (1985) and Guldin (1991, 1993) for Western assessments of Chinese anthropology.

6. The Ethnographic Futures Research (EFR) interview technique was developed by Robert Textor (1980). He further elaborated the technique in his interviews with prominent Thai intellectual elite (Sippanondha 1990; Textor, Bhansoon and Sidthinat 1984). I used the technique in several projects first with holistic healers and midwives (English-Lueck 1990a); then with the Chinese (English-Lueck 1990b); and finally with Silicon Valley educators (Darrah and English-Lueck 1993). Anthropologist Reed Riner has used it in a community study of Flagstaff, Arizona (1987).

7. There are a number of books and articles on educational and scientific policy in China. Many will emerge later in this book. A useful collection would include Conroy (1989), Epstein (1991), Goldman (1981), Goldman, Cheek and Hamrin (1987), Goldman, Link and Su (1993), Hayhoe and Bastid (1987), Lewin (1987), Orleans (1980, 1988), Simon (1987), Simon and Rehn (1988) and Volti (1982).

8. A great many books and articles have focused on the events in Beijing surrounding the turmoil of Tiananmen Square on June 4, 1989. Most are journalistic and focus on the perception of the dissenters (for example, see Salisbury 1989 or Han 1990). Note especially Kane (1990), Joseph (1991), Nathan (1990), and Yi and Thompson (1989). Spence (1990, 712–747) provides one of the clearest overviews. Unger (1991) presents a series of reports from areas outside of Beijing. Cheng (1990) is a comprehensive overview of the events in Beijing and its impact on the rest of China.

9. Although most of what is written here is based on my experience, Lull (1991, 182–207) discusses Chinese television in detail, not only during and after Tiananmen, but for the preceding years.

10. Myriad books have been written by foreigners about their experiences living and teaching in China; they are often witty but filled with angst. Margery Wolf provides an honest and insightful rendition of her experience doing anthropological research in China (1985, 28–55). Other reminiscences and intelligent analyses can be found in Barlowe and Lowe (1987), Salzman (1987), Holm (1990) and James (1990). Reference guides by Weiner, Murphy and Li (1991), and Turner-Gottshang and Reed (1987) are guides for potential foreign academics that nonetheless are filled with dry sojourner tales.

CHAPTER 3

1. For an exploration of the frontier concept as an intercultural process, see Bohannan (1967). Osborne (1977); Green and Perlman (1985); and Hudson (1977) discuss various applications of Turner's approach. Billington (1971) remains the best single synopsis of the Turner hypothesis, although you can consult the original (Turner 1986).

2. For discussions of the inner-outer frontier in China, see Cotton (1989, 39–41), Jagchid and Symons (1989) and of, course, Owen Lattimore, the author of the concept (1988, 20).

3. The name "Red Guard" was generated in the Qinghua University Middle School in Beijing (Cleverley 1985, 164). Kessen (1975, 151–170) describes "model" middle schools during the later part of the Cultural Revolution. The middle school is itself an institution designed to provide secondary education. Beyond the age of 12, the Chinese have lower and upper middle schools, roughly the equivalent of American middle and high schools. Increasingly, vocational and technical schools form a segment of the upper middle school. Key middle schools comprise the university preparatory track. Between 1978 and 1988 the enrollment in middle schools increased by 2.3 times (State Statistical Bureau 1989, 46). For more information on Chinese secondary education, consult Ross (1991) for a contemporary synopsis and Cleverley (1985, 236–240) for a general overview of middle schools.

4. Fictional works, largely autobiographical, on the Cultural Revolution include novels by Cheng (1986), Gao (1987), Liang and Shapiro (1983) and Liu (1989).

5. In the 1910s and 1920s Chinese schools were strongly influenced by missionary and Western—particularly American—models of education. The ideas of John Dewey (who first visited China in 1919) were especially potent (see Dewey 1968, originally 1916; 1989). He postulated that scientific inquiry, the ability to seek rational solutions to problems, is a vital part of democratic education. His view of education as an essential democratizing force was influential among the Chinese intellectuals so deeply disturbed by the low status of their country (Cleverley 1985, 44–54). During the May Fourth Movement of 1919, the concepts of "democracy" and "science" were intertwined in the rhetoric (1985, 49).

6. McCormick (1990), Ethridge (1990, 313–348) and Dittmer (1990) discuss the complexities of Zhao Ziyang and Hu Yaobang and their political relationships to both Deng and intellectuals.

7. The cultural portrayal of the June Fourth Movement can be seen in the language and treatment of student protests in issues of *Time* during that period (Benjamin 1989; Talbot 1989a, 1989b). John King Fairbank discusses the perception of Chinese by Americans in a broader context in his introduction to *China Watch* (1987, 1–9).

8. Eighty thousand Chinese students are estimated to be abroad during the decade 1978–1988. Probably many more than that are pursuing studies without governmental financial support and therefore do not figure in the standard statistics (Hayhoe 1991, 134).

CHAPTER 4

1. The statistics on student return rates are inconsistant and politically volatile. The vast majority do not appear to be returning. However, middle-aged scholars and state-supported scholars do have a higher rate of return. When directly asked, most scholars will say they intend to return (Link 1992, 244). To say otherwise would be imprudent.

2. Virtually all of the interviewees cited a litany of "leading fields" consistent with popular assessments. These diverse areas overlapped with the official designations of technological

priorities in China. The seven-year plan (1986-1990) highlights seven technologies—biotechnology, information, space, laser and automation technologies, robotics, energy technologies, especially nuclear reactors, and advanced materials (Simon and Rehn 1988, 180-183). This official recitation was echoed in the press. Phrases such as "science and technology can raise the productivity of agriculture" were direct quotations form news sources such as the *China Daily* (Anonymous 1989a, n.p.). Biotechnology was particularly portrayed to play a great role in future medicine (Anonymous 1989b, n.p.) and food production (Gu 1989, n.p.; Staff 1989, n.p.). The papers note the governmental emphasis placed on computers and software (Guo 1989, n.p.), space science (Anonymous 1989c, n.p.) and superconductors (Anonymous 1989d, n.p.).

3. As a consequence of the breakup of "Ma Bell" restricted resources resulted in a "lean and mean" strategy that limited available research and development funds. Thus, Bell Laboratories began to shift away from basic research priorities in the late 1980s and early 1990s. In 1993 declining profits resulted in corporate downsizing for both Apple and IBM. Diminishing resources forced a reshuffling of priorities away from basic research toward projects that would yield near-term profits (Davis 1993, 1F, 6F; Gomes 1993, 1A, 14A). This trend is mirrored in federal policy emphasizing the "D" in "R and D" (Marshall 1993, 1816-1819).

4. The "picture drawn on the wall" refers to "big character posters"—large pieces of paper covered with cartoons, slogans, poems and essays that can anonymously express various points of view. The Democracy Wall Movement in Beijing 1978 consisted of thousands of these messages pasted onto a wall west of the former Forbidden City (Spence 1990, 660). The posting of such "big character" dissent was a form of protest that extended back before the Cultural Revolution, even to the earliest protests in the twentieth century.

5. A hat, *maozi*, also carries the connotation of a political stigma. Stigma is often discussed in terms of the "hat" that is placed on them (Broaded 1991, 368-369). The "high cap" then would convey some irony.

6. This reasoning was part of a discourse popular in 1988 and early 1989. The idea that entrenched, feudal, "traditional" Chinese values inhibited efforts at modernization had been discussed in the controversial television series, "River Elegy" (see Lin 1993, 114; Link 1992, 156; Lull 1991, 213-214; Ogden 1992, 145). This series was mentioned in both casual conversation and interviews as a source for debate. Which values were to be preserved, which were too costly?

7. Merton's sociology of science has undergone several waves of criticism and transformation. Mulkay's classic (1969) essay challenges the idea of understanding science without its "extra-scientific factors." See also Stehr (1990, 287-291) and Lynch (1993, 59-67) for summaries of that debate.

8. This concept of "power distance" varies between American and "Asian" cultures (and within them as well). Hofstede defines the concept of power distance as the extent to which less powerful members accept the idea that power is distributed unequally (Hofstede 1984, 94; Hofstede and Bond 1984, 419). In high-power distance contexts "inferiors" accept the assumption that "superiors" are a separate, rather inviolate category. In low-power distance cultures, that assumption is questioned and authority is granted only when leaders can demonstrate legitimacy and expertise. In his 1984 work (also published in 1980) work Hofstede points out that high power distance is associated with cultures that value obedience in their children—namely, Confucian ones. The Chinese Culture Connection

(1987), a group of cross-cultural psychologists under the direction of Michael Bond at the Chinese University of Hong Kong, points out that the power distance concept is part of a larger package of values that place group integrity before a narrowly defined "self-interest."

CHAPTER 5

1. See Merton (1968, 607–610), Mulkay (1969, 23–24) and Lynch (1993, 61) for explanations of universalism and some of the criticisms attached to it.

2. The official position on science and technology has two thrusts. The first is the "spark" program aimed at spreading technology to rural areas through intermediate technology. Manure methane generators or convertible two-cylinder car/plows are examples of this approach. It is meant to be appropriate to small-scale applications, such as peasant family plots, and using technology that is cheap, reliable and reparable. The second drive is the "torch" program that promotes cutting edge high technology (Zhang Ping 1989). It is the advanced technology that is given the most public exposure since it places China among the most modern nations.

3. Rural schools rely on the *minban* system in which the local community finances and manages its own schools. The market system has undermined support since wealthy peasants can send their children to distant schools and the less wealthy cannot then sustain a financial base (Ogden 1992, 318).

4. Hsu discusses the notion of dyads in his 1971 essay on kinship and culture. He suggests that there are certain relationships are central to each culture's kinship structure. Central to his hypothesis is the "dyad," two linked persons within the kinship system. A husband-wife dyad (associated with Americans) cultivates discontinuity, exclusiveness, sexuality and volition as associated attributes. The Chinese central dyad, father-son, is associated with continuity, collectivity, authority and less clearly associated with sexuality (1971, 8–11, 29).

5. He (1991) provides one of the most comprehensive discussions of ecology and resource development in contemporary China.

6. A 1993 Harris poll suggested that 80 percent of American adults think there is too much violence on television (Anonymous 1993, 7A).

7. Link cites a set discourse in which intellectuals would bemoan their status, using such phrases as "The scalpel of the brain surgeon earns you less than the razor of the barber" (1992, 22–23). Such phrases would pass through the grapevine and then be replaced by others.

8. The discussion of models of distributive justice—based on need, equality and equity— extends back to 1975 (Deutsch). Hwang's research with Chinese people indicates that the kind of justice to be applied is based on the nature of the relationship of the people involved. Longer term relationships foster equality, and superficial relationships will select for equity (Bond and Hwang 1993, 258–259; Hwang 1987, 945; Leung and Bond 1984). In other words, within the in-group people avoid decisions that may be divisive, but that factor is less critical to more distant relationships. Then, equity is the means for determining fairness.

CHAPTER 6

1. Croll provides an historical overview of women's rights in China from the 1950 explosion of collectivized household tasks—dining halls, kindergartens, grain processing

plants, sewing centers—to the economic and social problems of the late 1950s and 1960s (Croll 1986, 231). Honig and Hershatter also provide a historic synopsis (1988, 2–6), as does Johnson (1980, 67–74). Honig and Hershatter discuss the legacy of the Cultural Revolution (1988, 23–31). Further discussion of the Marriage Laws of 1950 and 1980 can be found in Croll (1985, 122–127). Robinson provides a discussion of the opposing forces of economic growth, social inequality and population control (Robinson 1985, 32) as does Judd (1990, 42–43). Robinson also discusses the one-child policy as it relates to social problems such as female infanticide, wife-beating and abortions (1985, 54) as does Woodruff (1989, 112–113).

2. The hours spent in housework discussed by the interviewees are reinforced by descriptions in the literature on urban shopping (Whyte and Parish 1984, 176–182, 212–218). Women work on the average 1.5 hours more than men (Hooper 1991, 359), although male intellectuals spend more time on housework than other categories of men.

3. Educated workers are particularly vulnerable to residential changes. This issue was a frequent topic of discussion among intellectuals. If an engineer is needed in Lanzhou, one will be assigned there, but the spouse remains behind. Three hundred thousand couples have asked, but been denied permission, to reunite (Mathews 1983, 321). The term for couples separated by different residential assignments is *niulan zhinu*, referring to the tale of the weaver princess and her cowherd husband who are separated by the Milky Way when her divine mother recalls her to heaven. In late summer, the mythic couple is rejoined by crossing a bridge of birds over the stars, just as modern separated couples get to meet once a year at the New Year holiday. Choosing to accept a reassignment for work or school— which often leads to a teaching assignment in the granting graduate department—risks long-term separation. The government is aware of this problem and deplores it, but specialized workers are rare and economic planning drives the distribution of scientists, not personal convenience.

4. Robinson discusses the high demand for consumer technology (refrigerators, washing machines, etc.) which confirms the domestic role of Chinese women, while it is simultaneously seen by them as the key factor in raising the quality of life (1985, 42, 56–57).

5. Although there were television stations in a dozen cities in the 1960s, the Cultural Revolution dramatically slowed the spread of that medium. In the 1980s nearly every family bought a set—similar to the growth of television in 1950s America (see Lull 1991, 20–24 for a discussion of the scope of Chinese television). Kottak's study of Brazilian and American television viewing suggests that there are discrete phases in a culture's relationship with the media. The longer a society has television, the more integrated it becomes with the rest of the culture (1990). In China television is a novel mode of communication, intriguing and spell-binding. It is a consumer good of high prestige. For Americans, it is simply a ubiquitous part of life, no more remarkable than toasters. Yet it has restructured the nature of American symbolism conveying morality tales, providing education and generating a sense of local and regional community.

6. This set of traits comprises what has been called "human-heartedness" by the Chinese Culture Connection, that is, human-centered, not task-centered, behavior—including "kindness," "patience," "courtesy," and a "sense of righteousness" (see Chinese Culture Connection 1987, 158; Segall et al. 1990, 57–58; Gudykunst and Ting-Toomey 1988, 49). The notion of human-heartedness reflects a relationship-centered definition of self. Self is not individuated, but exists as a *ren*, a person in a web of connections (Bond and Hwang 1993, 220–221; Hsu 1985, 30–36).

7. Betrothal gifts were a traditional part of marital exchange in prerevolutionary China. At

that time, the betrothal gifts could be the indirect source of dowries. Dowries have been eliminated, but the betrothal gifts have reappeared with the economic reforms, particularly in the countryside. Even though young women's contributions to parental households are higher than ever, their earnings are funneled away from them, toward the gifts needed for their brothers. The value of the gifts has escalated in conjunction with the availability of expensive consumer goods. See Croll (1986, 124–125), Whyte and Parish (1984, 136–137) and Honig and Hershatter (1988, 141, 352).

8. Foster described this mechanism for leveling social discrepancies in his article "Peasant Society and the Image of Limited Good" (1965). The concept has been applied to Chinese peasants who express concern that no one should have an unfair advantage (Potter and Potter 1990, 238, 339).

CHAPTER 7

1. The notion of social trap evolved from a series of seminars at the Michigan Mental Health Research Institute in Ann Arbor (Cross and Guyer 1980, 2, 6). John Platt's 1973 *Science* article articulated the basic principles of social traps and social fences, and, based on behavioral learning theory, he also suggested potential ways out of such traps.

2. "There are many ranks in the classless society," quips an unnamed Chinese diplomat in Mathew's book, *One Billion*. Eighteen million people had some rank within the civil service system in the early 1980s (1983, 242). Nonestablishment intellectuals "still have some nominal 'official' status" as *ganbu* (Hua 1994, 116). Different occupations have hierarchies that finely order various levels of government officials—twelve levels for academics. The dividing line is grade thirteen. A ranking of twelve or lower makes one a *gaoji ganbu*, a high official who can garner and disperse special privileges.

3. The attitude demonstrated by this Chinese preschool teacher has been documented in Tobin, Wu and Davidson's study of such institutions in Japan, China and the United States. They note that Chinese educators see themselves correcting the small failures of the parents, and indeed, the parents expect the teachers to take this role (1989, 98, 195, 209). As governmental employees the teachers carry the mandate of the state into the classroom; they assume an aspect of the parental role that is attributed to the state.

4. Official service centers—such as the China Service Center for Scholarly Exchange— have been set up to provide services to those who go abroad, and entice them to return (Anonymous 1989f; Zhu 1990). The centers send teams to students abroad to lure them back with assurances of a useful position back in China. They are designed to allay the fear that the system is so bureaucratically inert that returning students will be unable to apply their newly won foreign skills and degrees. However, returnees' political concerns were not as easily addressed. After Tiananmen, particularly since President Bush, and eventually the U.S. Congress, allowed Chinese dissident students to extend their visas, students were reluctant to return to a less than optimal environment for intellectuals (see Ogden 1992, 94). Although the government "reaffirmed" that it will continue sending students through the open door and that it "will not impose any punishment" on those who expressed dissident opinions while overseas (Zhang Lin 1989), students were reluctant to return to China. For example, 20 percent of the Chinese students in Australia were not returning, even in the face of relatively harsh visa requirements (Maslen 1992, A30). The Chinese had launched a vigorous campaign to bring students back home. The September 1992 arrest of the returning student dissident, Shen Tong—author of a 1990 collection of personal essays on Tiananmen and chairman of

the Democracy for China Fund—highlighted the dilemma facing the returning student. His Harvard mentor Ross Terrill, who accompanied Shen back to China, was expelled (see Terrill 1992 for a discussion of the human rights issues implied by the Tiananmen conflict). Although Shen was ultimately released after two months, the incident indicated the Chinese government's internal contradiction between encouraging students to return, and yet needing to contain what they bring back (Ewell 1992, 25A).

Works Cited

Anonymous. 1989a. More agri-technology needed. *China Daily*. December 26: n.p.

——. 1989b. Bio-tech sure of big sales. *China Daily*. Xinhua News Agency. October 1: n.p.

——. 1989c. Hi-tech progress claimed. *China Daily*. Xinhua News Agency. August 31: n.p.

——. 1989d. Superconductors. *China Daily*. March 3: n.p.

——. 1989e. Jiang Zemin praises women's role in China. *China Daily*. November 17: n.p.

——. 1989f. Students encouraged to return. *China Daily*. November 28: n.p.

——. 1990. Shanghai college professors assess trends and situations in education. Fudan University conducts a sample survey on how education can extricate itself from its present situation. *Chinese Education* 23: 22–30.

——. 1993. 80 percent in poll say TV programs are too violent. *San Jose Mercury News*. August 9:7A.

Bantley, Francisca Cho. 1989. Buddhist allegory in the *Journey to the West*. *Journal of Asian Studies* 48(3):512–524.

Barlow, Tani and Donald Lowe. 1987. *Teaching China's lost generation*. San Francisco: China Books.

Barnes, R. H. 1987. Anthropological Comparison. In *Comparative Anthropology. Papers of the symposium on comparative method in social anthropology held at the University of St. Andrews*, ed. Holy Ladislav, 119–134. Oxford: Basil Blackwell Ltd.

Benjamin, Daniel. 1989. State of siege. *Time*, May 29, 1989:36–45.

Billington, Ray. 1971. *The genesis of the frontier thesis: a study in historical creativity*. San Marino, Calif.: Huntington Library.

Bochner, Stephan and Adrian Furnham. 1986. *Culture shock: psychological reactions to unfamiliar environments*. New York: Methuen.

Bodley, John. 1985. *Anthropology and contemporary human problems*. Second Edition. Palo Alto, Calif.: Mayfield Publishing.

Bohannan, Paul. 1967. Introduction in Beyond the frontier: social process and cultural change, ed. Paul Bohannan and Fred Plog, xi–xviii. Sourcebooks in Anthropology. Garden City, N.Y.: Natural History Press.

Bond, Michael. 1991. *Beyond the Chinese face: insights from psychology.* New York: Oxford University Press.

Bond, Michael and Kwang-kuo Hwang. 1986. The social psychology of Chinese people. In *The psychology of Chinese people*, ed. Michael Bond, 213–266. New York: Oxford University Press.

Bonnin, Michel and Yves Chevrier. 1991. The intellectual and the state: social dynamics of intellectual autonomy during the post–Mao era. *China Quarterly* 127:567–593.

Braudel, Fernand. 1979. *Civilization and capitalism 15th–18th century.* Translated by Sian Reynolds. San Francisco: Harper and Row.

Brislin, Richard and D.P.S. Bhawuk. 1992. The measurement of intercultural sensitivity using the concepts of individualism and collectivism. *International Journal of Intercultural Relations* 16:413–436.

Broaded, C. Montgomery. 1991. China's lost generation: The status degradation of an educational cohort. *Journal of Contemporary Ethnography* 20(3):352–379.

Cheng Chu-yuan. 1990. *Behind the Tiananmen massacre: social, political and economic ferment in China.* Boulder, Colo.: Westview Press.

Cheng Nien. 1986. *Life and death in Shanghai.* Toronto: Grafton Books.

Chin, Ann-ping. 1988. *Children of China: voices from recent years.* Ithaca, N.Y.: Cornell University Press.

Chinese Culture Connection. 1987. Chinese values and the search for culture-free dimensions of culture. *Journal of Cross-cultural Psychology* 18(2):143–164.

Cleverley, John. 1985. *The schooling of China.* Boston: George Allen and Unwin, Australia.

Clifford, James. 1986. On ethnographic allegory. In *Writing culture*, ed. James Clifford and George Marcus, 98–121. Berkeley: University of California Press.

Conroy, R. J. 1989. The role of the higher education sector in China's research and development system. *China Quarterly* 117:38–70.

Cooper, James. 1994. Allegorical imperatives: Cai Yuanpei and Chinese intellectuals in the 1980s. Seminar paper, Department of History. University of Hong Kong. January 20, 1994.

Cotton, James. 1989. *Asian frontier nationalism: Owen Lattimore and the American policy debate.* Studies on East Asia. Atlantic Highlands, N.J.: Humanities Press.

Croll, Elizabeth. 1985. *Women and rural development in China: production and reproduction.* Geneva, Switzerland: International Labor Office.

——. 1986. Rural production and reproduction: Socialist development experiences. In *Women's work: development and the division of labor by gender*, ed. Eleanor Leacock and Helen Safa, 224–252. South Hadley, Mass.: Bergin and Garvey Publishers.

Cross, John and Melvin Guyer. 1980. *Social traps.* Ann Arbor: University of Michigan Press.

Darrah, Charles and J. A. English-Lueck. 1993a. Anthropology in "The Tech": report on Fall 1992 activities and addendum. Silicon Valley Cultures Project. Department of Anthropology, San Jose State University.

Davis, Frederic. 1993. Where to now Mac? *San Jose Mercury News.* August 1:1F, 6F.

Deutsch, M. 1975. Equity, equality, and need: what determines which value will be used as the basis of distributive justice? *Journal of Social Issues* 31:137–149.

Dewey, John. 1968. *Democracy and education.* First published in 1916. New York: Free Press.

——. 1989. *Freedom and culture.* Buffalo, N.Y.: Prometheus Books.

Dittmer, Lowell. 1990. China in 1989: the crisis of incomplete reform. *Asian Survey* 30: 25–41.

Douglas, Mary. 1966. Purity and danger: an analysis of concepts of pollution and taboo. New

York: Penguin Books.

Du Ruiqing. 1992. *Chinese higher education: a decade of reform and development.* New York: St. Martin's Press.

Dudbridge, Glen. 1970. *The Hsi-yu chi: a study of antecedents to the sixteenth-century Chinese novel.* Cambridge: Cambridge University Press.

Ely, Margot, Margaret Anzul, Teri Friedman, Diane Garner and Ann McCormick Steinmetz. 1991. *Doing qualitative research: circles within circles.* London: Falmer Press (Taylor and Francis Group).

English-Lueck, J. A. 1990a. *Health in the New Age: a study of California holistic practices.* Albuquerque: University of New Mexico Press.

———. 1990b. China 2020: looking forward. *Futures Research Quarterly* 6:5-12.

English-Lueck, J. A. and Veeda Marchetti. 1987. You owe yourself a Nacerima: the role of the anthropological study of American culture in the future of anthropology. Paper presented at the American Anthropological Association meetings, Chicago, Illinois.

Epstein, Irving. 1991. *Chinese education: problems, policies and prospects.* New York: Garland.

Ethridge, James. 1990. *China's unfinished revolution.* San Francisco: China Books.

Ewell, Miranda. 1992. Dissident's sister condemns his arrest. *San Jose Mercury News.* September 3:25A.

Fairbank, John King. 1987. *China watch.* Cambridge, Mass.: Harvard University Press.

Fei Hsiao Tung (Xiaodong). 1981. *Toward a People's anthropology.* Beijing: New World Press.

Fetterman, David. 1989. *Ethnography: step by step.* Newbury Park, Calif.: SAGE Publications.

Foster, George. 1965. Peasant society and the image of limited good. *American Anthropologist* 67:293-315.

Gao, Yuan. 1987. *Born red.* Stanford, Calif.: Stanford University Press.

Geertz, Clifford. 1988. *Works and lives: the anthropologist as author.* Stanford, Cailif.: Stanford University Press.

Gilmartin, Christina. 1993. Gender in the formation of a Communist body politic. *Modern China* 19:229-329.

Gold, Thomas. 1991. Youth and the State. China Quarterly 127:594-612.

Goldberg, Robert. 1991. *Grassroots resistance: social movements in twentieth century America.* Belmont, Calif.: Wadsworth Publishing.

Goldman, Merle. 1981. *China's intellectuals: advise and dissent.* Cambridge, Mass.: Harvard University Press.

Goldman, Merle, Timothy Cheek and Carol Lee Hamrin, eds. 1987. *China's intellectuals and the state: in search of a new relationship.* Harvard Contemporary China Series: 3. Cambridge, Mass.: Harvard University Press.

Goldman, Merle, Perry Link and Su Wei. 1993. China's intellectuals in the Deng era: loss of identity with the State. In *China's quest for national identity,* ed. Lowell Dittmer and Samuel Kim, 125-153. Ithaca, N.Y.: Cornell University Press.

Gomes, Lee (contributing author) 1993 IBM bites the $8.9 billion bullet. *San Jose Mercury News.* July 28:1A, 14A.

Goodrich, Anne. 1991. *Peking paper gods: a look at home worship.* Nettetal: Steyler-Verlag.

Green, Stanton and Stephan Perlman. 1985. Frontiers, boundaries, and open social systems. In *The archaeology of frontiers and boundaries,* ed. Stanton Green and Stephan Perlman, 3-13. San Diego: Academic Press.

Gu Chengwen. 1989. China seeks more food from hi-tech. *China Daily.* December 29: n.p.

Gudykunst William and Stella Ting-Toomey. 1988. *Culture and interpersonal communication*. Newbury Park, Calif.: Sage Publications.

Guldin, Gregory Eliyu. 1990. Chinese anthropologies. In *Anthropology in China: Defining the discipline*, ed. Greg Guldin, 3–29. Armonk, N.Y.: M. E. Sharpe, Inc.

———. 1991. The organization of minority studies in China. *China Exchange News* 19:7–12.

———. 1993. Of disciplinary births. In *Urban anthropology in China*, ed. Greg Guldin and Aidan Southall, 3–7. New York: E. J. Brill.

Guo Zhongshi. 1989. Build-up in software exports a priority. *China Daily*. December 12: n.p.

Han Minzhu ed. 1990. *Cries for democracy: writings and speeches from the 1989 Chinese democracy movement*. Princeton, NJ: Princeton University.

Harrell, Stevan. 1991. Anthropology and ethnology in the PRC: The intersection of discourses. *China Exchange News* 19:3–6.

Hayhoe, Ruth. 1987. China's higher curricular reform in historical perspective. *China Quarterly* 110:196–230.

———. 1988. Shanghai as a mediator of the educational Open Door. *Pacific Affairs* 61(2): 253–284.

———. 1990. China's returned scholars and the Democracy Movement. *China Quarterly* 122: 293–302.

———. 1991. The tapestry of Chinese higher education. In *Chinese education: problems, policies and prospects*, ed. Irving Epstein, 109–144. New York: Garland.

———. 1993. Political texts in Chinese universities before and after Tiananmen. *Pacific Affairs* 66(1):21–43.

———. 1994. Observations on the changing situation in Chinese higher education. Contemporary Chinese studies seminar presented at the Centre of Asian Studies. University of Hong Kong. June 1, 1994.

Hayhoe, Ruth and Marianne Bastid. 1987. *China's education and the industrialized world*. Armonk, NY and Toronto: M. E. Sharpe and Ontario Institute for Studies in Education.

He Bochuan. 1991. *China on the edge: the crisis of ecology and development*. San Francisco: China Books.

Hofstede, Geert. 1984. Culture's consequences: international differences in work related values. Newbury Park, Calif.: Sage Publications.

Hofstede, Geert and Michael Bond.. 1984. Hofstede's culture dimensions: An independent validation using Rokeach's value survey. *Journal of Cross-cultural Psychology* 15:417–433.

Holm, Bill. 1990. *Coming home crazy: an alphabet of Chinese essays*. Minneapolis: Milkweed Editions.

Honig, Emily and Gail Hershatter. 1988. *Personal voices: Chinese women in the 1980s*. Stanford, Calif.: Stanford University Press.

Hooper, Beverley. 1985. *Youth in China*. Ringwood, Vict.: Penguin.

———. 1991. Gender and education. In *Chinese education: problems, policies and prospects*, ed. Irving Epstein, 352–374. New York: Garland.

Hsia, Chih-tsing. 1968. *The classic Chinese novel: a critical introduction*. New York: Columbia University Press.

Hsu, Francis. 1971. A Hypothesis on kinship and culture. In *Kinship and Culture*, ed. Francis Hsu, 3–29. Chicago: Aldine Publishing.

———. 1981. Americans and Chinese: passages to differences. Honolulu: University of Hawaii Press.

——. 1985. The self in cross-cultural perspective. In *Culture and self: Asian and Western perspectives*, ed. Anthony Marsella, George DeVos and Francis Hsu, 24–55. New York: Tavistock Press.

Hu Shi Ming. 1987. *Education and socialist modernization*. New York: AMS Press.

Hua Shiping. 1994. One servant, two masters: The dilemma of Chinese establishment intellectuals. *Modern China* 20(1):92–121.

Hudson, Jon. 1977. Theory and methodology in comparative frontier studies. In *The Frontier: comparative studies*, ed. David Miller and Jerome Steffen, 11-31. Norman: University of Oklahoma Press.

Hui, C. Harry and Harry C. Triandis. 1986. Individualism-collectivism: A study of cross-cultural researchers. *Journal of Cross-Cultural Psychology* 17(2):225–248.

Hwang Kwang-kuo. 1987. Face and favor: The Chinese power game. *American Journal of Sociology* 92(4):944–974.

Jacobson, Robert. 1991. China's policies called threat to university project. *Chronicle of Higher Education*, July 31:A27.

Jagchid, Sechin and Van Jay Symons. 1989. *Peace, war, and trade along the Great Wall: nomadic-Chinese interaction through two millennia*. Bloomington: Indiana University Press.

James, Sibyl. 1990. *In China with Harpo and Karl*. Corvallis Ore.: Calyx Books.

Jankowiak, William. 1993. *Sex, death and hierarchy in a Chinese city: an anthropological account*. New York: Columbia University Press.

Jiang Wandi. 1993. Development of women's rights in China. *Beijing Review* 36(46), Nov. 15–21:18–21.

Johnson, Kay. 1980. Women in the People's Republic of China. In *Asian women in transition*, ed. Sylvia Chipp and Justin Green, 62–103. University Park: Pennsylvania State University Press.

Joseph, William ed. 1991. *China briefing 1991*. Published in cooperation with the China Council of the Asia Society. Boulder, Colo.: Westview Press.

Judd, Ellen. 1984. Working class intellectuals in China. *Journal of Contemporary Asia* 14: 156–170.

——. 1990. "Men are more able": rural Chinese women's conceptions of gender and agency. *Pacific Affairs* 63:40–61.

Kane, Anthony ed. 1990. *China briefing 1990*. Published in cooperation with the China Council of the Asia Society. Boulder, Colo.: Westview Press.

Keating, Pauline. 1984. Middle-level education in contemporary China. In *China's changed road to development*, ed. Neville Maxwell and Bruce McFarlane, 141-148. New York: Pergamon Press.

Kessen, William ed. 1975. *Childhood in China*. New Haven, Conn.: Yale University Press.

Kingston, Maxine Hong. 1990. *Tripmaster monkey: His fake book*. New York: Vintage Books.

Kinoshita, June. 1995a. Government focuses funds, and hopes, on elite teams. *Science* 270: 1137-1139.

——. 1995b. Agriculture finds a niche; drug researchers seek help. *Science* 270:1147-1149.

——. 1995c. Incentives help researchers resist the lure of commerce. *Science* 270:1142-1143.

Knobloch, Edgar. 1972. *Beyond the Oxus*. Totowa, NJ: Rowman and Littlefield.

Kottak, Conrad. 1990. *Prime-time society: an anthropological analysis of television and culture*. Belmont, Calif.: Wadsworth Publishing.

Lan Chengdong and Zhang Zhongru. 1983-1984. Aspirations and inclinations of this year's senior high school graduates: A survey of three high schools in Shanghai. *Chinese Sociology and Anthropology* 16 (1–2):159–169.

Lattimore, Owen. 1988. *Inner Asian frontiers of China*. New York: Oxford University Press.

Laveley, William, Xiao Zhenyu, Li Bohua and Ronald Freeman. 1990. The rise of female education in China: national and regional patterns. *China Quarterly*, March 121:61–93.

Leung, Kwok and Michael Bond. 1984. The impact of cultural collectivism on reward allocation. *Journal of Personality and Social Psychology* 47:793–804.

Lewin, Keith. 1987. Science education in China: transformation and change in the 1980s. *Comparative Education Review* 31:419–441.

Liang Heng and Judith Shapiro. 1983. *Son of the revolution*. New York: Vintage Books.

Lin, Cyril Chihren. 1981. The reinstatement of economics in China today. *China Quarterly* 85:1–48.

Lin Jing. 1993. *Education in post–Mao China*. Westport, Connecticut: Praeger Publishers.

Link, Perry. 1992. *Evening chats in Beijing: probing China's predicament*. New York: W. W. Norton.

Liu Zongren. 1989. *6 Tanyin alley*. San Francisco: China Books.

Lull, James. 1991. *China turned on: television, reform and resistance*. New York: Routledge.

Lynch, Michael. 1993. *Scientific practice and ordinary action: ethnomethodology and social studies of science*. Cambridge: Cambridge University Press.

Ma Lizhen. 1989. Women: the debate on jobs vs. homemaking. *China Reconstructs* 38 (3) March:66–68.

Madsen, Richard. 1991. Contentless consensus: The political discourse of a segmented society. In *America at century's end*, ed. Alan Wolfe, 440–460. Berkeley: University of California Press.

Marshall, Eliot. 1993. R&D policy that emphasizes the "D." *Science* 259:1816–1819.

Maslen, Geoffrey. 1992. Australia stiffens entry regulations for prospective students from China. *Chronicle of Higher Education,* Nov. 18, 1992:A30.

Mathews Jay and Linda Mathews. 1983. *One billion: a China chronicle*. New York: Ballantine Books.

McCormick, Barrett. 1990. *Political reform in post–Mao China: democracy and bureaucracy in a Leninist state*. Berkeley: University of California Press.

McGough, James. 1979. *Fei Hsiao-t'ung: the dilemma of a Chinese intellectual*. Armonk, N.Y.: M. E. Sharpe.

Merton, Robert K. 1968. *Social theory and social structure*. Enlarged edition. New York: Free Press.

Mervis, Jeffrey. 1995a. The right ties can save lives and move mountains. *Science* 270: 1144–1147.

——— .1995b. The long march to topnotch science. *Science* 270:1134–1137.

Mervis, Jeffrey and June Kinoshita. 1995. Science in China: a great leap forward. *Science* 270:1131.

Moerman, Michael. 1988. *Talking Culture: ethnography and conversation analysis*. Philadelphia: University of Philadelphia Press.

Mulkay, Michael. 1969. Some aspects of cultural growth in the natural sciences. *Social Research* 36:22–52.

Nathan, Andrew. 1990. *China's crisis: dilemmas of reform and prospects for democracy*. New York: Columbia University Press.

Newnham, Richard. 1987. *About Chinese*. Revised edition. New York: Penguin Books.

Ogden, Suzanne. 1992. *China's unresolved issues: politics, development and culture.* Englewood Cliffs, N.J.: Prentice Hall.

Orleans, Leo. 1980. *Science in contemporary China.* Stanford, Calif.: Stanford University Press.

——. 1988. *Chinese students in America.* Washington, DC: National Academy Press.

Osborne, Brian. 1977. Frontier settlement in Eastern Ontario in the nineteenth century: A study in changing perceptions of land and opportunity. In *The frontier: comparative studies,* ed. David Miller and Jerome Steffen, 201–225. Norman: University of Oklahoma Press.

Overmeyer, Daniel. 1984. Review of *Journey to the West.* Volume Four. Translated and edited by Anthony C. Yu. *Pacific Affairs* 57:319–321.

Pelto, Pertti and Gretel Pelto. 1978. *Anthropological research: the structure of inquiry.* Second edition. Cambridge: Cambridge University Press.

Pepper, Suzanne. 1990. Post-Mao reforms in Chinese education: Can the ghosts of the past be laid to rest? In *Chinese education: problems, policies and prospects,* ed. Irving Epstein, 1–41. New York: Garland.

Plafker, Ted. 1995. National monitoring network does science—and a lot more. *Science* 270: 1151–1152.

Plaks, Andrew. 1987. *Four masterworks of the Ming novel: "Ssu-ta ch'i-shu."* Princeton, N.J.: Princeton University Press.

Platt, John. 1973. Social Traps. *Science* 28:641–651.

Potter, Sulamith and Jack Potter. 1990. *China's peasants: the anthropology of a revolution.* New York: Cambridge University Press.

Pye, Lucian. 1988. *The mandarin and the cadre: China's political cultures.* Michigan monographs in Chinese studies. Ann Arbor, Mich.: Center for Chinese Studies The University of Michigan.

——. 1991. The State and the individual: an overview of interpretation. *China Quarterly* 127: 443–466.

Rhoodie, Eschel. 1989. *Discrimination against women: a global survey of the economic, educational, social and political status of women.* Jefferson, N.C.: McFarland and company.

Riner, Reed. 1987. Doing futures research—anthropologically. *Futures* June:311–328.

Robinson, Jean. 1985. Of women and washing machines: employment, housework, and the reproduction of motherhood in socialist China. *China Quarterly* 101:32–57.

Ross, Heidi. 1991. The "crisis" in Chinese secondary schooling. In *Chinese education: problems, policies and prospects,* ed. Irving Epstein 66–108. New York: Garland.

Rossi, Alice, ed. 1985. *Sociology and anthropology in the People's Republic of China.* Washington, D.C.: National Academy Press.

Ruan Xihu. 1993. Present tasks of urban anthropology in China. In *Urban Anthropology in China,* ed. Greg Guldin and Aidan Southall, 8–13. New York: E. J. Brill.

Salisbury, Harrison. 1989. *Tiananmen diary: thirteen days in June.* Boston: Little Brown.

Salzman, Mark. 1987. *Iron and silk.* New York: Vintage Books.

——. 1991. *The laughing sutra.* New York: Vintage Press.

Schwartz, Shalom. 1990. Individualism-collectivism: critique and proposed refinements. *Journal of Cross-Cultural Psychology* 21(2):139–157.

Schwartz, Vera. 1987. Behind a partially open door: Chinese intellectuals and the post–Mao reform process. *Pacific Affairs* 59(4):577–604.

Segall, Marshall, Pierre Dasen, John Berry and Ype Poortinga. 1990. *Human behavior in global perspective.* New York: Pergamon Press.

Shen Rong. 1987. *At middle age*. Beijing: Chinese Literature Press.

Shen Tong. 1990. *Almost a revolution*. Boston: Houghton Mifflin.

Simon, Denis Fred. 1987. China's scientists and technologists in the post-Mao era: a retrospective and prospective glimpse. In *China's intellectuals and the state: in search of a new relationship*, ed. M. Goldman, T. Cheek and C. L. Hamrin, 129-156. Cambridge, Mass.: Harvard University Press.

Simon, Denis Fred and Detlef Rehn. 1988. *Technological innovation in China: the case of the Shanghai semiconductor industry*. Cambridge, Mass.: Ballinger Publishing.

Sippanondha, Ketudat. 1990. *The middle path for the future of Thailand*. With methodological and editorial collaboration with Robert Textor. Honolulu, Hawaii: Institute of Culture and Communication, East-West Center.

Skalnik, Peter. 1989. *Outwitting the state*. New Brunswick, N.J.: Transaction Publishers.

Smith, Tony. 1987. *Thinking like a communist*. New York: W. W. Norton.

Spence, Jonathan. 1990. *The search for modern China*. New York: W. W. Norton.

Spradley, James. 1979. *The ethnographic interview*. New York: Holt, Rinehart and Winston.

Staff Reporter. 1989. More grain gained with less water. *China Daily*. March 30: n.p.

State Statistical Bureau. 1989. *Changes and development in China (1949-1989)*. Beijing: Beijing Review Press.

Stehr, Nico. 1990. Robert K. Merton's sociology of science. In *Robert K. Merton: consensus and controversy*, ed. Jon Clark, Celia Modgil and Sohan Modgil, 285-294. New York: Falmer Press.

Sullivan, Richard. 1979. The medieval monk as frontiersman. In *The frontier: comparative studies*. Volume Two, ed. William Savage and Stephen Thompson, 25-49. Norman: University of Oklahoma Press.

Talbot, Strobe. 1989a. Fighting the founders. *Time* June 5, 1989:16-19.

——. 1989b. Defiance. *Time* June 19, 1989:10-13.

Tan Shen and Li Dun. 1993. Urban development and crime in China. In *Urban anthropology in China*, ed. Greg Guldin and Aidan Southall, 352-357. New York: E. J. Brill.

Terrill, Ross. 1992. *China in our time*. New York: Simon and Schuster.

Textor, Robert. 1980. *A handbook on ethnographic futures research*. Third Edition. Version A. Stanford, Calif.: Stanford University School of Education and Department of Anthropology.

Textor, Robert, Bhansoon Ladavalya, and Sidthinat Prabuhanitisarn. 1984. *Alternative sociocultural futures for Thailand: a pilot inquiry among academics*. Chiang Mai University: Faculty of the Social Sciences.

Thurston, Anne. 1988. *Enemies of the People: the ordeal of the intellectuals in China's Great Cultural Revolution*. Cambridge, Mass.: Harvard University Press.

Tobin, Joseph, David Wu and Dana Davidson. 1989. *Preschool in three cultures*. New Haven, Conn.: Yale University Press.

Tu Wei-ming. 1979. Confucianism: symbol and substance in recent times. In *Value change in Chinese society*, ed. Richard Wilson, Amy Wilson and Sidney Greenblatt, 21-51 New York: Praeger Publishers.

——. 1985. Self and otherness in Confucian thought. In *Culture and self: Asian and Western perspectives*, ed. George Devos, Francis Hsu and Anthony Marsella, 231-251. New York: Tavistock Publications.

Turner, Frederick Jackson. 1986. *The frontier in American history*. Tucson: University of Arizona Press.

Turner-Gottshang, Karen and Linda Reed. 1987. *China bound: a guide to academic life and work in the PRC.* For the Committee on Scholarly communication with the People's Republic of China. Washington, D.C.: National Academy Press.

Unger, Jonathan ed. 1991. *The pro-democracy protests in China: reports from the provinces.* Contemporary China Papers, Australian National University. Armonk, N.Y.: M. E. Sharpe.

Vizenor, Gerald. 1987. *Griever: An American monkey king in China.* Normal/New York: Illinois State University/Fictive Collective.

Volti, Rudi. 1982. *Technology, politics, and society in China.* Boulder, Colo.: Westview Press.

Wallace, A.F.C. 1972. Paradigmatic processes in culture change. *American Anthropologist* 74: 467–478.

Wang Jianliang and Nat Coletta. 1991. Chinese adult education. In *Chinese education: problems, policies and prospects,* ed. Irving Epstein, 145–162. New York: Garland.

Wang Jing. 1992. *The story of stone: intertextuality, ancient Chinese stone lore, and stone symbolism in Dream of the Red Chamber, Water Margin, and The Journey to the West.* Durham, N.C.: Duke University Press.

Wang Shuguang and Gao Yunzhu. 1989. *Qingnian shehui shenghuo xinli wenda.* Shenyang, Liaoning, The People's Republic of China: Liaoning Science and Technology Publishing House.

Wang Xiao-Lun. 1991. Cultural mediators or marginal persons? *Geographical Review* 81(3): 293–303.

Weaver, Gary. 1991. Reverse culture shock. *ASPIRENEWSLETTER* 1:5–7.

Weiner, Rebecca, Margaret Murphy and Albert Li. 1991. *Living in China: a guide to teaching and studying in China including Taiwan.* San Francisco: China Books.

Werner, Oswald and G. Mark Schoepfle. 1987. *Sytematic fieldwork: foundations of ethnography and interviewing.* Newbury Park, Calif.: Sage Publications.

White, Lynn III. 1994. Technocracy in China: biographical evidence on politicians and soldiers, c. 1980–1992. Seminar presented at the Centre of Asian Studies. University of Hong Kong. March 14, 1994.

Whyte, Martin and William Parish. 1984. *Urban life in contemporary China.* Chicago: University of Chicago Press.

Wolf, Margery. 1985. *Revolution postponed: women in contemporary China.* Stanford, Calif.: Stanford University Press.

Woodruff, John. 1989. *China in search of its future.* Seattle: University of Washington Press.

Wu, Cheng En. 1984a. *Journey to the West.* Volumes I. W.J.F. Jenner, trans. Beijing: Foreign Languages Press.

——. 1984b. *Journey to the West.* Volumes I and II. W.J.F. Jenner, trans. Beijing: Foreign Languages Press.

Wu, David Yen-Ho. 1994. Drowning your child with love: family education in six Chinese communities. 8th Barbara Ward Memorial Lecture. Hong Kong Anthropological Society. Kowloon, Hong Kong. May 11, 1994.

Yang Kuo-shu. 1986. Chinese personality and its change. In *The psychology of the Chinese people,* ed. Michael Bond, 106–170. New York: Oxford University Press.

Yi Mu and Mark Thompson. 1989. *Crisis at Tiananmen: reform and reality in modern China.* San Francisco: China Books.

Young, Linda. 1994. *Crosstalk and culture in Sino-American communication.* Cambridge: Cambridge University Press.

Yu, Anthony C. 1977. Introduction to The Journey to the West. Translated and edited by Anthony C. Yu. Pp. 1–62. Chicago: University of Chicago Press.

Zhang Lin. 1989. Students abroad "should not fear reprisals on return." *China Daily*. July 28: n.p.

Zhang Ping. 1989. Update on science, technology. *China Daily*. August 14: n.d.

Zhang Xinxin and Sang Ye. 1986. *Chinese Profiles*. Beijing: Panda Books.

———. 1987. *Chinese lives: an oral history of contemporary China*. Edited and translated by W.J.F. Jenner and Delia Davin. New York: Pantheon Books.

Zheng Defang. 1989. Unfair for women to bear brunt of reform. *China Daily*. March 9: n.p.

Zhou Guangzhao. 1995. The course of reform at the Chinese Academy of Sciences. *Science* 270:1153.

Zhu Li. 1990. Service center for scholars returned from abroad. *China Today* 39:28–29.

Index

About the Author

J. A. ENGLISH-LUECK is Associate Professor of Anthropology at San Jose State University. She is the author of *Health in the New Age* (1990) and is currently conducting research on Silicon Valley.

ISBN 0-89789-510-X

HARDCOVER BAR CODE